Writing Ann Arbor

Writing Ann Arbor

A Literary Anthology

edited by Laurence Goldstein

The University of Michigan Press
Ann Arbor

2008   2007   2006   2005   4   3   2   1

A CIP catalog record for this book is available from the British Library.

Library of Congress Cataloging-in-Publication Data

Writing Ann Arbor: a literary anthology / edited by Laurence Goldstein
       p. cm.
    ISBN-13: 978-0-472-09899-6 (cloth : acid-free paper)
    ISBN-10: 0-472-09899-3 (cloth : acid-free paper)
    ISBN-13: 978-0-472-06899-9 (pbk. : acid-free paper)
    ISBN-10: 0-472-06899-7 (pbk. : acid-free paper)
       1. Ann Arbor (Mich.)—Literary collections.   2. American literature—Michigan—
Ann Arbor.   3. Authors, American—Homes and haunts—Michigan—Ann Arbor.
I. Goldstein, Laurence, 1943–

PS572.A56W75   2005
810.8'03277435—dc22   2005050693

ψ

Contents

Part Three ☙ Matriculation

Part Four ☙ Spirit of Place

Laurence Goldstein

Introduction

The public history of a city can be written by a single author, but its inner history—the story of its cultural evolution, the ever-unfinished portrait of its shape-shifting identity—can only be written by a composite author. Jonathan Marwil provided us with *A History of Ann Arbor* in 1987; the present volume is a complementary account of how its citizens have periodically imagined this region of Southeast Michigan into life. Since its founding in 1824, and especially after the establishment of the University of Michigan in 1837, Ann Arbor has provoked a multitude of men and women into wielding their pens and keyboards with the aim of defining their alma mater.

Not every writer on the subject was (or is) a professor or alumnus of the university. As far back as 1836, Harriet Martineau, the British social reformer who traveled through the United States in the same decade as Tocqueville, remarked suggestively, "At Ypsilanti I picked up an Ann Arbor newspaper. It was printed badly, but the contents were pretty good. It could happen nowhere out of America that so raw a settlement as Ann Arbor, where there is difficulty in procuring decent accommodations, should have a newspaper." Martineau singled out the theme that writers ever since have returned to when they chose to characterize the city. It is a place distinguished by *intellectual culture*. I borrow this term from the eminent philosopher John Dewey's contribution to a student publication later in the century, when he was teaching at the University of Michigan. Of course, every university town (or city) sponsors cerebral activity, but Ann Arbor gets credited by the writers in this anthology with an extra-ordinary amount of intellectual vitality. Some of the rhetoric is raw boosterism, no doubt about it. But most of it is well-earned admiration for the city's scholarly and literary journals, bookstores and libraries, professoriat and student bodies, visiting speakers, scientific and technological laboratories, and socially progressive citizenry.

Ann Arbor's reputation as a "literary city" may be a default recognition that it is not an industrial or commercial center and that the failure of its efforts in the early nineteenth century to become the state's capital shaped its self-image in significant ways. Detroit, Lansing, Flint, Grand Rapids, and the expansive wilderness of the Upper Peninsula achieved real and symbolic power while Ann Arbor cultivated its identity as an arcadian retreat, though a crowded one. The University of Michigan became the most populous university in the country by the Civil War era, and the "college town" that grew up around it was destined to became a city sooner or later. The first novel with scenes set in Ann Arbor, by Justin McCarthy in 1875, disguised the town under the name New Padua and depicted it as hardly more than a few streets servicing the faculty and students. By the end of the century, a book of fiction could be titled *Ann Arbor Tales* under the working assumption that the name would be recognized throughout the nation. Thanks in good part to German immigration, the city increasingly took on a social, economic, and religious identity connected to European cultures.

After World War I, Ann Arbor became urbanized at a rate that discomfited the genteel part of the population, those who had cherished it as a village made up of fine old residences with large, lovely gardens and plentiful clothing stores and markets making up the downtown. Massive construction projects on and off campus, many of them initiated to accommodate the automobile, gave Ann Arbor the metropolitan profile of cities with much larger populations. New technologies nourished what became known as "The Research Center of the Midwest," including high-tech and pharmaceutical companies catering to the entire country. If residents off campus resented the increasing power of the university to set the agenda for the city, so did many instructors and students begrudge the increasing commercialization of public space, often for the benefit of faraway investors and developers. Town and gown conflicts were exacerbated in the 1960s when students put Ann Arbor on the map as a radical force in American life. When the activism represented by the first teach-in on the Vietnam War, Students for a Democratic Society (SDS), the Black Action Movement, and the White Panther Party, along with a notorious five-dollar fine for possession of marijuana, drew national attention to the city, even many conservative Ann Arborites felt a certain pride in challenging the status quo. They felt it again in the early years of the twenty-first century when the conflict over affirmative action resulted in landmark Supreme Court decisions. All of these volatile growing pains of an important cultural site nourished the vitality of literary production from the beginnings of the city's history to the present day.

Ann Arbor was first characterized in print as an asylum by Frederika Bremer, a Swedish traveler scouting out the contours of America, who described it in *The Homes of the New World* (1853) as "a peaceful retreat from the unquiet life of the world." More recently it has jokingly been called a six-square-mile world of ideas surrounded by reality. It may be useful to focus for a moment on that statement. That Ann Arbor is a realm apart from reality makes perfect sense when one considers the qualities of an intellectual culture. A world of ideas—of argument, of spirited discourse, of new and subversive formulations about everything—is indeed a glass house through which the inhabitants catch sight of a different world than the one presented to them by conventional wisdom. That is one function of a university. Living in a privileged place, one can become accustomed to thinking that the rest of the world conforms to the shape of one's own experience, rather like the old woman in Nancy Willard's novel *Sister Water* who thinks that everything she sees on television is happening in Ann Arbor. For students especially, the retraction of parental monitoring creates an enchanted and liberated space for powerful dreaming, for radical new forms of self-definition and community action. Sexual politics gets a lot of attention in the creative writing in this anthology, but there are defiant and influential assertions of communal political change as well. The students who rioted in favor of joining the Civil War in the 1860s and the students who demonstrated in opposition to the Vietnam War in the 1960s based their activism to some degree on the values fermenting on the campus.

So "reality" gets changed in the process and not just by being put in ironizing quotation marks. At a time when 70 percent of all Americans attend some institution of higher education, the surrounding world of hard knocks and lifelong opportunities is constantly reshaped by the ideas percolating in the university and pouring into the world outside the ivied walls. Surely the relationship is a symbiotic one. When John F. Kennedy visited Ann Arbor in 1960 to announce his idea for a Peace Corps on the steps of the Michigan Union, and when Lyndon Johnson came four years later to propose the creation of a "Great Society" during a commencement address in the football stadium, the dreams of an older establishment mingled with the radical ideas fostered on campus to generate an innovative and potent sea change in the cultural life of this nation and the world beyond. "The permanent and fruitful outcome of a college education should be the training of one's *human* nature," John Dewey insisted in the aforementioned essay. And Ann Arbor's writers have risen gladly to that pointed challenge by seeking to effect a merger of classroom concepts and policies of social betterment. From President E. O. Haven's prophecy in the mid–nineteenth century of a Christian civilizing force marching outward from Ann Arbor to the *Port Huron Statement* fashioned by the Students for a Democratic Society a century later, Ann Arbor has been the site of humanizing, indeed utopian, models for social transformation.

But there is more to being human than being intellectual. It would be a gross distortion of the literary record if an editor filled his anthology with writings about ideas, all-important as they are. It's fair to say that the majority of writings about the university, from first to last, focus on two other aspects of the academic condition: sports and recreational social life. There is no overestimating the passion for football, especially, in Ann Arbor, around the state of Michigan and in the hearts of alumni throughout the world. Football appears as a leitmotif in this anthology, first appearing in the nineteenth century (though it's interesting to note in a novel of 1899 that baseball had more respect on campus) and carrying forward into the fiction of Charles Baxter and Elwood Reid and the poetry of Donald Hall. (Alumnus Lawrence Kasdan rightly set his reunion film *The Big Chill* on the day of an important Michigan football game.) Because there are so many books available about football at Michigan I have represented only one actual game, in the lean journalistic prose of Pete Waldmeir writing about the historic victory of Michigan over Ohio State in 1969, "the greatest college football game of all time," in the words of Don Canham, athletic director of the University of Michigan. Likewise, "Homage to Cazzie Russell" by Richard Goodman composes a vision of basketball "perfection" as awesome as a theorem of Euclid or a lyric of Emily Dickinson.

And then there are the infinitely complex social relations, on and off campus, undertaken by young people spending four or more years of their lives in the privileged space of an academic milieu. I have chosen brief samples of fiction from the nineteenth century to demonstrate the earlier forms of what might be called *affiliations*, be they same-sex (fraternities, sororities, dormitories) or, more often, mixed-gender dynamics (dances, courtship, professional rivalries). I invite the reader to keep an eye on the slang, on the language in general, in which these early authors and characters speak their minds. The way of speaking about everything will change by the time we get to Allan Seager, Marge Piercy, and Wendy Wasserstein, but the forms of attraction and repulsion remain steady. Notice, too, how romance shades into intellectual culture in some of these writings, as in a novel of 1933 by Richard Meeker, called by its editor in

1987 "possibly the first novel published in America to show male homo-sexuality in a positive light," or a Joyce Carol Oates novella in which the push and pull of sexual desire has much to do with the way graduate students at a party promiscuously exchange their axioms and postulates. Nothing is more essentially Ann Arbor than a raucous argument about philosophy and literature at a pack-the-flat party.

When I mentioned to people during the last couple of years that I was assembling writings about Ann Arbor for an anthology, especially to acquaintances over forty, almost always the first response was, "Don't forget to include the scene in the underground tunnels in that Ross Macdonald book!" The reference was to Macdonald's novel of 1944, *The Dark Tunnel*, which was written shortly after the author received his M.A. at the University of Michigan. (He wrote a thesis on Coleridge.) When Macdonald returned to Michigan in the early 1970s to receive an honorary degree, he was invited to revisit the steam tunnels running under the main campus and declined. Macdonald's novel is so memorable, perhaps, because it grapples with the dark side of Ann Arbor, here figured as a Nazi presence and visible in later writings about the university as a forbidding cold war regimen of control, which, if not fascist, is portrayed as oppressive to the spirit of a free intellectual culture.

Some writers nostalgically depict Ann Arbor as a sort of utopian open society, a crucible of soul making that prepares the individual to withstand the pressures of the outer world. This view of the educational experience nourishes the iconography of the ivory tower. Other writers who revisit Ann Arbor in their memoirs see the matter with more complexity. Ann Arbor, in this view, is part and parcel of the everyday conflicts of the rest of the world, and what is most happily remembered is the vehemence with which the creative spirit struggled—in classrooms, in dorm rooms, in fraternity lounges, in the offices of the *Michigan Daily* or the Union or the Administration Building—against the temptation toward passivity and indifference. I have included two full-length essay-memoirs, by Arthur Miller and Dorothy Gies McGuigan, that render the nuances and subtleties of self-creation in an environment that is not always hospitable to the individual will. Excerpts from book-length memoirs by Tom Hayden, Sven Birkerts, and Ted Solotaroff likewise document how the values taking form in Ann Arbor strengthened the author when he left the city for larger venues—Los Angeles, Boston, and New York. Just as Alice Hamilton forged her social activism in the late nineteenth century by determined study and pragmatic actions, so the post–World War II students who lingered in Ann Arbor for several seasons armed themselves for the polemics they would write in later years. In each case, the author pays tribute to Ann Arbor mentors who guided them into a wiser adulthood.

Two *Michigan Daily* columns by twenty-first-century undergraduates conclude the anthology. Johanna Hanink's thoughtful response to the horrific events of September 11, 2001, models for us how one young writer registered the historical catastrophe, immediately, journalistically, on the pulse of her fragile belief system. The other, by Michael Grass, concludes the volume in the only way possible, by welcoming us (as imaginary freshmen) to the city of Ann Arbor.

Unlike the thankless task of editors such as Phillip Lopate, who in *Writing New York: A Literary Anthology* (1998) had to select a small number of poems from thousands of worthy possibilities, I encountered a relatively small range of first-rate poems. The poems enlarge our sense of the topography of Ann Arbor, taking us into neighborhoods, hospitals, art galleries, and other places unvisited by the prose writers. As with the fiction and essays, I kept to the rule that the work had to be clearly anchored in Ann Arbor, mentioning actual locations and not just set in a place that could be anyplace—even if the poem were written in and about Ann Arbor. Of course, rules are made to be broken, and there is some flexibility in the selection. For example, Robert Hayden does not mention Ann Arbor in "The Performers," but I can testify personally to the authenticity of his little drama: I, too, had an office on the seventh floor of Haven Hall in the early 1970s and well remember Hayden telling me of his delighted surprise upon swiveling in his chair one day and finding two window washers seemingly dangling in space in order to scrub his windows clean.

I have chosen to omit a famous poem popularly associated with Ann Arbor. Robert Frost's lyric "Acquainted with the Night" describes a forlorn figure walking through an unnamed city. "One luminary clock against the sky / Proclaimed the time was neither wrong nor right," he laments. Some partisans have identified this clock as the one on Burton Tower, but that is impossible since the tower was not built till long after the poem's date of composition. Others identify the tower clock as part of a downtown building in the 1920s, which Frost would have noted during his tenure as writer-in-residence. Frost remarked to Charles H. Miller, "I'm often asked which tower belongs to that poem. . . . It's true there was a clock on high in Ann Arbor, and I liked looking at it. And it's true that I wrote the poem in Ann Arbor. But the poem isn't about any one clock, or about Ann Arbor. It's about acquaintance with the night!" I'll let the poet have the last word on that subject.

Under the title "Authors and Wolverines" in the March 4, 1939, issue of the *Saturday Review of Literature*, Arnold Mulder wrote that "sober honesty compels the admission that authors—upper case authors—are about as rare in Michigan as the 'skunk bear' ever was and that the flowering of literary Michigan is still in the future." Sober honesty compels me to agree with Mulder that there is no major literary figure, no canonical masterpiece, in the annals of pre-1939 Michigan, let alone Ann Arbor. One looks jealously at a kindred anthology, *Berkeley: A Literary Tribute*, edited by Danielle La France in 1997, which boasts of writings by the likes of Lincoln Steffens, Frank Norris, and Jack London from the prewar period. When I began scouting for writing by the masters for this collection, I was told that Sinclair Lewis's novel *Arrowsmith* contained a hefty portion of scenes set in Ann Arbor. But that's not the case. Martin Arrowsmith attends a midwestern university called Winnimac, a portmanteau word combining Wisconsin, Minnesota, and Michigan, and there is no single reference to any location smacking of Ann Arbor—nor is the nearby big city of Zenith anything like Detroit. Authors who clearly had Ann Arbor in mind, based on their verifiable residence in the city, often took pains to disguise or radically distort its specific features in order to achieve some specious goal of "universality." With regret I excluded for this reason otherwise good writing by Lloyd C. Douglas, Chaym Zeldis, James Hynes, and others. Room had to be made, in any case, for that "flowering" of first-rate discourse about Ann Arbor that began to appear after 1939.

Nevertheless, I found much writing from the period 1824–1939 worthy of reprinting. If nothing else, these early documents provide a context or backstory for the themes that rush forth in full vigor during the last half century. It seemed useful to devote a full section of the anthology to scenes of matriculation at the university. The following two sections are somewhat arbitrary in their boundaries; they present thematic clusters that may have more continuity in the editor's eye than anyone else's. I was tempted to poach upon a sister publication, *The Huron River: Voices from the Watershed*, edited by John Knott and Keith Taylor in 2000. As numerous authors in that anthology point out, Ann Arbor cannot be fully brought to life without consideration of the river that runs through it. However, I have left the book entirely alone and direct attention to it here as required reading for anyone who enjoys the material in this anthology. I did poach one item, by Charles Baxter, from another anthology, *Ann Arbor (W)rites: A Community Memoir*, edited by Nicholas Delbanco for the Ann Arbor District Library (2004). In this charming collection, café owners, business people, social workers, journalists, public school teachers, and librarians mingle with young fiction writers and poets to convey the texture and flavor of the city.

I agreed to undertake the editing of this book in part because I had mentally and otherwise noted during my teaching and editing life most of the significant texts about Ann Arbor. In seminars with titles such as "Landscape and Literature" I had constantly made the point that the personal experience of local places is always enhanced by reading other people's versions of the same setting. The places we visit or live in are made more real by engaging textual versions of them. I am grateful to many sources that suggested avenues of inquiry, beginning with Mary Beth Lewis's article "Fictional Ann Arbor" in the 2003–2004 *City Guide* published by the *Ann Arbor Observer*. Andrea Beauchamp, Sue Burris, Nicholas Harp, Patricia Hooper, Lawrence Joseph, Jonathan Marwil, Scottie Parrish, Grace Shackman, and Alan Wald tipped me off to possibilities, and Kristen Bloomstrom turned up some useful sources for further investigation. I am grateful to LeAnn Fields of the University of Michigan Press for suggesting the project in the first place and then messaging me with suggestions thereafter. I am also grateful to the host of congenial spirits at the Bentley Historical Library at the University of Michigan who made key recommendations and guided me expertly through their holdings, especially Nancy Bartlett, head of university archives, and Francis Blouin, director of the Library, as well as Len Coombs, Karen Jania, Greg Kinney, and Bill Wallach.

Once, on visiting Oahu, I noticed the slogan printed on every issue of its chief newspaper: "Lucky you live Hawaii." I have lived in many places that sported the same kind of smug satisfaction with themselves. Ann Arbor is not immune from a kind of snobbery about its identity, and this book might be cited as further evidence of its amour propre. The truth is, every populated place on the globe has a rich inner life and a long tradition worthy of comprehensive portraiture. Aracataca, Colombia, must have possessed a profound identity in order for Gabriel García Márquez to have immortalized it as Macondo in *One Hundred Years of Solitude*. Lafayette County, Mississippi, nourished William Faulkner's astonishing reinvention of it as Yoknapatawpha, and Wahpeton, North Dakota, has served its native daughter Louise Erdrich as the inspiration for a series of outstanding novels. The writers who observe and then delineate their favorite locales help to bring those regions to enhanced and vivid life. Someday every remarkable place in the world will have its own anthology. Now it is Ann Arbor's turn—and the present offering is only the beginning.

Part One

Preliminaries

On the Name Ann Arbor: Several Views

[1850] The following evening we were at Anne Arbour, a pretty little rural city. . . . In Anne Arbour also the people were much pleased with themselves, their city, its situation, and way of life. The city derived its name from the circumstance that when the first settlers came to the place they consisted principally of one family, and whilst the woods were felled and the land ploughed, the labourers had no other dwelling than a tent-like shed of boughs and canvas, where the mother of the family, Anne, prepared the food, and cared for the comfort of all. That was the domestic hearth; that was the calm haven where all the labourers found rest and refreshment under the protection of Mother Anne. Hence they called the tent Anne's Arbour or Bower, and the city, which by degrees sprung up around it, retained the name. And with its neat houses and gardens upon the green hills and slopes the little city looked indeed like a peaceful retreat from the unquiet life of the world.

Frederika Bremer, *The Homes of the New World*, translated
by Mary Howitt (London: Arthur Hall, Virtue and Co., 1853).

The first settlers came about 1824, and lodged for some weeks under the shelter of their sleigh-box and a rude bower of trees covered with buffalo skins. This primitive arbor, or the beauty of the oak groves, furnished a name to the place, and the prefix Ann was given in honor of the names of the wives of the two pioneers.

Elizabeth Fries Lummis, *Summer Rambles in
the West* (New York: J. C. Riker, 1853).

Our town has a name unduplicated among the place names of the world. The story goes that a letter once arrived from farthest Russia with the mere superscription, "Mr. John Doe, Ann Arbor." Globe-trotters from Ann Arbor are often forced to explain that the name is not Ann Harbor, the assumption being, I suppose, that the town is a lake port and was settled by Cockneys.

Fantastic explanations have arisen from time to time as to "the real" source of the name. About 1900 one David Hackett, aged 92, is reported to have returned to these parts after spending seventy years in Texas. He stoutly declared that a beautiful young woman, frail, with heavy black hair and blue eyes, had been guiding people through the wilderness hereabouts long before the arrival of [John] Allen and [Elisha] Rumsey; that she mysteriously called herself Ann "Arbeur"; and that the settlers had honored her by inscribing her name on a rock in the middle of the Huron River. On his return he found the rock—but seventy years of exposure had erased the name!

The *Michigan Argonaut,* an old-time campus weekly, on March 27, 1886, presented another theory: that the Indian name for the locality was "Anaba," claiming to have the record of a pre-Allen fur trader, Col. D. W. H. Howard, who interpreted the name to mean "Good Youth." We discount this story as a bit of student spoofing. As for Indian names, what a blessing we are not saddled with "Kaw-Goosh-Kaw-Nick," the Pottowatomies' imitation of the sound of John Allen's sawmill.

It is accepted as a well-authenticated fact that John Allen and Elisha Walker Rumsey, our founding fathers, named the village in honor of their two wives. But there has always been considerable bickering about the arbor. Some old settlers insisted that the two men built an arbor, or even two arbors, one apiece; some say as a temporary shelter, others as an adornment just to pretty up the place. I doubt the latter idea especially. If they had any spare time between February 1824, when they first tramped about this lovely region, and May 25, when the plat was recorded in Detroit, surely they could have found more important things to do than building an arbor for mere decoration. There were chopping down trees and fashioning them into dwellings, breaking the ground and planting vegetables, following the surveyor up and down the proposed streets, and all this on a background of the time-consuming mechanics of mere existence in the wilds.

We lean toward the other theory, held by equally trustworthy pioneers, that the arbor was a natural one where wild grapevines had crowded gaily over wild plum trees; that it remained for many years near the southwest corner of West Huron and First Streets; that Mary Ann Rumsey had enjoyed doing her work there, as the warm spring days advanced (for Ann Allen did not arrive until October); and that the name was hit upon spontaneously one day by herself and John Allen, put to the vote by Calvin Chipman, their carpenter, and consented to by the less imaginative Rumsey, when the men were taking time off from cabin building for their noonday meal.

Lela Duff, *Ann Arbor Yesterdays* (Ann Arbor: Friends of the Ann Arbor Public Library, 1962).

Returning to Detroit, they registered their claim with the federal land office on February 14, 1824, Allen purchasing 480 acres, Rumsey 160. They chose a name for the site that acknowledged its generous stands of burr oaks, honored the common name of their wives, and beckoned evocatively—surely deliberately—to the tide of settlers expected in the territory. Annarbour, as it was then spelled, suggested a haven in an otherwise uncivilized landscape. Certainly it struck a more inviting chord than names like Allensville or Anapolis, which also seem to have been considered. Singular as a name, it retains to this day a subliminal enchantment.

Jonathan Marwil, *A History of Ann Arbor* (Ann Arbor: University of Michigan Press, 1987).

Ann Arbor (A Profile)

Neither city nor town,
even its location is ambiguous.
Of North and East and Middlewest it both is
and is not; in every case,
a hopeless candidate for the picturesque.

Trees and a few grand old
accidentally preserved houses
save it from total suburbanization,
give it the mildly authentic complexion
of secondhand furniture.

No setting for tragedy,
it is the scene, nonetheless, for more
than its surfeit of traffic would suggest.
Entrances and exits are frequent enough
to be anonymous; every year
the young adolesce in its residences;

the usual academic antipathies
enliven the cocktail parties,
while, driven from their garrets,
dim graduate students gripe in the beer joints,
leaving their wives to cope with babies
and contemporary interior decoration.

In all the tongues of the world
Its tone is Germanic and provincial.
Yugoslavs, Hindus, Japanese
fraternize in the supermarkets
where bean sprouts and braunschweiger
are equally available.

Love is frequently experienced
over jugs of California claret.
Politics are important,
and culture so cheap and convenient
that any evening you can expect
thin strains of Mozart
to issue from half a dozen windows.

The women who do not run for alderman
paint pictures, write poetry or give expensive parties
for the members of visiting symphony orchestras.
Their children are well-fed, rude and intelligent,
while alone in immense mysterious houses live the witches
who remember the coaches of the first city fathers.

A microcosm, something of a mosaic,
Always paradoxical, with scenery it has little to do.
And if you venerate antiquity or feel wiser
where there is history, you will, of course,
prefer Cambridge,
though even there the proportion of good people
to bad architecture is probably about the same.

From *The Collected Poems, 1955–1995*
(New York: Oxford University Press, 1996).

Ann Arbor, 1824 to the Present: A Collage

"Ann Arbor then had one house, a sort of frame, one story high. There was an additional log house, one story and a half high, no rafters nor roof on it. There was a tent north of the house. John Allen was putting up in the tent. Elisha W. Rumsey and wife occupied the house and entertained persons who came viewing land."

Thus did John Geddes remember Ann Arbor as he saw it for the first time in the summer of 1824. Although the settlement was then only five months old, it already had been designated by Governor Cass as "the seat of Justice" of Washtenaw County. "I presume that it is the most delightsome place for a county seat and an extensive village or city in the West," wrote Ezra Maynard on June 5, 1824. . . .

A traveler from Germany, Karl Neidhard, who visited Ann Arbor during the summer of 1834 wrote: "Six years ago he [John Allen] had considerably less than nothing. Now he lives like a prince in a magnificent house and his prosperity increases daily. No wonder! The half-acre lots which cost him seventy-five cents he is now selling for several hundred dollars."

Russell E. Bidlack, *John Allen and the Founding of Ann Arbor*,
Bulletin no. 12 (Ann Arbor: Michigan Historical Collections, 1962).

[circa 1830s] An old Indian used frequently to bring to Mrs. Dillon [of Ann Arbor] berries, venison, baskets, etc., which he wished to exchange for food or anything else she could get. Growing weary of his importunities, he was ordered to go away and not come again. While she was resting on a lounge beneath an open window one day, a swarthy face peered in above her and a guttural "boozhoo" sounded in her ears and startled her. She again ordered him away, but he insisted on having some food. Then she gave him a slice of bread and butter. But something had aroused his suspicions, and he asked her to taste of it herself, which she refused to do. He then went away muttering, threw the bread away, and was never seen afterward in that neighborhood.

Reminiscence of Mrs. Harriet L. Noble, in *History of Washtenaw County, Michigan* (Chicago: Chas. C. Chapman and Co., 1881).

[March 9, 1845] I arose quite unwell this morning on account of my toothache. Yet I was determined to be baptized today. It was a beautiful day. I went to the church and listened to a good sermon. The house was crowded to overflowing. There was a lot of students there—attracted no doubt by the curiosity of seeing me one of their number baptized. My tooth pained me during the whole day. After the sermon a vast multitude assembled on and by the bridge. Not only the Baptist congregation but the Methodist and Presbyterian congregations were there. Just before baptism a part of the bridge which was the most crowded fell and about 60 persons nearly all women and children were precipitated together into the river. As the bridge fell one yell arose from all the multitude—and then there was a rush—all were saved—and none were much hurt. All were wet and very much frightened. There was a great loss of fine clothes. It is a wonder that all escaped alive and uninjured. After the confusion had subsided seven of us were baptized. . . .

[March 11] . . . The accident at the bridge has led to much talk. A variety of stories was afloat about it—but the true one is that no one was seriously injured. It will have one effect as Elder Allen says it will make known the fact there is in Ann Arbor a Baptist church and that there are some who are willing to obey God.

Diary of George Washington Pray, Bentley Historical Library, Ann Arbor.

[circa 1857] The "campus," on which stood the four buildings then devoted to instruction, greatly disappointed me. It was a flat, square inclosure of forty acres, unkempt and wretched. Throughout its whole space there were not more than a score of trees outside the building sites allotted to professors; unsightly plank walls connected the buildings, and in every direction were meandering paths, which in dry weather were dusty and in wet weather muddy. Coming, as I did, from the glorious elms of Yale, all this distressed me, and one of my first questions was why no trees had been planted. The answer was that the soil was so hard and dry that none would grow. But on examining the territory in the neighborhood, especially the little inclosures about the pretty cottages of the town, I found fine large trees, and among them elms. At this, without permission from any one, I began planting trees within the university inclosure; established, on my own account, several avenues; and set out elms to overshadow them. Choosing my trees with care, carefully protecting and watering them during the first two years, and gradually adding to them a considerable number of evergreens, I preached practically the doctrine of adorning the campus. Gradually some of my students joined me; one class after another aided in securing trees and in planting them, others became interested, until, finally, the university authorities made me "superintendent of the grounds," and appropriated to my work the munificent sum of seventy-five dollars a year. So began the splendid growth which now surrounds those buildings. These trees became to me as my own children. Whenever I revisit Ann Arbor my first care is to go among them, to see how they prosper, and especially how certain peculiar examples are flourishing; and at my recent visit, forty-six years after their planting, I found one of the most beautiful academic groves to be seen in any part of the world.

Andrew Dickson White, Professor of History and English Literature at the University of Michigan, first president of Cornell University, and ambassador to Germany, *Autobiography* (New York, Century Co., 1905).

The students at the University of Michigan had been preparing for war since shortly before secession became an actuality. "Many who had planned for professional careers laid such things aside indefinitely and gave their every hour's spare time to military drills, counting all as uncertain or of little worth unless the Union were saved." Red, white, and blue became the favorite colors and the flag, which seems not to have been very prominent but a short time before, now came into display more often. This new patriotic surge was carried to extremes when a woman singer appearing with a group of entertainers at Hangsterfer's, the students' favorite hangout, came out one night draped in an American flag and sang the Star Spangled Banner. The students liked this so well that they demanded repeat performances each night. Several voluntary student companies were raised. The two or three students at the University from the South ridiculed the crude performances of these amateurs at war, but shortly these students left to fight with the South.

George S. May, "Ann Arbor and the Coming of the Civil War," *Michigan History* 35 (1952).

Your town, elevated and salubrious, is surpassed by none, equalled by few, in pleasantness of appearance, and in advantages both natural and social. Here factitious distinction founded upon ill-gotten wealth, too often joined with ignorance and pride, is not respected, and poverty is almost unknown, except a little occasioned by the use of intoxicating drinks by a few of our misguided people. The beauties of nature here are enhanced by art. Broad and regular streets, lined with neat and often elegant residences, embosomed in gardens and orchards, bespeak an intelligent and thriving people. Churches enough to accommodate at once all the inhabitants indicate proper attention to religion—while your spacious and palatial schoolhouses are an honor in which you surpass nearly all towns of your size and wealth, even in the oldest and best States of our country. In addition to all this, a University is situated in your city, which ought to be the pride of the State, a constant home of many intelligent and enterprising young men, from all parts of the country, where, you may say without boasting, the best advantages for thorough literary and mental culture that the country can secure are enjoyed. Have you not reason for yourselves and your children to be thankful?

E. O. Haven, President of the University of Michigan, *A Thanksgiving Discourse*, November 26, 1863.

[circa 1873] I have received all the letters you mention, but have only $16.00. Perhaps you have sent more and I have made some mistake. But I think not. Never mind. I'll pay it all back some time. I ought to settle my account here as soon as possible. If papa can send me money for the bills I shall be very glad. Provisions are very high, as usual in spring, and my bills are still more at the Club.

I have been just as economical as possible all the year, but of course the money you have been able to send hasn't been sufficient. We have had to burn a great deal of wood, as it has been and still is very cold; and my bill will be a little over $12.00. I had to get me a new pair of shoes.

You know I had only the cloth ones which I wore last summer. They lasted until this spring. I wore my blue hat just as it was all winter, and am wearing my old black one now. I got two yards of black ribbon and trimmed it myself. I bought a pair of cheap black kid gloves a few days ago, some lace for my neck and sleeves, and a fresh ribbon. I have got nothing I could do without; but you know I have to be dressed well all the time in the position I am in. I think I have all the books I shall need. They have cost me more than usual. But the most of the money you have sent has been paid for board.

If you can help me through this year I will try as best I may to take up the paddle and push my own canoe afterwards.

Letter from Alice Freeman Palmer, later President of
Wellesley College, from Ann Arbor, in George Herbert Palmer,
The Life of Alice Freeman Palmer (Boston: Houghton Mifflin, 1908).

[1901] "And when we shall have won this war—as we surely shall—we shall incorporate our present enemies, the Orange Free State and the Republic of the Transvaal, in the British Empire, conferring upon them, in due time the status of self-governing dominions, and bestowing upon their people the priceless benefits of the common law."

Boos and hisses followed this peroration just as they had punctuated the speaker's mention of British successes in the Great Boer War in South Africa, while tumultuous cheers greeted references to the successes of their enemies at Magersfontein and Colenso.

The speaker was the Honorable Winston Spencer Churchill, recently escaped from a Boer military prison in Pretoria and upon his return to England elected a member of Parliament by the constituency of Oldham; the date was January 9, 1901; the place, the auditorium of The University of Michigan in Ann Arbor; the audience, students of the University.

Still fresh in the minds of the audience were the national campaigns of 1900 and the charge of "imperialism" which the Democratic party had made to the policy of their Republican opponents with respect to the island possessions which Spain had surrendered to the United States by the Treaty of Paris.

An unfriendly, boisterous, and noisy crowd had confronted William Jennings Bryan, the Democratic candidate, when he appeared at the south portico of the old Ann Arbor court house for an address on the issues of the campaign. Mr. Bryan had bided his time until the crowd had momentarily exhausted itself, and then in that voice which in timbre and resonance no Stradivarius could emulate, he intoned, "If I were an imperialist I would call out a regiment and suppress you."

Taken by surprise, the crowd laughed, applauded, and then was silent, and Bryan proceeded with his denunciation of the Republican policy of imperialism. . . . This anti-imperialist mood had persisted among students, accounting for their unfriendly reception of Churchill.

I followed Mr. Churchill to his hotel—the "Cook House," as it was then known—and there approached his manager with a request for an interview for our college publication, *The Inlander*. The manager was not impressed; Mr. Churchill had just turned down an offer of $2,000 from a national magazine—if the college publication could raise that figure, Mr. Churchill might be interested—but, on my urging, he finally agreed to present my request to Mr. Churchill. In a few minutes he returned with the message that Mr. Churchill would see me, and he conducted me to his room.

Gustavus Ohlinger, "Winston Spencer Churchill: A Midnight Interview,"
Michigan Quarterly Review 5, no. 2 (spring 1966).

[circa 1910, drinking song still sung by the university glee club]

> I want to go back to Michigan
> To dear Ann Arbor town.
> Back to Joe's and the Orient,
> Back to some of the money I spent.
> I want to go back to Michigan,
> To dear Ann Arbor town.
> I want to go back,
> I've got to go back to Michigan.
>
> Father and mother pay all the bills,
> And we have all the fun,
> In the friendly rivalry of college life, Hooray!
> And we have to figure a hell of a lot
> To tell what we have done,
> With the coin we blew at dear old Michigan.

The Michigan Union Song Book, edited by Kent C. Haven '13,
University of Michigan Union, undated pamphlet.

The most vivid picture is of the enormous mass meeting in Hill Auditorium in April of 1917, preliminary to the departure of the Naval Reserve Unit [for service in World War I]. Never before had the American flag made such an impression on me as it did then, nor the Star Spangled Banner. Another war incident was a mass meeting for women held in the Natural Science Bldg., when we were discussing what Michigan student women should do. In the midst of the program, a Sophomore student, Rowena Bastian I believe, sprang to her feet, demanded the floor and started a fiery outburst against the horrors of war and urging everyone to join her against the present movement and for the Ideal of Peace. As President of the League, and presiding officer of the meeting, it was probably my first experience in trying to meet an emergency in public.

Margaret Reynolds, '17, memoir quoted in *Women's Voices: Early Years at the University of Michigan*, edited by Doris E. Attaway and Marjorie Rabe Barritt, Bulletin no. 47 (Ann Arbor: Bentley Historical Library), 2000.

[June 22, 1922, Robert Frost to John T. Bartlett] I'm still at Ann Arbor, Mich but the climax of annual improvements is about reached and it won't be many days before we book for home. . . .

This has been a year to wonder at. I don't know what I haven't done this year. I've had no assigned work as you may have heard. I've been supposed to have nothing to do but my writing and the University has been supposed to have nothing to do with me but take credit for my writing. In practice it has turned out humorously. I've been pretty busy dining out and talking informally on all occasions from club meetings to memorial services on the athletic field on Decoration Day. I have felt nonsensical at times. But it's the first year of an experiment. We want to find out if every college couldn't keep one artist or poet and the artist or poet and college be the better for the mutual obligation. There'll be less lionizing when the thing settles down and people get used to the idea. Miami University at Oxford Ohio has undertaken Percy Mackay[e] and Michigan University has undertaken me. That is as far as the idea has got yet. I'm probably coming back next year on a slightly modified plan. I am to be free to be clear away from the place for nine months out of the twelve. I've decided I would have to get very much done. I'll have a house here but it'll stand empty in memory of me most of the time.

Selected Letters of Robert Frost, edited by Lawrance Thompson (New York: Holt, Rinehart and Winston, 1964).

No address has greater power to stir me than 408 Thompson Street. It was at this magical address that I lived, on the second floor (front) of a rooming house in Ann Arbor, during the first year I spent at The University of Michigan. A short walk, and I was on the steps of the Library, or on the Diagonal, or in a little lunchroom called Van's; I was reading the books that were to mean most to me; I was seeing the friends who were to be remembered; I was having the cup of coffee and the toasted sweet rolls that tasted so much finer than they were. The world was just a few blocks around, and yet within it was everything I wanted to learn and everything the University wanted to teach me. Melvin T. Solve was there, and Lawrence Conrad, to tell me all there was to know about literature, and waiting for me somewhere in this tiny but comprehensive realm were history and philosophy and science—intimations of bliss. I did not doubt that this University, with its thousands upon thousands of students, knew I was on the campus, that Dean Alfred H. Lloyd, then Acting President, knew my name and was very specifically looking out for my welfare. I still don't doubt it. There are other places, surely, for other people, but for me there is one place, Ann Arbor, for there it was I discovered what life's bright possibilities were.

William Shawn '25–'27, Editor of the *New Yorker,* 1952–87, in *Our Michigan:*
An Anthology Celebrating the University of Michigan's Sesquicentennial,
edited by Erich A. Walter (Ann Arbor: University of Michigan, 1966).

[circa 1927] Annie climbed the wide steps and entered the library with the exultant reverence an art lover has entering the Louvre for the first time. She believed what Carl had told her—that there were more than a million books in the library.

The great vaulted rooms had the same grand smell the one-room library back there in Brooklyn had had: a mixture of ink, paste, leather, apples and wax; all dominated by a faint moss scent.

She went from room to room, floor to floor, stack to stack, reveling in books, books, books. She loved books. She loved them with her senses and her intellect. The way they smelled and looked; the way they felt in her hands; the way the pages seemed to murmur as she turned them. Everything there is in the world, she thought, is in books. Things that people said and did and the way they thought and acted even from away back. Away back! Long before Jesus was born, even. Everything that ever happened or could happen or didn't happen is in these books. Everything since the world began. . . .

Annie walked back across the campus, holding the books in her arm and swaying a bit, as she had seen the coeds do. Happily she believed she might be mistaken for a coed. She had to change her mind when some classes let out. Most of the coeds wore what was almost a uniform: dark pleated skirts, loose pull-over sweaters, a string of "pearls," saddle shoes and socks. Annie felt out of place in her city clothes. I'll never be one of them, she thought sadly. I'll never belong.

Betty Smith, Joy in the Morning (New York: Harper and Row, 1963).

[1930] We have had no drunken rows, no cases of wife beating, no children turned out of doors by drunken fathers, no disturbances of the peace and quiet of that beautiful city. We were told that if we abolished the saloons that grass would grow in the streets and business would be killed. Go out to Ann Arbor, and see the grass in the streets—if you can find any. But you can see the half a million dollars worth of commercial buildings that we have put up during the past three years in the business section—you can see the beautiful new subdivisions reaching out in every direction covered with fine residences; you can ride over the splendid pavements that we have put down; you can see every evening the laboring man and his family as well as nearly everyone else taking their evening ride in their automobile and enjoying the life that they could not enjoy when the saloon was taking a goodly portion of their daily wages. Never in the history of the city did whole families as a unit enjoy life as they are doing now. Go into our stores and ask the merchants whether or not their customers pay their bills more promptly than when the forty saloons were running in the city, and I don't believe you could find one in the whole city but what would give you an affirmative answer.

H. Wirt Newkirk, Mayor of Ann Arbor, from a
lecture on file in the Bentley Historical Library.

[circa 1932] Team morale was low. Then something happened to give us a needed lift. One of the best pass receivers on the team was a black track star named Willis Ward. He and I were close friends—we roomed together on trips out of town—and our friendship grew even closer during our senior year. Our next game was against Georgia Tech., an all-white school whose coach threatened to forfeit the contest if Willis played. Michigan tried to work out a compromise whereby both Willis and some Georgia Tech star would stay on the bench. Because I felt this was morally wrong, I called my stepfather and asked what I should do.

"I think you ought to do whatever the coaching staff decides is right," he said.

Still unsatisfied, I went to Willis himself. He urged me to play. "Look," he said, "the team's having a bad year. We've lost two games already and we probably won't win any more. You've got to play Saturday. You owe it to the team." I decided it was right. That Saturday afternoon we hit like never before and beat Georgia Tech 9–2.

Gerald R. Ford, *A Time to Heal: The Autobiography of
Gerald R. Ford* (New York: Harper and Row, 1979).

[February 9 and April 10, 1934, in a letter to his grandfather] Magazines have also gotten heavier, due largely to increased advertising by manufacturers of alcoholic beverages. Ann Arbor, which is very Republican, is dry again, and no beer is served after midnight. Nor are you allowed to dance and drink beer at the same time. But the state has opened a store where you can buy what you want during daylight hours. You see very little drinking. . . .

I feel so at home in my little Ann Arbor that I'm beginning to sink down roots here and have a hard time imagining my leaving it. But I am not doing anything very useful here.

Every now and then I feel strange when I think about how tiny my own country is and how large and wonderful America is. The best thing about America is that people here are not envious and they are not petty. Just imagine how much energy we waste at home [Sweden] by being suspicious of everything and everyone! Just think how unpleasant we make it for ourselves and everybody else by being pessimists instead of optimists!

Raoul Wallenberg, *Letters and Dispatches, 1924–1944*,
trans. Kjersti Board (New York: Arcade Publishing, 1995).

And so we arrived at Ann Arbor. It was not at all like Olivet. I had no idea it would be such an enormous place with so many students in it. All I really knew about Ann Arbor was that it was there that Avery Hopwood had left his money to found awards for those who were at the university and wanted to write in an original way. Poor Avery he had always wanted to write a great novel he did write something but they destroyed it, probably it was nothing but confusion at least so he said when I used to ask him about it and the man in the English Department who had charge of it asked me what advice could I give him about it. They did not know quite very well how to distribute the prizes.

The only suggestion I could make them would be that it would be rather amusing if they did with writers the way the Independent salon had done with painters. Suppose they let any one who wanted to write something write it and publish a huge volume of it every year not taking out anything and just see what it would be that they would be printing. But we do that he said we only take out what is manifestly not worth anything, ah yes I said but that is just it, who is to judge of that manifestly not worth anything. No the thing should be without jury and without reward which was the motto of the first salon d'independence, no one was a judge of what was or was not manifestly worth anything. It would have been rather fun if they had done it, I would have liked to read such a volume, but the minute anybody has judged of any of it anybody might just as well judge of all of it. Of course they have never done it. I do wish they had, it would have been a nice way to please Avery.

And then we went off in a plane back to Ohio.

Gertrude Stein, Everybody's Autobiography (New York: Random House, 1937).

[circa 1941] At breakfast we talked casually about Michigan, Wystan remarking on the faint bluish quality of the rural air. . . . Our house at 1223 Pontiac Trail was cozy when autumn rains pelted the windows, and during our talkative breakfasts Wystan puffed his Lucky smoke at the weeping panes and declared, "Lovely weather! Just lovely for writers and scholars." . . .

When we went to the then popular Flautz Tavern for beer and very good plain food, Wystan said, "This place is all right, but isn't there a *common* place where the, uh, workers go? A kind of beer hall?"

Yes, there was such a place, on Ashley Street near farm supply dealers, a big bare "café," and there we went on a gray autumn afternoon to sit among empty tables until a waitress approached, eyeing us warily. When I asked, "Have you any Canadian ale?" Wystan broke in, "Now, Charlie, none of that! We'll have just what the others are having! Two beers, please." The waitress's eyes had surveyed Wystan's unkempt Harris tweed jacket and unsoiled blue jeans, as well as my blazer with sport shirt, so she pinned onto us that invisible and damning label used by the Ann Arbor townspeople: "College crowd." . . .

Wystan was questing for his "common America," but I doubted that he'd find it on Ashley Street. Even my own authentic "commonality" was eroding in Ann Arbor. . . . [H]ere I was a Depression graduate, in the university of my choice, receiving Hopwood Awards and living in a comfortable studio house with an accomplished world poet. Of course I cherished my new status. And if Wystan quested for his "commonality" (allied in my mind with familiar Depression poverty) he was welcome to it. I willed it to him in discreet words while we sat self-consciously in this sad café.

Charles H. Miller, *Auden: An American Friendship*
(New York: Charles Scribner's Sons, 1983).

It was quite a coup in 1950 to get the foremost architect of the century to design a house for a young couple in Ann Arbor. [Mary and Bill] Palmer had no "in" with Frank Lloyd Wright; they just asked him. . . .

Mary wrote Wright a letter that concluded, "I hope you will design our house and we will not have to go to a lesser architect." Her mother, who lived in Raleigh, North Carolina, had told her that Wright was going to be lecturing at North Carolina State; so Mary suggested in her letter that they could meet there. Wright agreed.

The Palmers attended the lecture and then gave Wright a topographic map of their property. "He opened it and looked at it," Mary recalls. "Then he looked up, rolled it back up, and said, 'I'll design your house.' It was that simple." Not known for false modesty, Wright told them, "Wouldn't it be wonderful for your children to grow up in one of my houses?" . . .

Mr. Wright, as Mary Palmer calls him to this day, did not see the house until it was finished. She remembers his first visit: "He didn't look at the house. He went right to the piano and sat down and played." Asked what he played, she replies, "Something he composed extemporaneously."

Grace Shackman, "Design for Living," *Ann Arbor Observer*, April 2002.

⚕

Considering my indifferent academic performance in undergraduate school, I was admitted to the University of Michigan Law School with surprising ease. I took the aptitude test in August and by the first of September I was notified that I had been admitted. So I went back to Ann Arbor in September 1953.

One day in the first semester, I was totally confused in a course that we freshmen called "The Mystery Hour," where the faculty was experimenting in teaching Contracts, Equity, and Damages in one huge lump. I had understood virtually nothing of what went on in class, so I made an appointment with Professor William B. Harvey in hopes of clarifying the issues. He listened to my problem attentively. He was a small, precise man, whose Tennessee accent had been unaffected by his years of teaching in the North. He was also the law school's admissions officer.

Professor Harvey explained the essence of what he had been driving at, but although I paid close attention, his Southern accent distracted me. The South was a place I hated and feared and Southern accents from white faces made me cringe.

When I had sufficiently comprehended the course material, I expressed my nervousness over the fact that many people flunked out of law school the first year.

"I must have had the lowest undergraduate average in this class," I said to Mr. Harvey, fully expecting to be assured that that wasn't the case.

"That's right, Mr. Wilkins," the professor replied evenly.

My stomach turned.

"Well, why did you admit me?" I asked in a rage.

With no change in tone the Tennessean looked at me steadily and said, "If you had gone to some other college, you surely wouldn't have gotten in here. But we could check with your professors and we had some sense of your extracurricular activities. They all judged you to have far more academic ability than you displayed, so we took a chance.

"Now, why did we take a chance?" he continued, accent unabated.

"Well, it's because we here think the Negro people in this country need leaders—well-trained leaders. And we want to do our part in helping to train them. So we took a chance on you. Now that doesn't mean you won't have to do the work. You will. If you don't, you won't stay. But that's why we took a chance."

I left his office stunned by this Tennessee man who was the instrument of the law school's social conscience—the law school's affirmative-action program for 1953. So I worked hard enough to stay and did far better than I had done in undergraduate school.

Roger Wilkins, *A Man's Life: An Autobiography*
(New York: Simon and Schuster, 1982).

I think SDS [Students for a Democratic Society] was successful because its founding principle and its founding ideology was basically correct for the United States. It was non-dogmatic. It was understandable to people who had been brought up in this country. It spoke to people's needs and feelings. It linked them in a way which showed great perception. It had brilliant, indeed absolutely brilliant leadership. I'm talking of the Haydens, the Habers, the Flacks, the Rosses. I still consider those people among the most brilliant in the country from that generation. SDS was fortunate in pooling together an ideology and a group of people who could espouse that ideology in a way that was understandable to many people.

Barry Bluestone, in an interview with Bret Eynon, "The Turbulent 60's:
Ann Arbor in the Radical Vanguard," *Ann Arbor Observer*, February 1982.

For a while I considered using the name Pinocchio's. It had an Italian sound, and I remembered reading a statement by one of President Eisenhower's speechwriters that he used a lot of words containing p's because the letter sounds pleasing to the ear. . . . We must have gone through hundreds of different names. Most of them weren't even close.

One day in February, Jim Kennedy, who later became my top manager at Cross Street, came back from a delivery and burst in the door shouting, "Hey Tom, I've found our new name!"

"Yeah," I said. "What is it?"

"Domino's."

"That's it! That's it!" I yelled. I was so excited, I danced around like a kid. . . .

I had already talked to an advertising man named Sam Fine who was just launching his own agency in Ann Arbor. . . . He immediately began designing a logo for us. I had envisioned a black logo, because dominos are black. But he came up with a red domino and put three white dots on it, which he said represented our three stores.

"You can add a dot every time you add a new store," he said.

Tom Monaghan, with Robert Anderson,
Pizza Tiger (New York: Random House, 1986).

<p>

Mine is a pleasant, comfortable neighborhood in a pleasant, comfortable university town—Ann Arbor, Michigan. My neighborhood, called Burns Park, is a lower-upper-middle-class one, comprised of largish houses on quiet, shaded streets, inhabited largely by the professoriat of the University of Michigan, its apparatchiks and like-minded professionals. In its demographics, Burns Park is hardly a typical American middle-class enclave, as evidenced by the practice of one contentious colleague of flying the American flag on patriotic holidays so as, he claims, to annoy the neighbors. The level of education in Burns Park is much higher, of sophistication much greater, than the average suburban community: a residency requirement of, say, three college degrees per couple would not significantly diminish its population density. Subscriptions to the *New York Review of Books* outnumber substantially those to *Reader's Digest*, and now and again a book discussed in the former was written by someone in the neighborhood. Probably at least one member of each household watched *Middlemarch* on PBS and owns something by either Laura Ashley or Ralph Lauren. While one in nine Americans holds a passport, the ratio is much higher in Burns Park, where passports seem to be used with some frequency. In the little Italian village of San Gimignano a couple of summers ago, who should my wife and I run into but an artist acquaintance who lives a block away! Something of the ethnically unusual nature of the neighborhood may be suggested by the fact that, in the three years that I have been walking [a pony-sized Russian wolfhound named] Nina, three different people have stopped us to address her in Russian, which she listens to attentively and seems to understand—at least as well as English.

Like similarly constituted enclaves in Cambridge, or Palo Alto or Madison or Chapel Hill, Burns Park is resolutely secular. The Sunday morning ritual most devoutly observed, I suspect, is perusing the *New*

York Times, while weekly recycling represents our closest approximation to communion.

Gorman Beauchamp, "Dissing the Middle Class: The View from Burns Park," *American Scholar* 64, no. 3 (summer 1995).

Ann Arbor always feels smaller than it is, Anneke thought. Too big, at 120,000 people, to be an archetypal "sleepy college town," it nevertheless had avoided the ravages of urbanization. The University of Michigan, its core and raison d'etre, sprawled throughout the city, University buildings scattered in odd pockets from downtown to the outer neighborhoods.

It's the sort of city where the kid who hands you your fries at the Burger King has an IQ of 140 (and may some day walk on the moon); the sort of place where you can use the phrase "cognitive dissonance" in casual conversation. A city with an ego. Anneke remembered with amusement a time a few years ago when the football coach of another university had accused Ann Arbor of "arrogance." Shortly thereafter, bumper stickers blossomed on cars throughout the city, stickers that read "Arrogance is bliss."

Susan Holtzer, *Something to Kill For* (New York: St. Martin's, 1996).

Part Two

✿

Nineteenth-Century Perspectives

Grace Shackman

ℴℬ

from "The Underground Railroad in Ann Arbor"

*A few days since we had the rare pleasure, in connection with many
of our friends in this place, of bestowing our hospitalities upon six of
our brethren, who tarried with us some sixteen hours to refresh themselves, on their journey to a land of freedom.*
                                            —Signal of Liberty, May 12, 1841

The *Signal of Liberty* was the weekly newspaper of the Anti-Slavery
Party of Michigan. "This place" was Ann Arbor, where editor Guy
Beckley produced the paper from an office on Broadway.* The *Signal of
Liberty* was one of a series of Michigan papers that in the years before the
Civil War called for the abolition of slavery in the United States. On
May 12, 1841, it also provided a rare glimpse into Ann Arborites' prac-
tical efforts on behalf of escaped slaves: an article by Beckley and
Theodore Foster recording an escape from the Underground Railroad.

"Believing as we do that it is morally wrong to continue our fellow
beings in involuntary servitude, it is with the utmost pleasure that we
aid and assist them in their flight from southern kidnappers," Beckley
and Foster wrote. They described the fugitives as "from twenty-two to
thirty years of age—in good health and spirits and apparently much delighted with the prospect of a new home, where the sound of the whip
and clanking of chains will no longer grate upon their ears and mangle
and gall their limbs."

---

*Guy Beckley published the *Signal of Liberty* from an office in the Anson Brown Building on
Broadway (which today houses the St. Vincent de Paul store). His home, just a few blocks away
at 1425 Pontiac Trail, is the Ann Arbor structure most identified with the antislavery cause; it's
where school buses stop on historical field trips. A specific spot for hiding fugitives has never been
found in his house, although a back part has been torn down. It's possible that because Beckley
was so publicly identified with the Underground Railroad, fugitives were hidden elsewhere if a
danger was perceived. An ordained minister, Beckley moved to Ann Arbor in 1839, remaining
active in the abolitionist cause until his death in 1847.

According to a follow-up story on May 19, the escaped slaves successfully completed the final leg of their journey to freedom in Canada. "We take great pleasure in announcing to our readers that they have all landed, as we intended they should, safe on British soil," Beckley and Foster wrote. Today's Canada was still a group of British possessions then, and slavery was illegal, but slaveholders still had the right to apprehend escapees; in what is now Ontario, however, the attorney general had ruled that any person on Canadian soil was automatically free.

That promise made Canada the destination of choice for blacks who escaped in the South. The Underground Railroad was a network of sympathetic northerners who helped the fugitives on their way once they reached the free states. There are several stories about the origin of the Underground Railroad's name, but all point to situations in which slave hunters had been hot on the trail of fugitives, only to have the prey disappear as completely as if they had gone underground. Extending the metaphor, the escapees were referred to as "passengers" or sometimes "baggage," while the helpers along the way were "conductors" and the stopping points "stations." . . .

Two of the railroad's "lines" crossed in Ann Arbor, and from the *Signal of Liberty* article and other sources we know that fugitives passed through here on their way to Canada. But beyond that, there is much we do not know and probably never will. . . .

Beckley and Foster knew that their neighbors in Ann Arbor were divided over abolition. An Anti-Slavery Society was formed in 1836, and some religious groups, particularly Quakers and Wesleyan Methodists, were devoted to the cause. Ann Arbor's First Congregational Church was founded in 1847 by former members of First Presbyterian, who broke away in part because they wanted to take a stronger stand against slavery. But there was also a significant number who were not supporters of the cause.

"Our neighbors accuse us of being 'worse than horse thieves,' because we have given to the colored man a helping hand in his perilous journey," Beckley and Foster wrote. "We are also held up as transgressors of the law and having no regard for the civil authority."

As late as 1861, a speech by Parker Pillsbury, a noted abolitionist, was broken up by a mob. Speaking at a church at 410 North State Street (still standing, the building is now a private residence), Pillsbury had to escape out a back window, followed by his audience. The attack so unnerved other area churches that most of them closed their doors to another anti-slavery speaker, Wendell Phillips, when he came to town later that year. (The Congregationalists agreed to let him speak, but only after a special vote of the trustees.)

Despite these mixed feelings, no record has been found that Ann Arbor residents ever returned a fugitive slave. Slaves were in more danger from their former owners, and from bounty hunters, who sought to collect large rewards for their capture. The situation worsened after 1850, when a new Fugitive Slave Act was passed. It swept away all due process for blacks accused of being runaway slaves, increased penalties for helping escapees, and made it a crime for local law enforcers not to return slaves.

Even free blacks, of whom there were 231 in Washtenaw County in 1850, were not safe from the slave hunters. Laura Haviland, an abolitionist from Adrian, wrote about one such case in her 1881 memoir, *A Woman's Life*. In the 1840s, Haviland writes, she helped a fugitive couple named Elsie and William Hamilton. The Hamiltons left Adrian after their former owner appeared and tried to recapture them, moving to several other places, including "a farm near Ypsilanti, for a few years." According to Haviland, the Hamiltons had left Ypsilanti by 1850, but their former owner, believing they were still there, sent his son north to capture them. The son didn't find the Hamiltons, but he did find a family of free blacks, the David Gordons, who came close to the description he had of the Hamilton family. Claiming the Gordons were the Hamiltons, the slave owner's son demanded their arrest. Antislavery activists helped the Gordons confirm their freedom.

Most of the fugitives who passed through Michigan came from states directly to the south. (Slaves escaping from the more easterly southern states could go through Pennsylvania and New York, or on a ship along the coast.) "The fugitives came from various localities in the slave states, but most of those who passed on this line were from Kentucky, some were from Missouri and occasionally from the far south," reminisced Nathan Thomas, the conductor from Schoolcraft, south of Kalamazoo, in a letter he wrote in 1882. In another 1841 article, Foster and Beckley mention a fugitive "from the lead mines of Missouri."

The line Thomas was referring to went east and west across the state, roughly along the route of today's I–94. Fugitives usually came north from Quaker settlements in Indiana to Cassopolis, near Niles, where there was another Quaker settlement. They then traveled east through Battle Creek, Jackson, and Ann Arbor. A north-south route came from Toledo (where James Ashley, founder of the Ann Arbor Railroad, was an active member) to Adrian, an important hub where Haviland and a group of fellow Quakers ran a school, the Raisin Institute, for students of all colors. Refugees traveled from Adrian to Clinton and thence through Saline to Ann Arbor or Ypsilanti. From Washtenaw County, fugitives went on to Detroit, where they would cross the Detroit River at night in rowboats. Later, when the Detroit River was too closely watched, the route shifted northward to cross the St. Clair River. . . .

It is estimated that 40,000 former slaves and their families were living in Canada at the time of the Civil War. About half of them eventually moved back to the United States. They came over a period of decades to rejoin family, to return to a warmer climate, or to pursue jobs or education. In her memoir, Laura Haviland mentions a former slave named John White who after emancipation "removed to Ann Arbor, Michigan to educate his children."

Many Ann Arbor families trace their descent to these black Canadians. The local black Elks Lodge, according to member William Hampton, "was formed by a group mostly from Canada." Several well-known historic figures, including Charles Baker, co-owner of the Ann Arbor Foundry, and Claude Brown, who ran a secondhand store in the Main Street building that now houses Laky's Salon, came to Ann Arbor from Canada.

Ann Arbor Observer, December 1998.

Old Okemos

In May, 1859, Old Okemos, nephew of Pontiac, the Chief of the Pottawatomies, passed to the Indian heaven. He is remembered by the early settlers of Ann Arbor by his regular visits to town, his fine horsemanship, and the long train of squaws and ponies in single file following at his horse's tail, laden with the fruits of the chase, and the endless *mocock* of Indian sugar, ready for a trade for all sorts of traps and edibles. Even the females of the early settlers were quite willing to allow the old Chief, with his numerous progeny, a quiet smoke by the fireside, or a *wabunk* upon the kitchen floor, as an offset for the convenience of this traveling market of *suceasee* and *pokamin* (venison and cranberries), the staple article of his trade, for the Chief was merchant, as well as the governor, judge, jury, and general depository of the secrets of his tribe.

Old Okemos, though terrible in battle—as his cloven skull and numerous scars are proof positive that he had seen service—was gentle as a child when off duty. He made himself extremely interesting to the *Chomokoman papooses* who always gathered around him, and lost no opportunity of initiating them into the mysteries of the pure aboriginal language.

The evidences of aboriginal universal knowledge are extremely rare, because such knowledge is deemed among them a tribal secret which is felony to disclose. These evidences are, however, much more numerous than the public are aware of, from the fact that American archaeologists have grouped the various evidences of Indian skill, labor, or ingenuity, and upon these evidences have founded the visionary theory that the American continent was inhabited by a semi-civilized race, long since extinct.

Old Okemos was never known to forfeit his word or betray his friends but once, and then only when gratitude for numerous favors had induced him to betray his tribal secrets.

In the fall of 1827, Brown & Co. established at Ann Arbor a store for the sale of general merchandise. Old Okemos, after having bestowed upon the senior Brown the Indian christening of *Tichisquie* (Long-legs) became a regular customer. By virtue of being the principal trader, the Chief received numerous presents, and was allowed to spread his blanket and pass the night upon the store floor, while N. I. Brown, the clerk, slept near by. Upon one of these occasions, when the village had retired to rest, Okemos called up young Brown and informed him that he had a great secret to tell him. Holding to the light a silver half dollar, and pointing to the northwest, he proceeded to state that away in that direction, six days' travel, there was plenty of silver in the earth. Brown listened to him and agreed, upon his next visit, to purchase of him a horse and accompany him to the place of silver in the earth. Some two weeks after, Okemos came down alone, leading an extra horse. Necessary preparations were made during the night, and at day-light, next morning, Brown with blankets and provisions, and the Chief with an extra keg of fire-water, were on their way to the silver mine.

Taking their route to the northwest, toward the copper region, where silver has been found in small quantities, nothing of interest occurred until the third day, when the old Chief became moody and cross. Just before sunset he seemed to awake from a deep reflection—making the woods ring with his yells, and putting his horse to the top of his speed, was soon out of sight. Brown pursued until night, when dismounting, leading his horse and keeping the trail with his feet, he kept on his course. Late in the evening he came upon an Indian camp with Okemos in the center, and all of them intoxicated. Brown passed on a short distance, and, holding his horse by the bridle, passed the night. Going to the camp in the morning, he found the Indians in a sulky mood taunting Okemos with his treachery, and calling him a bad Indian. The old Chief, with numerous threats and flourishes with his scalping knife, ordered the "papoose" to *wachee wigwam*.

Brown, aware that the game was up, mounted his horse and made a long reach for home. At night, after holding his horse in the grass for a feed, he made him fast to a sapling, and testing the quality of his salt provisions, and rolling himself in his blanket, was soon in a sound sleep. Worn down with his long ride and vigils of the previous night, he did not wake the next morning until the sun was high in the heavens, when his horse, unused to be kept from the herd, had broken his fastenings and left. A slight meal of raw pork and crackers answered Brown's purpose, as he figured on his position—two days out from any settlement and without a horse. There was, however, no time to be lost. Throwing his provisions over one shoulder and his blanket over the other, he took his horse's track and started in search. A few hours of eager pursuit brought him up with the horse, which he succeeded in capturing. Finding it impossible to follow, on horseback, his back trail, he gave up the attempt and was soon lost in the woods, but traveled at the top of his horse's speed, not knowing whether he was in the right direction or not.

In the early settlement of Ann Arbor, widow Stratton, with her family, occupied the farm one mile south of the city. Her second son, Samuel Stratton, then some 20 years of age, was subject to occasional fits of insanity. When the fit was upon him, he would take to the woods, and, subsisting only on berries and roots, in one or two weeks starve it out and return entirely sane.

At the time of young Brown's hunt for the silver mine, Stratton had been absent about two weeks, his friends supposing he had wandered off a great distance and probably starved. Stratton says that in the afternoon he saw Brown riding in an opening, in a circle, at full speed, and knowing, from his actions, he was lost, took his station behind a tree to give him a good scare; so, as the horse came round, he broke out after him, yelling a million murders. He then left the circle and made a straight break for the woods. The pony, equally frightened with the rider, ran into a swamp, and sinking down, stuck fast. Brown gave it up; there was the devil, for he had seen him. Turning in his saddle to take a fair look, Stratton, nude as he was born, and out-grimacing the arch-fiend of evil, was standing at his horse's tail, and with a hoarse laugh roared out: "Brown, don't you know me?"

Stratton says, that as soon as Brown was able to speak, he quietly remarked:

"Look here, Mister, do you know the way out of these woods?"

"Of course," replied Stratton.

"Well, then," said Brown, "do you just take me home, and you shall have the best suit of clothes in the store."

"Done," said Stratton. "How's the provisions?"

Stratton swept the pile, at least four pounds of pork and crackers to match, and throwing Brown's blanket over his shoulders, they took a bee-line for home. Coming to a settlement the next day, Stratton stayed out, holding Brown's horse, while Brown went in, and after purchasing a suit of half worn clothes, ordered dinner for four.

"Why, do you think I'm so stingy?" said the old lady.

"Never mind," said Brown, "set on the victuals."

Afterward, when the old lady was looking on and observing the destruction of her winter stores, she exclaimed, "I shall charge for *four!*"

Finishing their meal they arrived in town late in the evening. Brown resumed the duties of his clerkship, and Stratton appeared the best dressed man in the streets.

Brown never abandoned his ideal silver mine, but sought it afterward above the surface. A few years after, he bought several of the most valuable locations in the Grand River valley, including the grindstone ledge in Eaton county, and the first stone coal discovered in the State; also a valuable tract of fine timber with water power upon Buck creek, Kent county, upon which he immediately erected mills, and ran the first raft of lumber on Grand River, thus commencing the Michigan and Chicago lumber trade, which has since increased to hundreds of millions.

Okemos, ashamed of his perfidy never after recognized acquaintance, or entered the store of Brown & Co., but took his *netos* and bartered his furs at the rival store of General Clark.

From *The History of Washtenaw County* (Chicago: Chas. C. Chapman, 1881).

E. O. Haven

☙

from "Address Delivered to the Medical Class at the University of Michigan, 1869"

The true relations of medical science to a great university may not be properly understood. A university does not establish a department of medicine and surgery primarily to supply the community with doctors, nor a department of law primarily to supply lawyers. Its true object is deeper and broader than this. A university is a part of the essential machinery of a perfect civilization. It is, in a certain sense, the heart of the State, where vital forces are to be gathered, and whence they are to go out again purified to the extremities. It is the sensorium, whither are to be brought by afferent nerves all elements of intelligence, to flow out again systematised and instinct with reason. The education of the schools cannot be perfect without institutions that are unlimited from above, where the freest thought and the most unrestricted investigation are both obtained and encouraged. From such universities will go out many men fitted to act as doctors, lawyers, ministers, teachers, editors, authors, engineers, chemists, farmers, navigators, artists, mechanics, and in all the various channels in which a disciplined mind works out its practical results; but to produce any of these particular classes of men is not its profoundest purpose. It is rather to grasp and present the thought which spontaneously takes this shape, and also diffuses itself among all classes of the people. The efficiency of a university is not to be estimated by the number of its graduates, but by its contributions to the cultivated mind of the nation. Its students should seek in it not merely access to a profession, or a recommendation that may be of pecuniary value to them, or social eminence, but knowledge and power. Its professors should contribute to the public welfare, not merely by increasing the number of respectably prepared professional men, but by healthily stimulating thought, and directing investigation. Degrees can be obtained in many places cheaper and easier than from us, but it should not be our ambition to increase the number of our alumni or students. We propose or should propose to secure the substance, leaving what is properly called accidental to adjust itself. Universities are the places where the abundant material gathered in actual practice and by toilers in special fields should be collected and generalised, and made to yield its best results. Nearly all of the first class authors in all branches of thorough investigation are university professors. Upon them self-made men, so called, as well as their students, depend for instruction, and by means of their books they give the fruit of their investigation to the community. Universities have therefore two great objects—the diffusion of science already acquired, and to make constant addition to the common stock. The former object it is not difficult to accomplish. Fluent repeaters of what every well informed man in the profession knows are easily procured. It is not difficult to establish a medical school whose simple purpose is, by two brief courses of lectures, to introduce young men into the rank of doctors, without any reference to their general education or fitness for such a responsible office. But to create a true university, with libraries and museums that shall contain all the information and means of illustration that the most accomplished scholars require, together with professors able to use this material, and who shall be utterly independent of mercenary motives, who shall not seek large classes so much as thoroughly disciplined students, and whose controlling ambition it is to promote the most comprehensive culture—this is no easy task. The teachings of our country are against it. Prevailing customs are against it. A tendency to superficiality, and a wish to wear honors without earning them, are against it. Many false motives must be resisted, and the counsels of trained conservatives, who look only for a constant reproduction of the past, must be disregarded.

It is desirable that the department of medicine and surgery of the University of Michigan should have its post-graduate studies and students as well as the other departments. It should be a place which the strong men of the profession should visit to prosecute their inquiries beyond the common range of elementary instruction. Results should be sought that will not be estimated by their quantity. Not to attract the applause of the people but to benefit them, should be our highest aim. Such a university is necessarily of a slow growth. It should increase with age, though its advancement may be especially rapid in a new country.

On this occasion, when the Regents and Faculties are together for the first time after the first considerable grant of pecuniary aid from the State to the university, I deem it peculiarly proper to express our profound gratitude for this manifestation of intelligent appreciation and approval. The representatives of the people have thus endorsed this institution. The State now asserts its right to the honor which this great school has conferred upon its name. It endorses the principle that a university is an essential part of its educational system. Granting the addition of more than two hundred thousand dollars to its permanent capital, it has substantially announced that so long as the university uses its means economically and efficiently it shall be sustained. I have no fears that this act will ever be repealed. On the other hand, as the State increases in population and wealth, and as our alumni go forth in increasing numbers to carry with them the intelligence and patriotism and preparation for increased usefulness and influence here obtained and strengthened, the act to which we refer will be appealed to as a wise and healthful precedent for still greater generosity. This department of the university will derive its share of profit from this wise public assistance. If a hospital is needed, and it can be shown that a hospital will succeed here, and that many patients will be attracted hither to avail themselves of the science and skill of our professors, then a hospital will be founded. A flourishing school of pharmacy has already been opened. From time to time such professorships as are demanded will be established. We have here no predetermined theory to carry out. We are not attempting to make the University of Michigan a German university, or the copy of any other. We do not commit ourselves to any narrow creed. We do not seek any "new education" that is illiberally "scientific," nor adhere to any old education that is illiberally "classical." We believe that narrowness of any kind, even though it is a reaction against other narrowness, begets bigotry. We believe in the safety and omnipotence of truth in a fair field. If any theorizers in the closet, or having only scanty facts to judge from, assert that various tastes and talents cannot be gratified and various good purposes be sought, in one great university, by various parallel or independent courses of study, not interfering with but actually sustaining each other, we place their lucubrations with all others of their kind, that have been proved false by actual experience.

That religion which embraces the essentials, while it allows a variety of taste to adjust the drapery, most commands our approbation. We are seeking to avoid old errors without falling into new ones. That some temporary disappointments and failures will not happen we cannot suppose, but judging from the past, we look for increasing success while we put our trust in God and his truth.

Young gentlemen, the university now enrolls you among her alumni. She has confidence in your ability and expects you to succeed. I doubt not that your reliance is not solely on science, nor on nature, but that you recognise as sustaining all things and infusing them with life, that infinite

Power and Wisdom and Justice whom we adore as God, and whose ministers we are, and whose beneficent purposes we hope to execute and enjoy both in this short life and in a life to come. Much as I rejoice in the external reputation and internal prosperity of this university, most of all am I grateful to God that in a university, requiring of its students subscription to no religious creed drawn up in human speech, and embracing in its numerous Faculty men of various professions and associations, and among its students many hundreds of young men from many States and even different nations, attracted hither solely by a desire for mental discipline and information, such substantial harmony of conviction and feeling on the great subject of morality and religion prevails, and that the combined public opinion of the University is so clearly against vice, and in behalf of the religion of Christ. So let it ever be, and more so. Let it be a place where human law is analyzed and the divine law obeyed; where the fearful mysteries of bodily and mental disease are investigated and all known remedies are studied, and where moral and spiritual health are duly prized; and where, while all the pathways of thought are traced out, they shall be found to terminate in the divinely announced fulfillment of all law and all teaching—love to God and love to man.

Pamphlet published in Ann Arbor by Dr. Chase's
Steamfitting House, 41 and 43 N. Main Street, 1869.

Justin McCarthy

from *Dear Lady Disdain*

New Padua is a university town. But let not any one be deceived by the name into fancying that New Padua is anything like Oxford, or Bonn, or even for that matter like Cambridge in Massachusetts, where the University of Harvard is situated. New Padua is the seat of what people in England would call a great popular college rather than a university; a college founded by the State, of which it is the educational centre, with special reference to the needs of the somewhat rough and vigorous Western youth who are likely to pour in there. The city of New Padua belongs to a State which not very long ago used to be described as Western, but which the rapid upspringing of communities lying far nearer to the setting sun has converted into a middle State now. The town is very small and very quiet; remarkably intelligent and pleasant. The society, and indeed almost the population, is composed of the professors and officials of the college, with their wives and daughters; the judges and magistrates; the railway authorities; the Federal officials; the students; and the editors of the newspapers. It is a sort of professional population all throughout.

The professors of the university are mostly men of mark and high culture. One or two are Germans, one or two Italians; one is French. Of the American professors, two at least bear names distinguished even in Europe, and one of these is our friend Mr. Clinton, who is Professor of Astronomy and is in charge of the Observatory.* Like almost all Americans, Professor Clinton is something of a politician. He contributes occasional

---

*Editor's note: The unmistakable model for Professor Clinton is James Craig Watson, Professor of Astronomy and Director of the Observatory at the University of Michigan. McCarthy would have become acquainted with Watson on one or more of his visits to the university during his lecture tours of the United States from 1868 to 1871.

President James B. Angell wrote of Watson: "In teaching he had none of the methods of the drill master. But his lecture or his talk was so stimulating that one could not but learn and love to learn by listening. Sometimes while discussing an intricate problem he would suddenly have an entirely new demonstration flash upon his mind as if by inspiration and then and there he would write it out upon the blackboard" (*The Reminiscences of James Burrill Angell* [London: Longmans, Green, 1912]).

articles to the *North American Review*, and writes not a little on European affairs in one of the New Padua journals.

It was this latter connection which enabled him to be of service to Nathaniel. When the young man had been a few days in his house, and he saw that there was really a certain amount of literary capacity about him for a great deal of energy, Clinton obtained for him an engagement on one of the New Padua papers, told the editor he would find a useful man in Nat provided he worked him hard enough to work all the nonsense out of him and get pretty quickly down to the good stuff at the bottom. Thus Professor Clinton started Nathaniel fairly in a new career, liking the lad with a sort of good-humored and half-contemptuous feeling, and continuing always kind to him. Professor Clinton's house was always open to Nat. Many a night when Clinton's wife and sister-in-law (he had no children) had gone to bed, he would start out with Nat for a long walk by the river, and would listen with kindly tolerance to Nat's theories and hopes, and ambition and nonsense. Professor Clinton had made in his own way all the success that was open to him, and he regarded it modestly, knowing that in the world's eyes it was not much, but finding it enough for him. It pleased him to do kind things and to note the human weaknesses of those whom he served, and Natty's absurdities had a sort of interest for him. . . .

One memorable day Nathaniel walked from the office of his journal towards the university grounds. These stood on an elevated plain a little outside the town, a simply laid out enclosure with broad oblong blocks of buildings, bare almost as a barrack, but deriving a certain picturesqueness from the situation. For standing on almost any spot of the university grounds one could look on the river winding between the hills and bluffs, and dotted here and there with little islets, each feathered and tufted with trees. The peculiarity of the scene was that the town was set back from the river and sheltered in between the bluffs, which made the river's bank, and an inland range of low and rolling hills. So when you stood upon the university grounds and turned your back upon the university buildings you saw only the river, lonely, with no sign of growing civilisation on its banks, looking as it must have looked when the red man shot along it in his canoe. The very soul and spirit of solitude might at certain soft sweet evening hours have seemed to abide there.

The melancholy beauty of the Indian summer was on the foliage and the water and in the sky this evening when Nat Cramp entered the university grounds. As he passed along a glimpse of the river attracted him, and he stood at the edge of the collegiate demesne and looked upon the scene. Its beauty touched him. He did not in general think much about inanimate nature; his own concerns occupied him far too much. His little self-conceits and strivings and humiliations filled his eyes and blinded them against the charms of trees and water, skies, stars, and flowers, as dust might have done. His poetry had always been only egotistical emotion put into inflated rhythm, and his eloquence was phrase. But he was for the moment stolen from himself by the quiet charm of that scene. The river flowing slowly eastward seemed to speak to him somehow of home, and there began to descend into his soul, mingled up with much feeling of baffled egotism and of hopeless love, a kind of salutary sense that he, Nathaniel Cramp, was in general little better than sham and an Ass. . . .

Society in New Padua seldom spread itself out much. People had pleasant evenings in each other's houses, where they ate ice-creams even in the depth of winter, and apples, and drank tea, and looked at engravings, and had bright, genial conversation—such genuine conversation, fair interchange of ideas on letters and art and things in general, as one only reads of now in England; and they went home early. The ladies came very plainly dressed on most of these occasions, and if a lady who had walked with her husband from her home appeared in the drawing-room in her hat or bonnet nobody considered it odd or unseemly. Only on rare occasions did the gentlemen come in evening dress. But this reception of the English travellers at the university rooms was to be quite an exceptional thing, and every lady who had been to Europe that year, or who had got any dresses home from Paris, was delighted to have an opportunity of making a little display. Really the feminine beauty of New Padua was well worth looking at, even in its undress. Perhaps it ought not be called New Padua beauty for there were no born New Paduans yet grown up. Twenty years ago there was no such place as New Padua.

The university had gathered a community about it from all quarters. The principal judge and his wife were natives of the State indeed, but came from its largest town a hundred miles away. The president of the university came from New York. His wife, still a fine woman, though passing her prime, was from Maryland. Professor Benjamin was from Ohio; his wife had drawn her early breath within sight of Boston Common. Our friend Clinton was a Vermonter, married to a lady from Illinois. The various foreign professors already referred to had some of them foreign wives; and the editor of the journal to which Mr. Cramp was attached had once been United States consul at Athens, and had brought home to New Padua a countrywoman of Sappho as his wife. . . .

Had he the time for such emotions he might have wondered at the transformed appearance of the library; at the lights, the flowers, the green wreaths and festoons of leaves—above all, the company. Could these be the quiet and unpretentious dames and demoiselles of New Padua, these ladies of the floating silks, the jewels, the bracelets, the laces, the wonderful structures of hair? Nat felt doubtful whether he should be justified in speaking to Professor Clinton's sister-in-law, unless she should previously recognise him—she looked such a different sort of personage in a blue silk dress and a train, and with white arms bare. True he had often seen the white arms still more bare than that, when she was engaged in her simple and undisguised occupation of helping to make bread and piecrust, and to cut up apples in Professor Clinton's modest household. What a grand lady she looks now, Nat thought. But indeed, she looked a lady always, he said to himself; and in her home of late he always called her "Minnie," as her folks and friends did. . . .

"Then you're settled here for good, Natty?"

"I don't know that, Miss Challoner; I like this place, and the people are kind to me—but it is narrow and small. Not much of a career here, Miss Challoner, for a man's ambition; and in this country one feels that he has a career open to him if he has intellect and courage," Nat added, with careless grandeur.

"Oh, I didn't mean New Padua. I didn't suppose you would stay here always, although it seems a delightful little place. So full of quiet and simplicity; and people only caring about books and education, and not about making money and getting on in the world. But I know, of course, that men must have ambition" (and Natty for the moment whimsically presented himself to Marie's mind in the form of one of those seals swarming up and down the rocks near San Francisco), "and I only meant that you were settled in the States."

From *Dear Lady Disdain* (1876; London and Glasgow: Collins' Clear Type Press, 1908).

Olive San Louie Anderson

❦

from An American Girl, and Her
Four Years in a Boys' College

The glorious hour has come at last—
Sophomores, we're sophomores!
—College Song-Book

"By Zeus! we're euchred, Sandy, and it all comes of introducing that topic of the girls. I can't play cards and discuss them too, so let's throw up the cards and make the discussion general. I propose the question: 'Our girls, are they a fizzle or not?—affirmative, Randolf and Sanderson; negative, Burton and Crooks; how's that Ran?'"

"Don't bother me with any questions about college-girls, for I'm sick of hearing them discussed. Every one I met all summer button-holed me about the girls in college; did I like them, and did they keep up in the class, and were they pretty and womanly, or homely and masculine, and had I fallen in love with any of them—till I swear I never wanted to see a petticoat again!"

"I was bored that way, too," said Crooks, "but I puffed 'em up, I tell you; for, on the whole, I think it was a good move for the institution to let 'em come."

This conversation came from an upper room in Fifth Street, where four gay young sophomores were assembled to have a good time, and talk over prospects for the year that had just opened. Randolf, the largest of the four, would have been handsome but for a supercilious and cynical look that he always wore; he was an excellent student, and plunged into everything with a sort of desperate enthusiasm, so that the girls, among themselves, had dubbed him "The Devouring Element." Charles Burton was two years his junior, a tall fellow, with a fine sensitive face and scholarly bearing, who, when the conversation took the present turn, sat with an amused smile, but said nothing, until Crooks, a jolly fellow, about whose face there was nothing striking, turned to him with—"Burton, we have not heard from you yet."

"Oh," said Randolf, with a curl of his mustached lip, "Charlie is in the situation of a fellow when he has married one of the girls in a family, and so is bound to stick up for all the rest, good, bad, and indifferent; of course, he will vote their whole ticket."

"As to that," said Burton, blushing; "I have not changed my first position in regard to co-education by acquaintance with the girls here, and if I had forty sisters I would have them all here."

"Come, come," said Frank Sanderson, a merry-faced boy with red cheeks and black eyes that sparkled with fun, "your talk is too general, and we must come down to particulars—that is, to the girls of '70. We'll take them in alphabetical order. I'll do Misses Allston and Bowers," and, lifting his eyes with a mock-heroic air, he said, "O my Muse, wilt thou vouchsafe to mortal man to sing the praises of his Mary Ann!" and then he continued: "I hear Miss Allston is a splendid dancer, and I'm dying to get an introduction to her; and isn't she pretty though, her lips look like fresh strawberries, and wouldn't I like to kiss her; and, in short, she is a decided success, for she gets her lessons first-rate—not one of your digging sort, but light, airy, fairy-like, you know. Then Miss Bowers enjoys the distinction of being the homeliest girl I ever saw, but she doubtless has the feminine virtues in excess to make up for it—scholarship faultless, etc. There, Crooks, you take Misses Collins and Davidson."

"Well, boys, I'm going to get out my Greek for to-morrow," said Randolf, going to the table and taking the lexicon and a copy of Homer, "for Old Toughy will invoke the Muses in a different way, if we don't know all the Homeric forms"; and he pretended to hear no more of the conversation.

"I'm not poetical like you, Sandy, so I'll do mine in plain prose," said Crooks. "Miss Collins strikes me as being a very sensible sort of girl, and don't you remember her elegant translations in Thucydides? I used to wish that I could run words off my tongue as she did; as to Miss Davidson, I don't know much, for she did not recite in my section, but she has magnificent hair and complexion, which will carry her through. But *my* favorite among the college-girls, is Nelly Holmes."

"Stop! you are ahead of time," said Sanderson, "for we next come to the *chef-d'oeuvre* of the class of '70, the Queen of the Amazons, the 'coming woman,' Miss Will Elliott, and no one of us can do the subject justice but Randolf," and he nudged Crooks's elbow. Randolf looked up and frowned.

"Don't get me started on her, for I can't bear her style."

"She admires *you* anyway, and that shows good taste, for she was anxious to have an introduction to you last year," said Burton, winking at the others.

"She does?" said Randolf, feeling flattered; "well, I'll not throw myself under her chariot-wheels; why, I'm afraid of her: she is brilliant and all that, but so cold and sarcastic and independent, and then she has such a way of aping boys; her very name is boyish—'Will'; if she wants to shorten Wilhelmine, why don't she have it Mina or Minnie, or something feminine? Then her hats are always the same boyish style. You know we fellows don't like to see anything in any woman that we would not want to see in the woman we would marry; and I'd as soon think of marrying an iceberg or the north-pole as Miss Elliott. She is the first girl that I can't understand; she sets herself on a pedestal, and she may stay there, for all o' me."

"I think you entirely misjudge her," said Burton, warmly; "for I had an excellent opportunity of becoming acquainted with her last year, and I do not think there is another girl in the class that has more real womanly feeling than Miss Elliott; and as to her independent ways, I admire them, for they are out of the common run, and her hats are peculiarly becoming to her style, the broad brim and high crown *à la Kossuth*. It seems to me it is time for us to lay aside the prejudice that requires women to be cast in the same mould. I think Miss Elliott a splendid specimen of a sound, healthy girl, morally and physically."

"So say we all of us," said Sandy. "By-the-way, I hear she has lost a favorite sister; you remember she was called home before last term was out; perhaps that will soften her to the consistency Randolf likes."

"I shall be careful not to get into her clutches," said the latter worthy.

"How nonsensically you talk," said Burton, "Will Elliott, of all others, is the last to want to clutch you or any one else. I think her independence of masculine help is perfectly sublime. Ran wants a girl to twine around him, for he is still befuddled with the oak-and-vine picture."

"Don't let us show so much disposition, boys," said Sanderson; "I hear Misses Fitzgerald and Baker are not to return—one has gone to Europe, and the other's father has failed, so that leaves only seven of the fair sex."

"I say, Burton," said Crooks, "are you and Nelly Holmes going to hold up the Unitarian choir this year? You are a lucky fellow to have the chance of singing off the same book with her twice every Sunday."

"It's plain to be seen where Crooks's trouble lies," said Sanderson, "but let's have something to drink"; and he poured out a glass of cider from a pitcher on the table, and raised it to his lips, saying, "Here's to the pioneer girls of the University of Ortonville—long may they wave!"

"What do you think?" said Crooks; "Brown, the medic, told me to-day that several women have matriculated in that department, which certainly looks like business."

"Gracious Heaven! Female medics?" said Randolf; "the male medic is bad enough, but from the female medic may Zeus preserve us!"

"You think," said Burton, a sarcastic smile playing round his lips, "with the scientific preacher in one of Charles Reade's novels, that woman is high enough in the scale of creation to be the mother of God, but not high enough to be a saw-bones?"

In another part of the town, at 45 Clinton Street, four sophomore girls were settling themselves for the year in two suites of upper rooms in the family of Mr. and Mrs. Lewis, a middle-aged couple, who proved to be a father and mother to the girls, and made a home for them which they always left with regret, and returned to with pleasure.

People were not so afraid of taking college-girls this year; in fact, the Meyerses and Hodges, in Thompson and Jefferson Streets, actually advertised for girls. They had heard that girls were not so noisy as boys; that they took better care of their rooms; that they did not smoke and injure the wall-paper, nor spit tobacco-juice on the furniture; that they did not reel up-stairs half-seas over, and go to bed in their hats and boots. In short, college-girls were no longer ostracised, except in families where there were marriageable daughters, where, of course, nice young men were preferred.

The four girls in Clinton Street are Will and Clara, Nelly Holmes, and her room-mate, Laura Davidson. There are two sitting-rooms, and two bedrooms, cozy and nice; and they have just finished unpacking their trunks, and are putting up their book-shelves and little brackets that they have brought from home, to add to the pictures and other things with which the rooms are decorated. Before one of these pictures Will stands with folded arms. "I like this one," she said, pointing to a fine steel engraving called "Pharaoh's Horses." "What magnificent heads, with flowing manes, fiery eyes, and nostrils dilating as they are driven into the sea by the royal charioteer! But what a queer one *this* is; see, it is one of Cole's 'Voyage of Life,' in which youth is starting out. There he stands at the prow, with beautiful long hair, and innocent, hopeful face; is it a boy or girl? either, I guess; behind him, in the stern, sits old Father Time, with his scythe and hour-glass ready to cut him down at the wrong time; and see, stretching away in the dim distance is the river of life, running in among the trees, and banks lined with beautiful things; but he does not see them, for his eye is fixed on that vague shadowy object which looks like a temple of some kind, for there are towers on it; but it is all so dim, like a dream: is that what we are all chasing, I wonder?— *Mater sanctissima!* there goes eight o'clock, and I have not looked at my Trig nor Greek yet—have you Nell? I don't want to begin the year by flunking."

"By what?" said Clara, pausing, with a duster in her hand.

"Why, haven't you heard the boys talk about flunking? I think it is one of the most expressive words in the English language; it means a failure, a fizzle, a want of ability to answer when you are asked. Now, how very incomplete it sounds to say: 'The prof called on me, and I was unable to respond from want of knowledge of the subject; or, not being conversant with the topic, I was obliged to remain sitting!' but just to say I 'flunked,' covers the whole ground, including the dreadful feeling of shame and the desire to get through a very small place that must come from a failure in recitation."

"I wish," said Clara, "that you would not fall into the boys' manner of expressing things, for they are so full of slang."

"I don't at all agree with you, for I think that a judicious use of slang is very effective, and I intend from time to time to transplant some of the choicest of the boys' phrases into my own; it is greatly superior to girls' slang; why, one of my girl-friends went to Vassar, and came home full of such as 'I'm dying to know it; I'm furious to see him,' and the most trifling things were horrible, or splendid, or gorgeous, and every other sentence began with, 'I vow!' and, if you don't see that boys' slang is superior to that use of English, I don't admire your taste. For instance, 'cheese it,' 'that squelches me,' 'I'm smashed on her,' 'up on your ear,' or 'that's cheeky'—jewels every one of them, 'five words long, that sparkle upon the stretched forefinger of all time forever'; then, when you add to these the many invocations of the Olympian Zeus, and other classic oaths, you have at once a diction elegant and imposing," continued the provoking Will.

The next time that Clara was alone with Nell, she said: "Don't you think the freedom of our life here is having a bad effect upon Will? She seems to take so naturally to boys' ways."

"I'm not alarmed about her," said Nell, "and I like every one of her odd ways; she is a character rarely met out of books, and is decidedly refreshing. She is the most delightful mixture of boy and girl that I ever met: she has all the daring, independence, and strength of a boy, and yet the grace and tenderness of a woman. Isn't it too funny to see her try to sew? She has no more idea how to use a needle than if it were Neptune's trident."

"Yes, and for that very reason she needs taming and curbing a little, for she is inclined to be too boyish."

"Well, I don't want to see her tamed, and she sha'n't mend any stockings or gloves as long as I can get into her trunk—the dear old bother!"

From *An American Girl, and Her Four Years in a Boys' College*
(New York: D. Appleton and Company, 1878).

John Dewey

☩

A College Course:
What Should I Expect from It?

What should I expect from a college course? is, I believe, the question, my courteous editors of the *Castalian,* which you wish me to answer. It will not be out of the way, I suppose, to take the "I" who is the subject of this expectation as meaning you, me, anybody, what Walt Whitman calls "the common, that is, the divine average." There are certain things which I presume we should all pretty much agree upon. A man ought to expect a body, a physical tool, which is sound, and pliable to his purposes. He ought to have learned the rights of the body, and that these rights cannot be destroyed, nor the body cheated of them. The expectation of so many students in so many generations that the mind can be cultivated along with a systematic and continued neglect, or abuse of the physical system should be abandoned, by one and all, in the year 1890. There are certain intellectual gifts which the average student, and he below the average, should expect, while the very best student may beware lest he fall short. A certain range of information, a certain amount of learning, a mental discipline, that is, a quality of mind at once flexible and concentrated in dealing with new material, a certain attitude of mind, a mental openness and eagerness—these things should be expected almost as a matter of course. And certainly there are some moral results which should come too. One ought—whether one does or not—to expect a training of will, a cultivating and maturing of character, a reverence for truth wherever found, freedom from self-conceit and respect for the opinions of others, sympathy for their purposes, a highness of aim in the affairs of one's life agreeable to the opportunities enjoyed, belief in whatsoever things are true and lovely and of good report. Because such expectations are so normal and so obvious, if I should attempt to enforce them I should probably run either into the Scylla of mere moralisms, or into the Charybdis of a straining for the novel. And yet in attempting to say anything upon this topic, I do not imagine that I shall, after all, do more than repeat these same things—*Nur mit ein bischen andern Worten.* Whether I shall come to my goal with less of the ballast of commonplace or of the top-sail of paradox on account of a roundabout course may perhaps be doubted.

One thing, then, that a University education should do for a man is to rid him of his provincialisms. We all—or almost all—of us come out from a sphere of life somewhat narrower than that into which we come. The question is whether in this emergence we come out of our shells, or bring them with us. Certainly the boy or girl who comes to college judging all things from the standpoint of the way they think and do "in my place," ought to have his horizon of outlook pushed out a little further, and his standard of measurement lengthened. There may be touches of provincialism in manner which nothing but actual contacts will destroy, or which will always remain as the outer tokens of a sturdy, genuine and "home-keeping" spirit. But the voyage one takes in entering college life is a voyage to a far port, and through many countries foreign in space, in time, in manner of speech and thought. If such travelling of the spirit does not remove the narrow and small cast of one's opinion and methods it is failing of its aim. The Germans call the period of youthful culture a period of "self-alienation," because in it the mind gives up its immediate interests and goes on this far journey. Let a man learn on this journey to lay aside the suit, the habit, of mental clothes woven and cut for him in his native village, and to don the foreign costumes. If he be called to wear again his old suit, he will wear it the more easily and naturally for knowing something of the fashion of other men's garments.

And when one gives up his provincialisms let him make the renunciation complete. Partisanship, of whatever sort, or however disguised, is but provincialism of a larger growth and more imposing mien. The lesson is harder learned; the sacrifice seems greater. It is easy to take boisterousness of thought and expression for earnestness of conviction; the thoughtless assimilation of opinion from an authority already, probably, second-handed, for strength and originality of mind. To be in doubt, to suspend judgment, to await the conviction which can come only from the fact—all this seems weakness. The breadth of sympathy which feels that the world of truth is a sphere which comes into itself again, the fairness of judgment which will know both sides, and the thoroughness which will know even the inside—all this seems like needless painstaking, like unpractical theorizing, in a word, what the newspaper writers call "Mugwumpery." But all this ought a man to expect from his college course. Its name is Freedom.

And finally, a student should expect from his college course a sense of the due proportion and right values of the various interests which may claim his attention. He should find out where their center of gravity is, and this, not as a matter of theory, but as a practical insight which may serve him instinctively in the affairs of life. He should have ingrained within him the subordination of all learning, of all the sciences and all the arts, to social relationships and sympathies. Cardinal Newman, in one of the few educational books of the world which are neither priggish nor impractical, *The Idea of a University*, says that if he were asked to choose between a university which gave degrees upon examination in all subjects to students without residence and without tutorial supervision, and a university which had no professors or examinations at all, but simply brought a number of young men together for three or four years and then sent them away again, he should "have no hesitation in giving the preference to that university which did nothing, over that which exacted of its members an acquaintance with every science under the sun." And his reason is that an education without the *human* element would produce a generation frivolous, narrow-minded and resourceless, while the contact of "a multitude of young men keen, openhearted, sympathetic, and observant" would constantly bring out new ideas and views, fresh matter of thought and distinct principles for judging and acting. Above all it would secure a training in the relations and uses of those elements of knowledge necessary for our social being. Free contact of men and women will, at least, produce a "community constituting a whole, it will embody a specific idea, it will represent a doctrine, it will administer a code of conduct, and it will furnish principles of thought and action." In a word, it will develop an ethical atmosphere, and this will secure, as far as it goes, a real intellectual training, for it induces the recognition that "knowledge is something more than a sort of passive reception of scraps and details; it is something, and it does a something."

I have made my quotation somewhat extended, but the idea conveyed seems to me the root of all right ideas about University training. The permanent and fruitful outcome of a college education should be the training of one's *human* nature. This training alone is really practical and preparatory for life, for it alone is ethical. It is the only basis of a genuine intellectual culture, for only as all the studies of a college course find a unity in the human, in the social, do they become more than scraps and fragments. Relationship to man, to his interests and purposes, takes the dust of specialism out of its barren isolation and vitalizes it into germinant principles. With all his getting, then, the college student should require of his college course that it give him that sense of the proportions and right values which can come only of centering all studies in their human relationships.

But all this is rather intangible, you will say, to one who wishes some definite instructions as to what he should expect from his college course. Undoubtedly; but the kingdom of heaven, in learning as in other matters, cometh not with observation. The general effects, the internal results, those which give the set and fix the attitude of the spirit, are the real effects of the college education. The average graduate may have no ready answer to the inquiry five years after his graduation, what use he now makes of all his learning, of his Greek, his Mathematics, his Old High German and his knowledge of Kant's *Critiques*. If he is wise, his thoughts will take somewhat this form: "All this is a matter of no account. The thing of importance is whether I have my interests trained to alert action and ready and wide vibration. Am I avoiding stagnation, both the apparent stagnation of mental idleness, and that stagnation which simulates the form of action but is the mere vacant repetition and imitation of the thoughts of others? Above all, are my sympathies with whatever touches humanity, nearly or remotely, broad and dominant? If so, the Philistine may return to Gath; my college course has fulfilled its purpose, I have the *unum necessarium*—the one thing needful."

From *The Early Works*, 1882–1898 (Carbondale and Edwardsville: Southern Illinois University Press, 1969). First published in the *Castalian*, published by the Independents of the Senior Class, University of Michigan, V (1890).

Alice Hamilton

꜔

Two Letters to Her Sister Agnes

To Agnes Hamilton

Ann Arbor
March 6th 1892

Dearest Agnes,

I have just been out to mail Mother's letter. Yours will probably have to wait until I go to the College to-morrow morning, so if you do not get yours as soon as she does, don't think it is because it was not written on Sunday. You and Madge have probably just come home from Communion service. I wonder if you are up in Jessie's room talking things over and wondering what I am doing and if I am very lonely. Well I am not, not very. Things are so interesting that I have not time to be. Only I shall have to talk all Summer without stopping, to make up for these long silences. I went to Communion service this morning too. Mrs. Prescott took me to church and I stayed to communion afterwards. It was a nice service, not like ours of course, but much nicer than at Farmington. It made me feel as if I belonged to church and I was glad it came on my first Sunday. Mrs. Prescott is very lovely to me, but I try to keep out of the way as much as possible. She is a thorough lady and the doctor is dear, but I fancy they have not very much money and they never took a "roomer" but once before. The house is exceedingly tasteful and shows so much cultivation, especially in the pictures and the lovely harmonies in the walls and curtains and there are any number of queer old things that look as if they came from Europe. My room is very pleasant. It is a southwest one, the southern window looking out on a big oak grove across the road and the western one, a broad window just above my writing table, looking way across the valley to "Germantown" on the other side. This part of the town is filled with professors and is not very thickly built up. It remind[s] me very much, as indeed all the town does, of Cambridge. It is much larger than I expected. In some ways it isn't at all like a college town. Of course you meet swarms of students everywhere, but you are not stared at at all and you can go wherever you please and meet other girls everywhere in the campus, in the buildings and everywhere. So it is ever so much nicer than in Cambridge.

To-morrow I am going to my first lecture, on Materia Medica, at half past nine. Then comes one on Surgery, then one on Obstetrics and that finishes the morning. After that I suppose I shall drag what is left of me to dinner and study during the afternoon, if I have any courage left to study with. I have not the slightest idea what my standing will be, whether I shall find myself utterly deficient or pretty well advanced. It is so queer to be one of so many and of such very little importance. I am absolutely nobody, for the first time in my life, with no family name or reputation to fall back on, just one of the multitude with no more deference shown me than any of the others. I saw three "female medicals" on Friday when I was with Mother and more forlorn, micky looking specimens you couldn't find in the overall factory. But I met a nice one this morning, a Miss Bishop and she promised to pilot me around tomorrow.

The meals are going to be very nice. I don't mean the eating part, which is quite good though, but the people. I sit at one end with one man on one side and five on the other. Mrs. Hertel sits next to the one man, then come three girls and one more man. One of the girls is foolish, one is quite pretty and the other ordinary-looking, but the two last seem very nice. Several of the men do too. When I come to know them better I fancy I shall enjoy my meals very much. They are all literary students and I can imagine their horror when Mrs. Hertel told them they were to have a "medical" among them.

My back is tired writing or I could go on for ever so much longer. I wish I had somebody with me just to tide me over to-morrow. After that it will not be quite so bad.

Very lovingly
Alice

To Agnes Hamilton

[Ann Arbor]
January 22nd 1893

Dearest Agnes,

I mean to begin this letter to-day, but it may not get finished till next Sunday, unless I decide to make it very short, for there are no odd moments any more which can be filled in with writing letters. The mid-years come in three weeks and everyone is putting on extra steam and cramming early and late. We have petitioned for extra quizzes too, which adds to the rush. I am just as sure as sure that I shall be conditioned in at least three things, but there is no use groaning over it, or talking either. There is a case out at the hospital now, whom I am rather worked up about. It is one of the obstetrical cases, her baby will come in a few weeks. She is an exceedingly pretty girl and seems to be much better bred than the other girls in the ward, with whom she has nothing to do at all. I had not noticed her much until she was referred to our department for an inflammation of the joints. Then I was sent to take her history which she gave in a defiant sort of way, with her eyes on the novel she was holding, and with just as short answers as she could. Dr. Dock discovered that she is infected with a disease that bad women very often have and that renders her approaching confinement very dangerous, almost surely fatal. It seems so dreadful, for she is so young, so utterly alone and has probably been so wicked. I told Kate about her and she exclaimed over the beautiful opportunity I had of getting at her, but, Agnes, I cannot get at her at all. I simply don't know how. I would give anything to be able to reach her, and not only her but the other women in the ward too. There are three more, one whose baby is born and whose husband has deserted her; and two wretched looking girls, who might have been chambermaids in some fourth-rate boarding house. They turn away when I come in and seem to shun any notice, yet I am sure anyone who knew how could be a comfort and a strength to them. You know I told you when I was at home how provoking it was that the nurses would not let us have anything to do with the patients, except in the line of our work. Well since Fanny and I have been so much with Dr. Dock for the last month, the nurses have come to look upon us with much respect and now I can go in the wards where I please and talk to whomever I wish and I just wish I could not. For then I could put the blame on someone else and now it is all my own fault. Sometimes I think that if I were used to speaking plainly and having people speak plainly to me, it would come easily, but don't you think that the way we all have of never putting into words things that we feel at all deeply about, is a disadvantage in a way? It simply is a mental and physical impossibility to me to do what comes as easily as can be to some people.

To change the subject, has that very rude cousin of ours ever acknowledged the—I forget just what it was that we sent him—but whatever it was? Because he has not to me and if he has to you, please write and tell him to divide his gratitude evenly.

This has been a more Sabbath like Sunday than the last two. Fanny and I decided to take turns staying out at the Hospital and to-day was my turn, but fortunately Dr. Dock came early and I got away a little before twelve. When she announced that she meant to go to church he said in a nasty little way that he was glad his staff was not neglecting its spiritual interests and he hoped that she would worship for the rest of us. I wish he were a little more reverent. I went the rounds with him and then stained specimens for him to examine, until just about twelve, when I had time to skip down to the church for Dr. Prescott's Bible class. Mr. Gelston, the minister, is ill and three of our professors have offered to take the Bible class off his hands for the next three months. Dr. Prescott has it this month and his subject today was the limitations of human knowledge in the field of chemical science. It was very beautiful and so many came to hear him that the room would not hold them and they had to move into the church. After dinner I went with Kate to see a Mission school that has been started down in lower town, where she has a class of girls. On our way back we stopped at Mrs. Lombard's, for she had asked us to come in and have a cup of tea. Mr. Bourland and Mr. Budgett, the nice Englishman who assists Dr. Lombard, came in by and by, and we had a very nice time. Mrs. Lombard's rooms are charming, the tea was real tea, which Mrs. Hertel's is not, and there were macaroons and chocolates besides. I am so glad to have Mrs. Lombard learn to know Kate, for they will like each other so much. One of the Delta Gammas told me to-day, that she was perfectly sure Kate had refused Dr. Warthin last Summer. I am rejoiced to know it, but I wonder at his forgiving her, as he seems to have done. This letter began with an announcement that it was to be very short, but it seems to be lengthening out someway. I must write to Mother now, though.

Very lovingly
Alice

Who do you suppose could have sent me "Japanese Girls and Women" *anonymously*. It was sent from Putnam's and there is no card or name anywhere. I am mystified.

Barbara Sicherman, *Alice Hamilton: A Life in Letters* (Cambridge: Harvard University Press, 1984).

Stanley Waterloo

༄

from The Launching of a Man

In autumn, when the sky is clear, the scene about one of the largest and greatest universities in the world is assuredly a fine one. The huge buildings give a dignity to the campus and the sun glorifies a thousand windows, as it does the reddening leaves of the trees along the broad thoroughfares and upon the distant hills. Nature and man have in their work combined to make a splendid picture—even the freshman should be glad in his new and unaccustomed home—but, of all there is to be seen, nothing may compare with the young men. They come from the mountains of the far Northwest and from the distant land of grapes and oranges on the western slopes of the Sierras, from Florida and Oregon, from every state in the Union, and from Canada; youth of varying tradition, training and appearance, but all led by the same ambition and destined to attain, by companionship, a schooling perhaps as broadening as that gained from the learned professors to whom they listen daily.

Different in gait, in dress, and in pronunciation, are these knowledge-seeking youths. It requires no keen eye to distinguish the Texan from the Pennsylvanian, or the Californian from the Tennesseean, but, as the four years of study and association slip away, the members of the great mass conform more and more in garb and walk and manner, and there goes forth, finally, into the world, a group of resolute, clean-cut Americans who think little of state lines and are as lacking in dialects as in prejudices. The influences about them have been such as to make strong men. The breeze across the hills is not more wholesome.

It was October and the flurry of the opening of the collegiate year was over. The returning students had become domiciled and the new ones who had passed examinations were settled down to the life which was to them a novelty, a life the varied experiences of which were all before them and entered upon with mixed delight and doubtfulness. Already the freshmen had decided among themselves that their class contained material to make it famous in future annals of the University, and lacked no confidence that the year of their graduation would be one of importance to the country. Their very existence was, it is true, unnoticed by the seniors, but the juniors were most friendly, and as for the sophomores, they were, at best, but as the dingoes of Australia or the dogs of the Deccan, creatures whose friendship was impossible and who were to be looked upon, at best, with apprehension. In college the adversaries of each class are the classes immediately before and behind it, the oppressors or the oppressed.

Sufficient time had not yet passed for completion of the curt pourparlers in open air preceding the usual merely surface class vendetta which comes up like a mushroom between sophomores and freshmen, but the soil was tilled and waiting and the harvest promised to be plenteous. The crisis was imminent, but affairs among the interests outside of study required attention. There were class elections and Greek letter fraternity matters, and, particularly pressing, the necessity for work by the base-ball, foot-ball, and cricket teams. In the first of these young Sargent was deeply interested. He had distinguished himself the year before and had now been elected captain.

Foot-ball was growing in favor in the University. There is no better discipline of body and of temper than that gained in foot-ball, and even those who were not enthusiastic over the game often became members of the two half-trained teams who made great clamor in their contests. There existed then no such strict rules as have come to regulate the game of late, and, though accidents were rare, there were many noble contests. Asked what the rules were by a Rugby man who had entered the University, the captain of one team responded blithely: "There are none to speak of, save that no man is allowed to use an axe." The ball was sometimes of rubber, and its existence was always brief.

To cricket pertained more dignity, because of a group of opponents existing outside, and of most admirable metal. These were, almost without exception, middle-aged Englishmen living in towns along the principal railroad line passing through the University town. They had been cricketers in the old country, and their hands had not forgotten their cunning, their legs their sturdiness, nor their heads their wisdom in the field. They would come, these graybeards; and the University eleven, reinforced by picked men from the base-ball team, would meet them manfully, but too often with most inglorious results to the rash youngsters. In vain the best bowlers would send the ball whizzing fiercely at those craftily-guarded wickets, in vain the best catchers would hover about the field; slowly but surely those old farmers and shopkeepers would add to their score, and the showing made was always good.

But it was when the University men had come to bat and the veteran bowlers were arrayed against them that the youngsters learned what fine work appertains to the game so popular across the water. Those toughened and still keen-eyed old men would deliver balls which conducted themselves in a most sinister and mysterious way. They would come hurtling like cannon shot, they would roll lazily along the ground in a manner most deceptive, or they would start apparently far aside from the wicket and then turn like a serpent and find it surreptitiously and suddenly. Most improving to a vaunting spirit were these games with the old British experts, who usually, though not on all occasions, gained the victory.

And what suppers followed the contests, when the graybeards, flushed with conquest and ale and made affable by much eating and smoking, told such tales of wonderful feats in youth as would have suited an Indian chief about to give his personal history just before a scalp dance!

These things were all well, but it was the "national game" which commanded the real attention of those students who were training body and mind together at the old University, which placed the captain of the first nine upon a pedestal, the captains of other and minor nines great men, and gave to every member of those organizations a standing which was most enviable. Sargent had won his position fairly and bore his weight of honor with more or less modesty and meekness. He had been a ball-player from his childhood. Born in the country, he had played "two old cat" with other farmer boys, and later, in the bustling town of the Saginaw Valley, where he had prepared for college, he had become captain of the high school nine and developed an executive genius which even surpassed his value in the field. He gained a place in the University nine almost immediately after his entrance to college and had done such work in many a hard-fought game as had marked and elected him for the place he held. He was an enthusiast and hard trainer. "The Czar" they called him. . . .

There were daily contests now, between the first nine and the others; for the season of matches was at hand, and to the sophomores who were among the players even the noble and necessary work of disciplining freshmen lost much of its importance.

From *The Launching of a Man* (Chicago and New York: Rand, McNally and Company, 1899).

from Ann Arbor Tales

The various and varying newspaper accounts of the [hazing] affair awoke Ann Arbor from its peaceful slumber and for a space the town lived. For two days interest developed with the passage of the hours. Speculation became general. Opinions were as many as those who offered them; until there was not a man or woman from the Cat Hole to Ashley Street who did not advance a theory, new or old.

A like puzzlement, but one tempered by more original conjecture, characterized the attitude of the undergraduate body as a whole. For two days Catherwood had not appeared upon the campus, but at all hours friends and mere nodding acquaintances called at his rooms only to be refused admittance by Mrs. Turner, whom he had bade inform all callers that he was ill, very ill, quite too ill to be seen.

Little Green was one of these callers. He had expected the refusal of admission which Mrs. Turner, with many apologies, gave him and straightway he telegraphed his papers that Catherwood was dying as the result of the great bodily injuries he had received at the hands of his unknown undergraduate assailants. For little Green knew by instinct what many a reporter requires long years to learn—that a "story" is "good" just as long as there is a drop of "life" blood left in it, and not an instant longer.

Little Green fairly reveled in the commotion he had caused. The regular college correspondents, anæmic, frightened little fellows, were at a loss to know who had beaten them in their own papers. It was little Green's game, absolutely his, and he purposed playing it alone, aided and abetted in the achievement of this purpose by the various telegraph editors whom he sought to serve. And so far as the faculty was concerned, the frequenter the dispatches, the more woefully addled did the professorial brain become.

Out in the state, and in adjoining states, wise editors, looking down, as it were, from some high place, wrote venemous and vicious editorials in which the legislature was called upon to pass laws abolishing hazing in institutions of the commonwealth by making the practice of it a felony, punishable by imprisonment. Parents in the further west with sons and daughters at Ann Arbor feared for their children's lives. School boards passed resolutions. Guardians wrote to the heads of various university departments asking if their wards were quite safe, alone and unprotected in Ann Arbor. A New York newspaper, on the second day, dispatched its most ingenious "woman reporter" to the scene of action and in three hours the sprightly creature had woven a fictional fabric beside which the tale of Ali Baba was the glowing, gleaming truth. She revived all the half-forgotten stories of ancient hazing rites, dead these many years, and wrote of them as of contemporary practice. And the imaginative artist in the home office illustrated her vivacious article elaborately, seeking to convey to the eye horrors of undergraduate torture that words were useless to describe.

Skeletonized, the story was wired across the sea and the ponderous *Times* gave forth an editorial in which it averred that such refined cruelty had never been heard of in English academic life; not even in the palmiest days of Rugby and of Eton at the height of the fagging system.

Amidst the wild excitement, little pink-cheeked Green grinned at his reflection in his mirror and exclaimed:

"Gad! You've got 'em goin', Greeny; you've got 'em goin'. Greeny, *you're it!*"

From *Ann Arbor Tales* (Philadelphia: George W. Jacobs and Company, 1902).

Part Three

☙

Matriculation

Dorothy Gies McGuigan

☙

A College Romance

My parents both went to the University, and it was in that serene and golden era just before 1914, the year in which the nineteenth century came to an end. Among the sheaf of tickets at my father's June Week was one good for "An Automobile Ride through the Kindness of the Ann Arbor Civic Association," with the added note: "As the number of machines will be limited, seats will be assigned in order of class seniority." The class historian was Marjorie Hope Nicolson, and she spoke earnestly of "the great bond of love of the mother who had taken them to her heart, made of them one strong, indissolvable union"; she described her classmates as "a band of youthful adventurers who turned away from the world without." That much was certainly true; in all the swelling oratory of June Week—as in the pages of *The Michigan Daily* for the years just preceding—there is scarcely a hint that an explosive world existed outside the cocoon of the campus.

Three days after my father graduated, Archduke Francis Ferdinand was killed in Sarajevo.

Can you see him, my father, as he came to Ann Arbor for the first time in September of 1909, a boy from a tiny town in the Thumb, uncomfortable in the stiff starched collar he had only just taken to wearing, far too shy to ask directions, lugging his suitcase up the hill from the depot in the direction of the rooming houses that bordered the campus?

He certainly did not have any very clear idea of why he was there. It was, in fact, a miracle of no small proportion that brought him, not an especially brilliant boy, but I think a very nice one: the first boy from his town to go to the University, quite likely the first in the entire county.

It was my proud, ambitious grandmother, who sent away to Best's in New York for her little girls' party shoes and took the train alone to Saginaw to see Sarah Bernhardt and Sothern and Marlowe—it was she who had determined that her eldest boy, the apple of her eye, would go away to college. My grandfather, with his modest hardware business, had acquiesced—somewhat lukewarmly. It was not an easy project to bring off. The local school had only ten grades, and my father had had to be sent away to board with a widow in Saginaw to finish high school. To complicate things further there was grandfather's "rich" bachelor cousin Ed, who had left school in the third grade, and by penurious saving and canny investment acquired a small fortune in land in downtown Pontiac. Whenever Cousin Ed came to visit, he would raise fresh doubts in grandfather's mind about the wisdom of the whole project.

"What good's it going to do him, Joe? Better let him get out, and work. Good for him. Look at me. Gonna cost you plenty before you're through."

The University a half century ago, already one of the biggest in the country, but gentle still, insular, pastoral, the surrounding town impinging less suffocatingly, the campus for all its haphazard design, very soft, very green, very open. Round beds of flowers studded the lawns in spring; eastward on a hill above the treetops could be seen the shining dome of the Observatory, on which was mounted Professor Hussey's thirty-seven-inch reflecting telescope. Between it and the campus lay an expanse of parklike green called "Sleepy Hollow," which the University had just acquired as a playground for its girls.

The autumn of my father's advent, the autumn of 1909, there was much in the air that was new. Old buildings had been refurbished and painted, new buildings were going up—engineering, dental, chemical, and a maddening marble mausoleum, the Alumni Memorial, known to disgruntled students as D'Ooge's Palace after the distinguished professor of Greek who had been instrumental in getting it built. They had begged for a commons or clubhouse instead of a tomb for alumni records, but the promoters of the new building felt it would be desecration to allow eating and card-playing in a monument dedicated to our fallen soldiers.

There was a new course on campus in railroads. It was taught by the economics faculty assisted by members of the engineering and law faculties, and there had been a virtual stampede to enroll in it. What could be more thrilling than anything having to do with trains?

And there was a new president; James Burrill Angell was just retiring. Eighty years old, he still taught classes, might be seen, cane in hand, slowly traversing the Diagonal, a frail old man with gray beard, tipping his hat to young ladies.

It was President-Emeritus Angell who gave the welcoming address to new students on Sunday afternoon, October 12, in the auditorium of old University Hall:

> Those of you who are here for the first time find yourselves suddenly cut loose from all restraints. There is a strong temptation to think there is an opportunity to take a sort of moral vacation. It is a real temptation and one against which you should be guarded. I hope the whole body of students may be cooperative in the pursuit of all that is best in life.

Immediately after followed a talk by a gentleman from the Presbyterian Board of Home Missions in New York on "The Contribution of the Bible to the Growth of the Nation," and after that Bishop Charles Williams of the Episcopal Diocese of Michigan addressed the gathering on "The Need of Religious Education, Particularly in State Universities."

President Angell might well be dubious about their pursuit of the best in life—or perhaps their *definition* of the best in life. Mothers worried then, as they do now, about the fate of darling sons dispatched so far from the tender influence of home; worse yet, legislators in Lansing were apt to express themselves in vituperative terms about certain recent happenings in idyllic Ann Arbor.

The previous year a mob of a thousand students had wrecked the Star Theater, a nickel movie house the proprietor of which had offended by ejecting a disorderly student. They had smashed windows, demolished the piano and furniture, and wrought havoc for good measure in the adjoining saloon. "The mayor, fire department and the few policemen the town affords," wrote one reporter, "were powerless in the hands of the students." President Angell had been sent for and had pled in vain with the students.

In a recent election, though many Michigan counties had gone dry, Washtenaw County had remained firmly wet. Edwin E. Slosson writing of the University in the *Independent—a Weekly Magazine* remarked, "If the saloons are not to be banished from Ann Arbor, as they have been from Cambridge, Berkeley, and Urbana, they should at least be kept decent."

Moreover, the hazing of freshmen by sophomores had become so crude and so ruthless that the faculty Senate in the autumn of 1909 placed a ban on the practice until a new set of rules could be drawn up. In his article Slosson spoke of "hair-cutting, face painting, house-raiding, and kidnapping" as "epidemic," adding that freshmen were frequently "treed and egged and put through such stunts as sophomoric ingenuity could devise."

Despite the faculty ban, hazing went merrily on that autumn. Numbers of luckless freshmen, identified by the little gray caps they had to wear, were subjected to the various species of torment and ridicule then fashionable; according to *The Daily*: ". . . with coats turned inside out, marched into different nickel shows and forced to do an impromptu vaudeville stunt. . ." For more sadistic practices two sophomores had to be expelled.

Stern rules were laid down to govern the class games between freshmen and sophomores on Black Friday, the second after the opening of classes. It was decreed that for the Pole Rush—when both classes tried to climb greased poles and grab the banners of the opponent—"participants must wear tennis shoes"—football cleats having proven to be singularly damaging to an opponent's face—and that "entering of private houses for the purpose of capturing opponents is strictly forbidden."

My father looked back on the operation of hazing with considerable contempt; he went to watch but not to participate in the pole rushes.

I could wish that his letters from his first year at the University had been saved, though perhaps they said no more than most freshman letters; he had got the box of fudge his mother had sent, and could she spare another five?

He admired the dazzling girls who emerged from the sorority houses about campus, lovely creatures in tucked and embroidered shirt-waists, in white and cream-colored dresses, their hair pouffed in Gibson girl style. He spoke of one or another of those dashing girls long after as "the beautiful Miss Mills" or "the handsome Miss Adams." I asked him once if he had ever taken Miss Mills out.

"Oh gosh no," he said, "I crossed to the other side of the street when I saw her coming."

He adored the theater, and he went to everything offered that year. The Whitney showed *Graustark*, Frank J. McIntyre in *The Traveling Salesman*, Trixie Friganza in *The American Idea*, and a play called *The Climax*, heralded in the ads as "the Purest Play of the Day. For Mother, Father, Wife and Daughter. An Offering that Pulls at Your Heart Strings."

The new Majestic, on Maynard Street across from the School of Music ("Theater beautiful," its ads described it), offered something called "refined vaudeville." For twenty-five cents (thirty-five cents in the boxes) one could see "Lolo the Mental Marvel. A Genuine Sioux Indian Girl in a Wonderful Exhibition of Telepathy and Thought Transference." Or there might be even gayer delectation: "Tilly Whitman (Oh You Fat

Girl!) and Those Dancing Girls (Beautiful Eyes!).” At the Bijou some-one called Lois Love performed “Singing, Dancing, Contortion,” and “Mysterious Mack and His Automobile” cavorted on the stage.

For more intellectual nourishment, then as now, a student could attend the Lecture Series, hear a lady named Mrs. Maud Ballington Booth talk on “The Lights and Shadows of Prison Life,” and Peary describe his trip of the year before to the North Pole.

By his second year my father had made a few friends, begun to feel at home. He played trombone in the Varsity Band and in the University Symphony, and he joined a fraternity.

He took pains to dress correctly. An ad in the *Daily* of a local haber-dashery showed a young gentleman in evening clothes mounting a lad-der, with the caption: “It’s easy to climb the ladder of social and business success when your garments bear evidence of sound judgment and re-fined taste. We consider your build and complection (*sic*).” My father bought a dress suit and went to fraternity parties.

His instinct for wearing what was right led to a bitter quarrel with his mother as she packed his trunk for his departure for his sophomore year. He insisted adamantly that in Ann Arbor young men wore only BVD’s in winter as well as summer, and not the objects the ads described as “Woollens light as air—Keep warm, let your skin breathe!”

My mother came to the University in the fall of 1910. If it was some-thing of a miracle that my father was here, it was doubly a miracle that my mother was.

Her Dutch immigrant family had been in America scarcely ten years, and they had been years of sheer, unmitigated hardship. My mother’s father developed tuberculosis soon after they came and could not work indoors; a new baby arrived; the older boys foraged in the country for firewood to heat the house. None of them knew English; my grand-mother studied her children’s schoolbooks at night; to the end of her life she spoke a slangy schoolchild’s English with a delicious Dutch accent.

My mother, a big girl of ten or twelve when they came to America, had been put back to the first grade in school; by the end of the year she had advanced through six grades and was at the top of her class. She was a whiz at math; in high school she turned out to be a whiz at Greek and Latin; all her teachers urged her to go on to college.

But there was simply no money. My mother worked for well-to-do families in Battle Creek after school and on Saturdays, dutifully turning over her earnings to her family. My mother’s father respected learning, sat at night sipping his brandy and reading Jules Verne in Dutch. But the

University—that was for the rich, and education anyhow was chiefly for boys; daughters could get on very well without it.

My mother, with a kind of cheerful and invincible determination, taught country school after high school, managed a year or so at Ypsilanti Normal, taught again, and arrived in Ann Arbor in the autumn of 1910 with her tiny savings and a couple of new dresses her mother had made her.

So far as I can discern my mother's college years were blissfully happy. An older brother who ran a train between Battle Creek and Chicago lent her money to finish.

She was delighted with everything she found, most of all, the delectable array of courses from which she could choose. She plunged at once into philosophy, and it seemed to her the special mark of a lucky fate that she landed in Professor Wenley's quiz section. Though they did not yet know each other, my father was also taking Professor Wenley's basic philosophy course; the two sat on opposite sides of the lecture hall.

He must have been an extraordinary man, Robert Mark Wenley, for he was able to associate the profoundest concepts with the familiar and the everyday, to make his students perceive that their own problems were problems of philosophy and that only through philosophy might they be solved. My parents spoke of him with reverence, and often, years later, something would bring to mind a remark by Professor Wenley.

In the spring of my father's sophomore year, he was patently flunking his German. There was no grading system yet at the University; one either passed or failed. My father could simply make nothing out of Schiller's *Wallensteins Tod*. A kindly professor suggested that he get some tutoring, and gave him the names of two or three able German students.

On a sunny afternoon in April my father presented himself at my mother's rooming house.

"Did he pay you for tutoring him?" I asked her once.

"Oh my goodness no," my mother said. "He didn't have any more money than I did. He brought a box of chocolates the first day he came, and I remember he opened the box and ate most of them while we talked."

She did get him through Schiller.

The next autumn, my father's junior year, they enrolled in two or three classes together—Professor Cooley's Sociology, I know, and Professor Rankin's Rhetoric.

In fine weather they canoed on the river, went ice skating in winter, my mother a little ashamed of her Dutch skates, which were different from the other girls', of wood with long runners that curled up in front. "It was wonderful skating then, and there was always a crowd on the river."

They danced at Granger's Academy on Huron Street on Saturday nights. "Your father hated it. When we came out, he always said, 'Well, that's over with!' I loved it though."

Easy to see what attracted those two. My mother, with her clear, very blue eyes and pink and white skin, and her sheer, unmitigated delight in everything.

From the beginning she admired him—his nice manners, the stylish way he dressed. He was always having small adventures, with landladies and shopkeepers and girls at the ticket window, and he could turn them all into delightful and funny accounts. He was a charming conversationalist, but the kind that blooms only in small groups, with close friends. My mother listened to him and thought he was a most extraordinary young man.

With the sophistication of two years of the Whitney and Majestic, he took her—she had never in her life seen a play—to *The Merry Widow*, and Belasco's *Girl of the Golden West*, and Henry Miller in *The Great Divide*, and Mrs. Leslie Carter in *Du Barry*.

They walked everywhere, of course. Four livery stables in town furnished carriages and buggies, but it cost $1.50 for a couple to and from an event before twelve, $2.00 after twelve—nearly as much as a week's room rent.

It was a wonderful year or two.

In the spring of his junior year my father hired a buggy and they drove to Whitmore Lake and back, and he asked her to marry him.

He hadn't any prospects or the remotest idea of where or what he intended to do in his life. He thought vaguely about writing. His literature and rhetoric courses had been exciting to a boy nourished on G. H. Henty and *The Youth's Companion;* he tried to screw up his courage to ask for admission to Professor Scott's Rhetoric 23, a kind of club then for hopeful young writers. He didn't think he was good enough, and I think he never applied. My mother says he was not sufficiently encouraged by his professors. *She* read his essays and pronounced them remarkable.

My father drifted into business. His youthful marriage forced a choice; he wrote advertising for shoes, for ladies' dresses, for basement sales. He had an ear for the singular word, an eye for the eccentric manner, but very little interest in the process of making money. He changed jobs often, out of frustration and boredom; we moved again and again.

Even as children my sister, my brothers, and I were aware that for our parents the University loomed, immense, monumental, a frame of reference for everything that came after, an enormous irretrievable experience, their Golden Age.

The photograph of my father's fraternity hung above his chiffonier where he could look at it each morning. Their college books moved with us each time, the notebooks in my mother's clear, logical hand, the German and Latin texts, even the fateful *Wallensteins Tod*.

My father was most happy, clearly, at home at night, reading aloud to us out of that marvelous array that had once spread before him. We heard Mark Twain and Poe and Plato and Shakespeare, all the new plays as soon as they were in print, and older unfashionable ones like *The Great Divide*, *The Witching Hour*, *The Copperhead*. In the mornings, to get us out of bed, my father would play a few bars of a Sousa march on the trombone, very jollily, and if we still did not stir, the end of the trombone might be thrust, ice-cold, under the covers. In the evening, while my mother got supper on the table, he put on the wind-up Victrola "Gems from the Pink Lady" or "Gems from the Chocolate Soldier."

His dress suit hung in the closet in a cheesecloth bag, with mothballs. I saw him wear it only once that I recall, on a memorable New Year's Eve, sometime in the 1920s. Something must have happened to produce that gala evening, for my parents had no social life, rarely went out or entertained. On that New Year's Eve they went to something called *Chauve Souris*. My father had bought my mother a dress; I know that he bought it and not she, because it was utterly extravagant and headily fashionable, of dark blue tricollet, bare-armed, with deep fringe that began at one knee and swooped down to the ankle on the other side. My mother had her hair marcelled. My father appeared before our admiring eyes in all the splendor of his newly pressed tails, and there was a great joke about his tie, which he had left all askew on purpose so that we would shriek and drag him to a mirror and then to my mother to put it to rights.

Sometime, very late, or perhaps early, I heard music and got out of bed and crept to the top of the stairs. In the living room below, on our worn carpet, my parents in all their finery were slowly, dreamily fox-trotting to a record of "Three O'Clock in the Morning."

As for my mother, during the years we were growing up, she ironed seven thousand shirts, cooked fifteen thousand meals, most of the time cheerfully, only occasionally lost her temper and rattled pans and slammed doors and let fly a Dutch expletive. Evenings she helped us with homework, made us see the world of difference between *Iste Catiline!* and *Ille Cicero!*

Grandfather's bachelor cousin Ed, who had been so discouraging about my father's education, paid us a visit sometimes as he had my grandparents, very close with money still, the slowest tipper in Lower Michigan, grumbling about rising taxes and multiplying schools. He was just saved in my mother's eyes from total damnation by his good-natured tolerance of children; once he took us to two different movie houses in one afternoon, and another time on the Giant Roller Coaster at Seabreeze, clutching his battered old felt hat with both hands and muttering "Jesus God!" through clenched teeth when he could get his breath.

One day I had brought my Latin book to where my mother was ironing, and Cousin Ed demanded:

"Now will you tell me just what good does that stuff do the kid?"

My mother began to explain patiently all the advantages of a good foundation in the classics.

"Well," insisted Cousin Ed, "but what good did Latin ever do you? It don't help you iron or bake a good pie."

"Well, I could go back to teaching Latin, for one thing."

"That's it! that's just it!" cried Cousin Ed in triumph. "That's just what I mean. Them colleges teach Latin to raise more Latin teachers, and *they* teach to raise *more* Latin teachers, and it just keeps the darn system going!"

My mother was too angry to answer and the steam sputtered where she dabbed a wet finger on the iron.

In 1928 my father started a little business of his own, manufacturing clever and imaginative display fixtures for department stores. Money began to come in, quite a lot of it, and it seemed just possible he might bring the whole thing off, after all; there were travel folders and steamship ads on the dining room table, and my parents talked of taking us to Europe.

Then suddenly, of course, nobody had much money at all. We had absolutely none; no money and no job, and my sister starting college. My father, swallowing his pride, took a job in the store that had hired him when he first left college twenty years earlier. We moved back to Ann Arbor. It seemed quite natural that my brothers and I should go to college there, after all. And of course, even in the worst days of the depression—and there were bad ones—my parents had never doubted that all their children would finish college.

My father died before his fiftieth class reunion rolled around. He would not have gone in any case; he could not bear to see things change, or that people should grow old. But I went with my mother to her fiftieth reunion; it was much gayer than I expected, full of delightful, spry old gentlemen, some on their second and third wives.

My mother is eighty-two now and has moved back to Ann Arbor. One day not long ago she showed me a book a friend had sent her, *Fragments from Sappho*, and asked me to translate the Greek words that appeared on the cover. "Oh but I can't! I don't know Greek."

"At least try it," she urged, "they are really the same words, almost, as the Latin." She read them aloud and went on to quote from memory a passage from Sappho. "I wonder," she said thoughtfully, "if my hearing weren't so bad, I might just go back to class again and brush up a little on my Greek."

From *Our Michigan: An Anthology Celebrating the University of Michigan's Sesquicentennial*, edited by Erich A. Walter (Ann Arbor: University of Michigan, 1966).

Richard Meeker

☩

from Better Angel

On the whole the two got along unusually well; and by the end of his freshman year, Kurt had been taken on as an accepted adjunct in all the goings and comings of the Graylings. His presence at Sunday dinner, at the occasional party that Chloe or Derry would give, at family outings and picnics was taken as much for granted as Derry's own. He liked it. In the evenings both Derry and his sister studied, and Mrs. Grayling read, or crocheted interminable yards of edging for pillow slips and towels, her long dark face almost sullenly intent in the glare of the overhead light she always insisted upon using. The friends he made on the campus were accepted by the Graylings as well, and their friends by him. So the change from Barton to Ann Arbor had been, after all, less revolutionary than it had promised to be. The whole environment of his extradomestic life, to be sure, had changed. But otherwise he had simply substituted a new family for an old one. There was still a home in which he was free to do as he chose, a piano to play when he liked, all the quiet certitude of family that he had always known. . . .

The spring of this first new year away from home had brought to Kurt a third frightening experience, yet one mixed with a new and unholy joy. Mrs. Grayling had been unwontedly peevish, and Derry, as usual at such times, had gone into a sulk. He had come into the room where Kurt was reading, thrown himself across the bed with a sigh that seemed to say, "Be sorry for me if you dare!", sullenly refusing to answer Kurt's questioned, "What's the matter, Derry?"; and had gone promptly to sleep. Mrs. Grayling, weeping volubly, had shut herself in her room, and Chloe, exasperated by her mother's behavior, and her brother's, had gone to the library. Such scenes were disturbing, but Kurt was growing accustomed to them and somewhat reconciled, for he knew that another day would see everything set to rights again.

Derry wakened late in the afternoon, and at Kurt's suggestion, had gone to supper with him at the cafeteria, and then to an early evening movie. They had come out into a night full of warm moonlight, and walked without talking much after Derry's initial "What do you say we walk a ways?" out of town beyond the last almost-defeated gleam of street light, and sat down on a hillside. They had been quiet at first. Then something in the white silence of the May moon had melted down the reticence their eighteen years of living had built up. Talk, slowly undertaken, had drifted little by little to forbidden things, to exchanges of confidences—and, at last, to the thing Kurt had fought so stoutly for the last four years, complicated now because shared with another.

After it had happened, the joy of it turned to fear. Not to bodily fear this time—he knew better now—but to religious fear, a fear for his soul's damnation. It was enormous, his guilt, and its enormity grew upon him through the walk home and through the endless sleepless hours of the night. Unprecedented, this act, and unmentionable. No one, he was sure, had ever been guilty of so heinous a sin. He seemed, as he thought confusedly about it, to stand alone, beyond possibility of forgiveness, blackened eternally, and he envied and marveled at Derry for the matter-of-fact way in which he took it. He should hate Derry, he knew; yet he knew, too, that he did not. When a few nights later it happened again between them, he knew, although he stubbornly refused to accept the fact of his knowledge, that he was caught in a new snare, inextricably—a snare which he did not understand and for the explanation of which he had no slightest intimation of where to go.

He went home in June. His pleasure in being there, in seeing in the *Barton Observer* the item, "*Kurt Gray, the son of Mr. and Mrs. Elmer Gray, valedictorian of his class in the local High School last year, returned Tuesday from Ann Arbor, where he is at present Barton's only representative at the University,*" was shadowed by his consciousness of guilt, of his hypocrisy, and by his longing for Derry. At home it was so, and at church, where he was welcomed as a valuable addition to its somewhat anæmic life. He played the organ, he talked at the Epworth League about the status of religion among university students, with all the time the consciousness of his unfitness upon him and the realization that it all seemed much less important to him than it had a year past. Upon him too was the consciousness that his religious faith was much less sure than when he left. Freshman biology had taught him things about the origins of life against which he at first rebelled, but which in the end he was too clear-headed not to accept as true, or at least as more credible than anything he had hitherto learned. He wanted desperately, as he told Chloe so much later, to believe in something, always to believe in something. His attempt to adjust his knowledge to his faith, his mind to his heart, his thought to what he wanted to think, was in him a real and bitter struggle and one from which he emerged slowly—clinging stubbornly, tenaciously, to the last tatters and remnants of a faith he knew was inadequate, because, as yet, he had found nothing to replace it. . . .

How strange and twisted it all was. There was Chloe with her cool gray eyes, her smooth black hair, and her mind which he felt he knew so well—her mind tempered and adjusted to a spiritual sympathy that was constantly amazing him. . . .

Then there was her brother, with his eyes gray too, but scornful; his dark hair tangled, his mind alert, objective—as incapable of fine sympathies as of deceit. Derry, with this mental equipment that was as clear and free of subtleties as a lump of polished glass, yet that constantly puzzled and repulsed him by its very concreteness. Derry, with the man-body he knew so well; the cool white skin, the firm chest, the lean belly and strong back, the thick thighs and calves, the wide blunt-fingered hands. There was a loneliness in Kurt, an emptiness, that throbbed and pulsated in the night. It made him think again of the darkness in which he used to cower.

The past few months had seen growing in him a beginning of understanding. He had read for the first time the new psychology—Brill, Jung, Freud, Ellis, Carpenter; he had discovered Wedekind. From them he learned that his sin and Derry's was not the unique sport he had believed it to be. There were others, it seemed (at least in Europe there were) of his sort. Plato he reread with a new interest. The high idealism of the Phædrus and the Symposium had captured him and engulfed him as a flood. Now that there was a whole summer of inaction ahead, he could begin to formulate into ideas, maybe, the feeling that had been growing in him.

He was in love with Derry. He belonged to that strange class of humanity, the singularity of whose position appealed to the romantic in him at the same time that it overwhelmed him with its pathos. "I am the love that dare not speak its name," he read. He divided his time between his music and a stumbling search for knowledge. There was in him a yearning for the vicarious companionship of others like himself. Of an actual companionship other than Derry's, he never dreamed. It was as if he had been initiated into some secret fraternity, and, at every discovery of some new communicant in ages past, he felt a thrill of pleasure. There was Plato, beyond a doubt. There were Cellini, and Michelangelo, and Shakespeare. There was, he felt almost certain, Shelley.

From *Better Angel* (1933; Boston: Alyson Publications, 1987).

Arthur Miller

ϙ

University of Michigan

My first affection for the University of Michigan was due, simply, to their accepting me. They had already turned me down twice because my academic record (I had flunked algebra three times in my Brooklyn high school) was so low as to be practically invisible, but the dean reversed himself after two letters in which I wrote that since working for two years—in a warehouse at fifteen dollars a week—I had turned into a much more serious fellow. He said he would give me a try, but I had better make some grades. I could not conceive of a dean at Columbia or Harvard doing that.

When I arrived in 1934, at the bottom of the Depression, I fell in love with the place, groggy as I was from the bus ride, because I was out of the warehouse at last and at least formally a part of a beautiful town, the college town of Ann Arbor. I resolved to make good for the dean and studied so hard my first semester that in the history exam my mind went completely blank and the professor led me out of the class and told me to go to sleep and to come back and take the exam again.

I loved it also because of the surprises. Elmo Hamm, the son of a potato farmer in Upper Michigan, turned out to be as sharp a student as any of the myopic drudges who got the best grades in New York. I loved it because Harmon Remmel, the son of an Arkansas banker, lived in the room next to mine, and from him I got a first glimpse of what the South meant to a Southerner, a Southerner who kept five rifles racked on the wall, and two .38's in his valise, and poured himself bullets in a little mold he kept on his desk. (In his sophomore year he disappeared, and I found out he had been unable to bear it any longer once duck-hunting time had rolled around again.)

I loved the idea of being separated from the nation, because the spirit of the nation, like its soil, was being blown by crazy winds. Friends of mine in New York, one of them a cum laude from Columbia, were aspiring to the city fireman's exam, but in Ann Arbor I saw that if it came to the worst a man could live on nothing for a long time. I earned fifteen dollars a month for feeding a building full of mice—the National Youth Administration footing the bill—and out of it I paid $1.75 a week for my room and squeezed the rest for my Granger tobacco (two packs for thirteen cents), my books, laundry, and movies. For my meals I washed dishes in the co-op cafeteria. My eyeglasses were supplied by the health service, and my teeth were fixed for the cost of materials. The girls paid for themselves, including the one I married.

I think I sent more students to Michigan than anybody else who ever went there.

It was a great place for anybody who wanted to write. The Hopwood Awards, with prizes ranging from $250 to $1,500, were an incentive, but there was something more. The English Department had, and still has, a serious respect for undergraduate writing efforts. Professor Kenneth Rowe, who teaches playwriting, may not have created a playwright (no teacher ever did), but he surely read what we wrote with the urgency of one who actually had the power to produce the play. I loved the place, too, because it was just big enough to give one the feeling that his relative excellence or mediocrity had real meaning, and yet not so big as to drown one in numbers.

I remember the June of each year when the Hopwood Awards were announced, and the crowds would form to hear the featured speaker— some literary light from the book world—after which the presentations were made. How I hated those speakers for holding up the awards! And those prizes meant more than recognition. In my case at least, they meant the end of mouse-feeding and room-sharing and the beginning of a serious plan to become a playwright. Avery Hopwood made millions by writing bedroom farces like *Getting Gertie's Garter* and *Up in Mabel's Room*; if my sense of it is correct, never was so much hope created in so many people by so modest an accomplishment. I have never sweated on an opening night the way I did at Hopwood time.

I do not know whether the same thing happened at Harvard or Columbia or Yale, but when I was at Ann Arbor I felt I was at home. It was a little world, and it was man-sized. My friends were the sons of diemakers, farmers, ranchers, bankers, lawyers, doctors, clothing workers and unemployed relief recipients. They came from every part of the country and brought all their prejudices and special wisdoms. It was always so wonderful to get up in the morning. There was a lot learned every day. I recall going to hear Kagawa, the Japanese philosopher, and how, suddenly, half the audience stood up and walked out because he had used the word Manchukuo, which is Japanese, for the Chinese province of

Manchuria. As I watched the Chinese students excitedly talking outside on the steps of Hill Auditorium, I felt something about the Japanese attack on China that I had not felt before.

It was a time when the fraternities, like the football team, were losing their glamour. Life was too earnest. But I remember glancing with sadness at the photographs of Newman, Oosterbaan, and the other gridiron heroes and secretly wishing that the gladiatorial age had not so completely disappeared. Instead, my generation thirsted for another kind of action, and we took great pleasure in the sit-down strikes that burst loose in Flint and Detroit, and we gasped when Roosevelt went over the line with the TVA, and we saw a new world coming every third morning, and some of the old residents thought we had gone stark raving mad.

I tell you true, when I think of the library I think of the sound of a stump speaker on the lawn outside, because so many times I looked up from what I was reading to try to hear what issue they were debating now. The place was full of speeches, meetings, and leaflets. It was jumping with Issues.

But political facts of life were not all I learned. I learned that under certain atmospheric conditions you could ice-skate up and down all the streets in Ann Arbor at night. I learned that toward June you could swim in a certain place without a suit on and that the Arboretum, a tract of land where the botanists studied plants and trees, was also good for anatomical studies, especially in spring under a moon. I had come to school believing that professors were objective repositories of factual knowledge; I found that they were not only fallible but some of them were damn fools and enough of them seekers and questioners to make talking with them a long-lasting memory.

I left Ann Arbor in the spring of 1938 and in two months was on relief. But, whether the measurement was false or not, I felt I had accomplished something there. I knew at least how much I did not know. I had found many friends and had the respect of the ones that mattered to me. It had been a small world, gentler than the real one but tough enough. It was my idea of what a university ought to be.

What is it now [1953]? You can see at once, I hope, that my judgment is not objective, if only because my memories of the place are sweet and so many things that formed those memories have been altered. There are buildings now where I remembered lawn and trees. And yet, I told myself as I resented these intrusions, in the Thirties we were all the time calling for these dormitories and they are finally built. In my day bequests were used for erecting less useful things—the carillon tower whose bells woke us up in the morning, the Rackham Building, a grand mausoleum which seemed to have been designed for sitting around in a wide space.

There are certain facts about the university today that can be disposed of right off. In almost every field of study, a student will probably find no better training anywhere than at Michigan. Some say that in forestry, medicine, creative writing, and many other fields it is really the top. I wouldn't know, I never went to any other school.

The student will need about a thousand dollars a year, which is cheaper than a lot of places. He will get free medical care and hospitalization; he will be able to borrow money from the university if he needs it and may take nearly forever to pay it back; he will use modern laboratories in the sciences and an excellent library in the humanities; as a freshman he will live in new dormitories, and the girls will have to be in bed at ten-thirty; if he flies to school he will land at the Willow Run Airport, the safest in the country, owned now by the university; he will have a radio station and a television station to try his scripts, if he writes, and if he is more literary than that he can try for a Hopwood Award in poetry, drama, the essay and the novel.

He will meet students of many backgrounds. Two-thirds will be from Michigan and a large proportion of those from small towns. About nine hundred will be foreign, including Japanese, Turks, Chinese and Europeans. If he is Negro he will find little discrimination, except in a few Greek-letter fraternities. Most of his classes will be large in the first years, but his teachers have regular visiting hours, and with a little push he can get to know them. He will not be permitted to drive a car or to keep liquor in his room.

On many winter mornings he will wake to find great snows, and there will be a serene hush upon the campus and the creaking of branches overhead as he walks to his class. In spring he will glance outside at a blossoming world and resolve to keep his eye away from the girl sitting beside him. By June, the heat of the prairies will threaten to kill him and he will leave just in time.

If he has the talent, he may join the *Michigan Daily* staff, and the *Daily* is as close to a real newspaper as he will find in any school. On its own press, it prints about 7,500 copies a day, has the Associated Press wire service and syndicated columnists, and its student staff is paid twelve dollars a month and up. The university athletic plant includes a stadium seating nearly 100,000 people, indoor and outdoor tennis courts, swimming pools, and so on.

If a figure can convey an idea of complexity and size, it costs about

$40 million a year to keep the place going. There are now better than 18,000 students and nearly 1,200 faculty, and the figures will rise next year and the year after. The school has just bought 347 acres for new buildings. More facts may be had for the asking; but in any case, you couldn't do better for facilities.

Things seem to be getting *done* now. For instance, on the north side of the campus the Phoenix Project is going up, the only thing of its kind in the country. It was conceived by an alumnus in the advertising business who discovered, while traveling through Europe, that we were being accused of using the atom for war only. Returning here, he began a campaign for alumni contributions to create an institute which will accept no government money, do no war work, and instead of operating in secrecy will attempt to discover and disperse the knowledge of the atom that will, some say, revolutionize human life. Research projects are under way, although the scientists are not yet housed in one building, and already a method has been found by which the dreaded trichina, often found in pork, is destroyed. One of the men in charge of the project told me that the implications of Phoenix will reach into every science, that it has already moved into botany, medicine, dentistry, and eventually will span them all.

There is an enormous growth in all kinds of theater since I was at Michigan. Somewhere, sometime this year on campus, you could have seen *Brigadoon*, Gilbert and Sullivan, a German play, a French play, Aristophanes, Pirandello, *Deep Are the Roots*, *Faust*, *Madame Butterfly*, *Mister Roberts*, and more, all acted by students. A professional theater has done Camus, Bridie, Shakespeare, Saroyan, Yeats, Gertrude Stein, Sophocles, Synge and the Norwegian Krog. A symphony orchestra and a jazz band play student compositions frequently; there is a practically continuous art show going on, with both traveling and local exhibitions on view; the best foreign and art films are shown once a week, and the joint is jumping with concerts. All this is proof that a considerable number of people in Ann Arbor are looking for more than technology and are eager to feed their souls—a fact sometimes doubted by many in and out of the university.

The increase in students goes far to explain the impression of great activity, of building, of research, the scores of research projects, and of course the great increases in the faculty, especially in the English and Psychology Departments. But the changes are also qualitative. As one small sign, the music school has a few teachers who actually compose. The old idea of the university is not passing away, it is being worked away, it seems; the study of phenomena is giving way to the creation of useful things. *Generation*, the literary magazine, does not merely publish essays on music but new scores, as well as poetry, photographs and stories.

The university has the feel of a practical workshop these days. In my time a great deal of research and thesis writing was carried on by people who were simply hiding from the Depression. When you asked undergraduates what they intended to major in, and what career they meant to follow, you saw an oblong blur float across their eyes. These days nearly everybody seems to be quite sure. I knew graduate students who lived in an abandoned house with no electricity or heat and never took the boardings off the windows for fear of discovery, and one of them had been around so long he had gone through every course in the lit school but Roman Band Instruments. The lucky ones got an assistantship at $600 a year and even so looked like they had dropped out of a novel by Dostoyevski. Now, in some departments, a man doing his dissertation hooks into a research project and earns $2,400 a year and sometimes gets secretarial help in the bargain.

The Psychology Department, for instance, which used to have about a half-dozen members, and was year in year out trying to discover the learning processes of rats put through an enormous maze, now spreads out over a whole floor of offices, and spends tens of thousands investigating mass behavior of *people*, of all things, problems of industrial psychology, and in the words of one troubled researcher, "how to make people do what you want them to while thinking they are doing it because *they* want to."

From the physical, quantitative point of view, it seems to me that if by some magic this university of 1953 had suddenly materialized on a morning in 1935, let's say, we would have decided that the millennium had arrived. The mere fact that every morning the *Michigan Daily* displays two columns of invitations from corporations and government bureaus to students to apply for positions would have been enough.

The millennium is here, and yet it isn't here. What's wrong, then? I have no proof for this, but I felt it many times in my stay and I'll say it: I did not feel any love around the place. I suspect that I resent the Detroit Modern architecture of the new administration building and the new Haven and Mason Halls, and the fluorescent lighting and the gray steel furniture in the teachers' office cubicles. Can steel furniture ever belong to anybody, or can anybody ever belong to steel furniture? Is it all right to need so much administration that you have to put up an office building with nothing but administrators in it? Maybe it's all right, but God, it's not a university, is it? Why not? I don't know why not, it just feels like an insurance company, that's all. And yet, with eighteen to twenty thousand students, I suppose you've got to have it. Somebody's got to count them. But there is no love in it.

There is a certain propriety around the place that I found quite strange. Or was it always that way and I didn't notice? I do not remember teachers lowering their voices when they spoke to you in the corridors, but they do that now. At first I thought it was my imagination, and I asked a few men about it, but they denied that they do it. Still, they are doing it. The place is full of comportment. Maybe I have been around theatrical folk too long but it seemed to me that everybody had turned into engineers—in my day all engineers wore black suits and short, antiseptic haircuts. The curious thing is that now the engineers affect buckskin shoes and dungarees or tan chino work pants.

The lists of help-wanted notices alone would have solved the problem of my generation. And yet in talking with a certain high administrative official, it quickly became evident that the millennium had not yet arrived. I found it hard to believe that this gentleman had been elevated to administration, because when he was my teacher several hundred years ago he used to drop his coat on the floor sometimes and forget about tying his tie correctly, and his suits were usually rumpled. He just wasn't executive. Now his suits are pressed and finished worsted not tweed, but the smile is still warm and the eyes crinkle with a great love for humanity. He is very proud of the school, but there is a cloud. There is a cloud over the whole place which is hard to define, and here is part of it. I do not quote him but summarize what he said:

There is less hanging around the lamppost than there used to be. The student now is very young and he has little background. He generally comes with high respect for Michigan's academic standards. The school takes the top half of the in-state students and the top twenty percent of the out-staters. Fear of the competition is one reason why they absorb themselves in the pursuit of grades. Another is that they do not want to lose their Army deferments. Finally, in the old days a corporation would interview a C student because he might have other valuable qualities, while today the selections are almost statistical—they see the very top of the class and no others. The students know this and are more methodical about grades to the neglect of other interests.

The implication seemed to be that they are more machinelike and perhaps even duller. Or perhaps he meant only that some spirit had departed.

What spirit was he referring to? I think I know. The word *university* used to imply a place of gentle inquiry, an absorbing waste of time from the money point of view, a place where one "broadened" oneself. And I think he meant that everything is being *defined* now, it is all becoming so purposeful in the narrow sense of the trade school that some of the old separation between university and commerce, university and vocation, university and practicality in the narrow sense, is disappearing.

One symptom of this is the growing and dangerous rivalry with Michigan State College. In my day State was an agricultural college, and the University of Michigan was "The Harvard of the West." Today State is challenging the university for supremacy in all departments, even threatening to rename itself Michigan State *University*. Dr. John A. Hannah, State's vigorous president, has been able to raise enough funds to build a row of impressive dormitories along the main road. The public can see and count the things it is getting for its money. The university cannot compete for the public's appreciation—and support—on the basis of invisible accomplishments like culture and broadening. Consequently, a new and in my time unheard-of slogan is going around the faculty gatherings. Service to the state is the idea. Do things they can *see*. My friend spoke with startlingly serious irritation, real misgivings, about State's victories over Michigan in football. It has come even to that.

As in everything else, therefore, the competition must be carried through on the level of the lowest bidder. Michigan State has always been able to show that where one blade of corn had grown now there were two because of its new insecticides, and the cows were happier for its vaccines. Michigan State went on television, got its own station, so the university decided to win friends and acquire *its* station.

A professor of English was speaking to me in his office. I must note the incongruity of this particular man sitting in this particular office. In my time this man was, how shall I say, dusty. We were all afraid of him because in his classes you either knew your stuff or you didn't. His subject had made him pale and austerely exact. A great poem was a structure that had to be turned and turned until you understood its time, its place, its rhythms, and the telling reference in every line. Only a powerful love for the poem itself could have generated his kind of energy in teaching it. He is the kind of man who just does not go with fluorescent lighting and long hallways with little cubicles opening off them, and rivalry toward Michigan State. Or so it seemed long ago.

I asked if he noticed any difference between the present student and school, and the student and school of fifteen years ago. A repressed anger crackled in his eyes.

"It's *all* different. Take the study of literature. Who are its judges? The psychologist is looked to for an analysis of motivations. But even that isn't as bad as looking at a book or a play to discover what kind of Oedipus complex the author had. The sociologists are deferred to as the only men who can really say how typical the situation is in society, and the anthropologist also has a few words handy. Now, I am only an amateur in these disciplines. They are the experts. And what about the literary people? They are becoming experts in their own way. We have what are called The New Critics. The poem to them is a thing in itself. If the diction is exact, the imagery consistent, the writing original and the form consonant with the breadth of the matter, that's the end of it. It is as though the values of humanity——"

The Values. A certain few themes kept coming up wherever I went, and The Values were in the center. The impression gained from certain quarters is that, in 1953, it is thought sufficient to have described a piece of existence, whether it is a book or an isotope. The conflict is being played around certain connected themes. One is The Values. Another is Apathy.

Another English teacher told me: "The student today has no spine. He thinks he is here to receive something that is wrapped up, easily digestible and complete. He is not really working anything *out*."

The *Michigan Daily* keeps bewailing "apathy" among the students. One reason is that it cannot find enough men to man its positions. The Values and Apathy.

I went back to the *Daily* building and looked up the papers of my day, '34 to '38. I was surprised and amused to read that the Michigan student was a lizard, apathetic, uninterested in campus affairs.

So it gets more complicated. The student is apathetic, but the *Daily* thought he was apathetic in 1936. In those days we laughed at research-for-its-own-sake and now people are disturbed because everything has got so practical, provable and dangerously unvague.

A psychology professor told me: "The student *is* different. The back-talk is feeble. They *are* passive. Imagine a graduate student asking me to tell him what his dissertation subject should be. I couldn't believe my ears at first, but it is happening regularly now. And more than that, they expect me to lay out the lines of their research, and when I try not to do it, they are astonished. They regard themselves as instruments. It is as though they thought it a waste of time to speculate, to move into unknown territory, which is just what they should be doing."

Another psychologist said: "The most embarrassing question you can ask a researcher is, 'Why are you doing this?' He can tell you its immediate application, but whether it is good or bad to apply it or whether it could be a disastrous power to put in the wrong hands either is not his business or else he is just hoping for the best."

I began to feel after a while that something was chasing everybody here. The Necessity to Keep Doing. A fantastic number of discoveries being made and a gnawing worry about What it is All For. I think the Phoenix Project is one answer, a statement of the university's conscience.

One example of this atmosphere of pursuit is the television question.

A professor of English: "Now we are going on television. Why? Allegedly to spread education among the people. But is that really why? It is not. It is because Michigan State is winning friends and influencing people, so we must. Did you know that they send out calendars reading, 'Come to Michigan State, The Friendly College'? We are now going to be 'friendly'! Can you really teach people on a university level through TV? My subject is hard. It requires that a student work to understand it. Isn't it inevitable that we will have to make it easier and easier and lower our standards in order to compete? The TV audience is profoundly passive. It is looking for a massage, not a message. And in addition my subject has 'controversial' aspects. Can a teacher maintain the courage to speak his heart in the face of the pressure groups and the mass ignorance they can arouse against him? I don't believe it. We are being asked to become entertainers, and the time will come when a professor will be cast for voice, looks and camera manners. Oh, you can laugh, but it is absolutely in the cards. We are going to have to put ourselves over, we are going to have to sell Michigan. The neon age of education is upon us. And don't confuse this with democracy. It is the triumph of the leveler, and the man in charge is an advertising man."

I could go on endlessly because in nearly every conversation these themes kept cropping up. But there are many who deny their validity.

A physicist: "I know they are all beefing about passivity, but I don't find it in my field. They are as hep and alive as they ever were. Some of this 'apathy' is really a kind of maturity. Kids don't join things so much now, because they are more serious. There is, of course, the problem of values. The atomic boys found that out with a jolt. It is not enough to discover something, one must work on the problem of its use. And you can be sure that a scientist who has the brains to work in nuclear physics is intelligent enough to worry about values. So much so that some people risked a great deal and went to the government to implore them to understand what the atom implied. Don't think for a minute that we are automatons without conscience. Nothing is farther from the truth."

Another English professor: "I can't tell any great difference between these kids and any peacetime class. I think what some of the others are complaining about is really based on our experience with the veterans who left here about 1948. It's true, they were thrilling people to teach. They were serious but inquisitive, they were after the facts, but they knew that a philosophy, a standard of values, was of first importance. But the prewar classes didn't measure up to the veterans either."

I met students in the restaurants, in dormitories, classrooms, hallways, and in the union, the center for nonfraternity students. If there were no two alike, they nevertheless had certain common feelings that came up to the surface very quickly. Michigan means freedom to them. It has nothing to do with academic freedom but a release from home and the neighborhood or town they came from. This is as it always was, but I had forgotten what an adventure it was to leave home. One afternoon I sat with the girls on the veranda of the Martha Cook dormitory. Martha Cook is brick and ivy, lawns and old trees, and windows you remember as leaded but which are not, mellow wood, and an outline of Tudor-out-of-Yale.

The Girl From Massachusetts: "Oh, gosh, yes. I would never dare do at home what I think nothing of doing here. What, exactly? Well, I don't know, but I go out with fellows my parents wouldn't approve of. You couldn't be friendly, really, with a Chinese or a Negro in my town. Not really, you couldn't. You can here."

The Girl From New York (the intellectual): "Well, that's not quite true. It's very complicated."

The Girl From Ohio (who will marry a law student after graduation and settle in Rio, where he will practice): "I think it's enormously freer. It's like, well, it's an explosion, almost. I started in literature, then I went to botany, and now I'm in music." And brother, she was. As they used to say, she was bursting with life, sitting there in blue jeans, her heels tucked against her buttocks, her knees up around her cheeks, and a sunburned face sucking in everything that was said and ever would be said. But the others thought she was hasty in planning to settle outside the country. I was surprised. I had thought they would all be thrilled at the prospect of foreign lands. It took a minute for them to say exactly why they thought her hasty.

"There might be a revolution there," they finally agreed. It would be better to stay home.

Maybe they were just envious. But they weren't apathetic, if that means dull, without thought. The Depression means to them what World War I meant to us; that is, an old-fashioned thing. Time after time I got the same image—"It couldn't happen that way again. The government wouldn't let it, I don't think." They seem to feel that society is under control; it is so enormous, and it *is* operating, that there is just nothing to think about in that department. They feel there is enormous opportunity for anybody; that men are rewarded pretty much according to their abilities, and time and time again said the same line, "It's up to me."

The famous panty raids that swept the country started at Michigan last year and these girls had witnessed that strange crusade. It seems that some guy was blowing a trumpet in one of the men's dorms, and somebody else yelled at him to stop, and the trumpet player dared the other guy to make him stop, but instead of fighting they decided to invade the women's dormitories and steal panties. A crowd gathered and kept getting bigger all night as one dormitory after another was entered. Martha Cook was among those that "fell." The girls were quite gay about it and told the story as though they kind of wished more of the same would happen now and then.

The story sounded as though it might well have happened at any time, the Thirties included, but to my ear there was nevertheless a strange note in it. It did not sound like a simple sexual outburst. As the girls spoke, I had the feeling that the panty raids were one of those phenomena which are only superficially sexual and were directed more as a challenge to the atmosphere of paternal repression which is, and always was, quite strong at Michigan.

An administrative official arranged a luncheon for me with a dozen or so student leaders. I feared this would be a polite waste of time and it is no reflection on the man to say that they were under wraps in his presence. As they themselves told me later, the paternalism of the administration is not conducive to student expression. It was always a rather heavily administration-dominated school, but in the old days they had a fight for their money. I remember one hell of a racket when Fred Warner Neal, probably the most prolific reporter the paper ever had, resigned from the *Daily*—which gave him a full column on Page 1 to write his resignation—because the administration had forbidden him to write some story or other. And I remember he was reinstated. I remember committees demanding to see the president whenever they didn't like something, and I remember a few times when they won the argument, or half won it.

These dozen, being interested enough to head up the student legislature, the interfraternity council and so on, were the contemporary
equivalents of the people who made the noise in my time. While the
official was with us they weren't very noisy; it might have been a meeting of young bankers. But he had to leave soon and we were alone and
it started coming.

"People are afraid to say anything."

Afraid of what?

"Well, for instance, a lot of people are tired of paying high prices for
books. We want a university bookstore, but we know we'll never get one
because the bookstores will raise hell and, besides, the administration
won't pay any attention to us."

But you're evidently not afraid to make the demand.

"No, not exactly afraid——"

What do you think would happen if you tried to rally support on campus for a demand like that?

"You mean, like to have a meeting or demonstrate?"

They all looked uncomfortable. Some laughed nervously.

One boy said, "We'd be called communists."

You mean that truly?

"Sure. But the worst thing would be that back home the papers would
pick up our names and there might be trouble."

You mean they'd think you'd been turned into Reds here?

"Some people would think so, but it's not exactly being called communists, it's different."

What exactly is it?

"Well, it's that when you went to, let's say, the local plant for a job, and
if they found out about it they would—well, they wouldn't like you."

Oh.

A girl: "I live in a cooperative house." And really, she blushed. "I'm
getting ashamed to mention it because people on campus ask me why do
you live with those collectivists? But it's cheaper, and anyway they're
not collectivists." They all laughed but they knew that what she was
saying was true.

A boy hitherto silent: "I know for a fact that everything you do is
being written down and sent to the authorities."

Like what?

"Never mind, I just know it."

I had, the day before, been sitting in the *Daily* building going through
the 1934–38 papers. A middle-aged man with eyeglasses and a thick

neck took out a file and after a while began noting things down. A reporter came over to me and whispered that this man was a state policeman, and his job was to check up on subversives in the school. The reporter said that he and the others on the paper were always trying to tell the man that the people he was listing were not Reds, but he went right on, in a very affable way, listing anyone who was connected with anything "controversial."

It is necessary to add that at the luncheon, the very broaching of this subject reddened some faces. They were bravely willing to discuss it, and really quite eager to, but if they were not in fear I do not understand anything.

"That's why everybody wants to get into Intelligence."

What's that?

"I'm telling you the facts."

"Oh, go on, they just feel they won't get shot in Intelligence."

"There's a lot of jobs in the Army where you don't get shot. I swear, they all want to get into Intelligence."

So that they can investigate other people?

"No, they don't want to investigate other people, but they feel once they get in there they won't be bothered any more."

Would you like to get into Intelligence?

Laughter. "Sure, I'd take it."

And he blushes. That is, he blushes, but he would take it although he's against it.

There are more evidences of gumshoeing around the campus, but it would be false to picture the place as being in fear of any specific thing. The important fact to me is that the gumshoeing is disliked, sometimes scorned, but accepted as perfectly natural. Sometimes the old liberalism will crop up, however. Not long ago the university prohibited a communist from speaking on campus, and Professor Slosson went to the hall where the man had to make his address, debated with him, and from all accounts slaughtered him.

Compared to my years at Michigan there does seem to be a blanket over the place now. The tone is more subdued, if one measures tone by the amount of discussion, argument and protest openly indulged in. In my day we were more likely to believe that what we thought and did would have an effect upon events, while the present student sees himself separated from the great engine that is manufacturing his and the country's fate.

But it would be inaccurate to think that these boys and girls are inert.

I sat in on a graduate seminar in political science one afternoon at which five students and a professor were discussing the subtlest relationships between political ideologies over a span of three centuries. It is a long time since I witnessed such complete concentration upon essentials, sharpness of mind, and freedom from cant and sloganeering. In the Thirties such a discussion would have verged on partisanship after an hour, but it never did here, and that is a big change, I think.

They know now that the old easy solutions are suspect, and they are examining rather than exhorting each other. In this sense they are more mature than we were, yet they are also more separated and removed from the idea of action. But action is immensely more complicated than it was and more difficult to conceive; for instance, one of the heaviest loads they bear is the Army draft. In my day we could rally and vote against conscription because it was only a threat, while today there is nothing to be done about it, and it makes futile many of their plans and weakens as well the very idea of controlling their own destinies.

I do not know how things will work out at Michigan any more than the next man does. It may be the faculty men are correct who see a profound shift of values which will make of Michigan a place not unintelligent, not overtly browbeaten, but a school of obedient pragmatists where each individual walks in blinders toward his niche in government or giant corporation, his soul unswept by the hot blasts of new ideas and vast social concepts. The very bigness of Michigan, the size of the investment in it, and the mutual suspicion that is gripping so many people are forces that would help such a process along. And there is a deeper, less-noticed frame of mind which goes even farther to create such an atmosphere, and I think of the faculty man-of-goodwill, in this context, who was talking to me about a certain administrator who paid no attention to the students' ideas or complaints or suggestions. "It's a pity," said this faculty man, "that X's public relations are not better." Whether X might in fact have *been* authoritarian and unheeding was evidently beside the point. The fault to remedy was X's inability to put himself over. It is in such remarks and attitudes that one sees the absence of an idealism I clearly remember at Michigan and in its place a kind of pragmatism that threatens to create a race of salesmen in the tawdry sense of that word.

I cannot promise that it will not end this way: a chromium-plated silence, a highly organized, smoothly running factory for the production of conformism. I only know that in my time it was supposed to be a training ground for leftists or, from the opposite viewpoint, a cave of vigilantism, and it turned out to be neither. I know that when I recently sat with individual students they spoke like seekers, their clean, washed faces as avid for truth as I suppose we were so long ago. I know that they do not think of themselves as a "silent generation" or as a generation at all but simply as "me." I know that in their rooming houses and dormitories the old bull sessions go on into the mornings, but I also know that what so many of them really feel—and here, I think, lies the difference between the generations—they are not saying in public nowadays, if it seems to question that this is the best of all possible worlds. It is simply not done in 1953.

When I stood waiting for the plane at Willow Run I tried to summon up the memory of the other time I had left Ann Arbor, in the fall of 1938. I had had a ride to New York with a young salesman of saddles and riding equipment who had just passed through Ann Arbor. He had been in contact only with the upper echelons of the community—certain high officials, industrialists, a regent or two who owned horses. He had sold a lot of saddles in Ann Arbor. He was leaving with the impression of a fairly ritzy school. For myself, I had not known a single soul in four years who had mounted a horse.

As he started the engine I waved to a girl who was standing in front of the Women's League, a girl that I dared not dream I would ever have money enough, or security of soul enough, to marry. As we drove east, through Toledo, Ashtabula, the red-brick roads through the Ohio farmlands, I tried to tell him what Michigan really was. It was the professor who, with selected members of his class, held séances during which the spirits of Erasmus, Luther and other historical figures were summoned and listened to. It was the fraternity boys sitting on the porches of their mansions, singing nostalgic Michigan songs as in a movie, and it was three radicals being expelled. It was, in short, the testing ground for all my prejudices, my beliefs and my ignorance, and it helped to lay out the boundaries of my life. For me it had, above everything else, variety and freedom. It is probably the same today. If it is not, a tragedy is in the making.

—1953

From *Echoes Down the Corridor: Collected Essays 1944–2000*, edited by Steven R. Centola (New York: Viking Press, 2000).

Allan Seager

֍

from A Frieze of Girls

Every freshman rented a room somewhere. Every freshman had a program of study. These were essential, not important. It was fraternities
that were important. Nearly every freshman emitted a kind of cloudy
yearning to be pledged. Some were modestly willing to take any pledge
pin they could get. Others went around smirking because they were lega-
cies, merely waiting on a formality. Others, like myself, were fussy. During the first week I learned that the fraternities my friends belonged to in
the South were not very highly regarded here. SAE, for instance, which
at Sewanee was jammed with aristocrats, did not rank much higher than
the YMCA. There were Yankee outfits new to me like the Dekes, Psi Us,
Chi Psis, and Sigma Phis which seemed to have more class. And "class"
was the right word. I wanted to be identified with the right people and I
didn't think a couple of swimming medals would quite do it.

Had I known then that an ancestor of mine had sailed from Plym-
outh, England, in 1630 and settled in Connecticut, I could have rested
secure in another kind of snobbery, but all I knew was that my grandfather had originated in Vermont and had taken up veterans' land in
Michigan after the Civil War. Beyond him my family might have sprung
from acorns, for all I knew. And I had very little money. I had to depend
on my yearning and a few friends who didn't know me very well because
I had been in the South for nearly ten years. One's sixth-grade pals
change almost out of recognition in ten years.

I accepted invitations from inferior houses because the meals were
free. It was understood that they looked you over for two meals, and if
they asked you for a third, you could expect an offer to join. One night
during my first visit to one of them, I was hustled upstairs and shut in a
small room with the football captain, who had been sitting there all
alone. He was wearing his sweater with the big M on his chest. He gave
me a lot of prepared malarkey about "working for Michigan," insisting
that the best place to do this was in his particular club. Statements like
this embarrass me and did then. I didn't want to work for Michigan. I

wanted Michigan to work for me, although I was polite enough not to say so. As he talked his face had a faraway look as if he did not keep his clichés handily in his head but down in his stomach and laboriously regurgitated them. It tired him and at last he reached a dead stop. I had begun to say, "I've got to be going," when he silently whipped a pledge pin out of his pocket and tried to stick it in my lapel. He was a good deal heavier than I and he nearly made it, but I got away safely.

If I cast my mind back over those years casually, I can say like everyone else that my college years were the happiest of my life. However, I kept a diary and when I look at the entries for the early days of my first semester, the truth comes back. I was numb with anxiety. The right people weren't rushing me. It was a rainy fall and in the diary I am always stalking around in a smelly green slicker with wet leaves stuck to my shoes, worrying, and when I was not walking I lay on my bed waiting for the phone to ring. I didn't know what was the matter with me. I looked hardly any different from other pledges, and my poverty, or what I thought was my poverty, didn't show. I considered, I thought quite seriously, running away to sea or going to Australia to raise sheep. Then with an oily celerity I was asked to lunch twice at one of the houses I had secretly chosen and pledged the third night. I relaxed. I felt worthwhile.

It didn't take me a week to find out that I didn't like the brothers very well. I couldn't admit this even privately and it made me criminally aloof. My adviser, an elegant senior, lectured me on my "attitude" whenever he could find the time, but he never had much to say since I never had much to say. (It reminded me of my grade-school days in Memphis, when, hating the place, I tried to get through every day without saying a single word. I made it only once.) I performed my freshman duties, waking the upper-classmen in the morning and answering the phone with as little talk as possible. And I didn't hang around the fraternity house trying to be a popular pledge because someone would find me an errand to run if I did.

Slowly I learned that the house was split down the middle into the Christers and the drunks. (I do not believe this schism still exists. I think they are all drunks. At least they were fined twenty-five hundred dollars a year ago for keeping a bar in the cellar.) The Christers were the more conscientious about everything, the drunks the more interesting. Although I was out for swimming, I resolved to line myself up with the drunks.

We had what is called in the South "a big old boy" from the hills of West Virginia whom the football coaches had their eye on. He was a twenty-three-year-old freshman. He weighed around two hundred and thirty and his fist looked like a peck of potatoes. Like most wrestlers and football players he had a sweet nature and with a docile somnolence he acquiesced in the brothers' attempts to teach him to play bridge all one winter. He did not quite learn the game properly as he always bid "two spades" no matter what cards he held, but he was always glad to play. He also took a mild interest in his textbooks, riffling the pages delicately with his great hands to see if there were any pictures, and if he found one, he would go, "Whooee! Looka hyuah now!" in a pleased falsetto.

He called all girls "poon tang" indiscriminately but he was gentle and smiling with those he met. He couldn't dance a step and didn't try, but parties were always crowded and he was very happy to hug some girl in a corner while the music played. If, however, misled by his open face and his gentleness, she went into a room alone with him, she came sprinting out thirty seconds later, disheveled and shrieking with disillusion.

While our house was not an athletic house, it was believed that athletes did no harm, and, in fact, it was wise to keep a couple in residence to back up our claim that we were a well-rounded group. Everyone knew that it was going to be hard to keep Maxcey around for very long. While it was not true that he was totally analphabetic, the printed word gave him a rough time. He could read, muttering every word and pointing to it with his toelike fingernail, but it was so hard for him and he was so relieved to finish any sentence with an approximate accuracy that it was like a ritual. We used to gather to watch him read, each of us forming the words silently with his own lips, mutely cheering him on, a mutual frown forming at every impediment, and an exhalation and wide general smile at the period. A successful paragraph would raise a ragged cheer, and Maxcey—proud as he could be—would clasp his hands over his head and cry "Heah now!"

I suppose everybody in the house had a crack at tutoring him one time or another. Maxcey was as patient as a turtle, obviously ashamed of his own deficiencies, and he meekly accepted correction from snotty youths he could have broken in two. His first two years we were aided by the Athletic Department, who steered him into courses in Physical Education where, to pass, he had little to do but ripple his muscles, but we feared his junior and senior years, when he would have to take academic subjects. We cooked up quite a few schemes to help him out. One we discarded might have worked. It was to register a moderately intelligent brother under Maxcey's name in two or three of his courses. Maxcey was delighted and offered to pay any *Doppelgänger* handsomely. (Maxcey had a lot of money some alumnus had sent him.) We didn't use this plan because we surmised that the authorities would throw everyone concerned out of school if they caught us. As it was, we put him into courses that at least two other brothers were taking. They moved him to class every day, lent him their notes, and explained what was going on as well as they could. At exam time they made cribs for him, either writing in block letters on a small roll of toilet paper which he could feed across his belly, from one pants pocket to another, tear and stuff into the pockets if the professor came snooping around, or packets of notes given to freshmen with instructions to lurk in the men's toilet nearest the exam until Maxcey came in when they were to read the notes to him as quickly as possible. The freshmen got fairly tired of this but it helped Maxcey. He staggered through his program, dragging a tail of C-minuses after him.

In his junior year Maxcey signed up for a course in Speech, charmed because he thought that all he would have to do was talk, but the professor threw him a curve. Maxcey had to learn the anatomy of voice production, and the differences between larynx and pharynx took relays of frantic helpers because Maxcey had heard of the lynx, the furry denizen of the forests, and that lynx kept creeping in.

It was a second-semester course and the grade depended chiefly on a term paper. The subject was the endocrine glands. In the month of April Maxcey was never seen without a book on the endocrines in his hands. The football coach had told every member of the squad to keep a football on his desk during the year and to squeeze it and fondle it while studying so as to get the feel of it. I think this was what Maxcey was doing with the book; I didn't see him read it. The paper didn't get written and Maxcey asked the professor to give him an Incomplete and he was so genial the professor did. Maxcey went off to work as a stationmaster at some whistle stop in the West Virginia mountains for the summer. When he returned in the fall, he still didn't have the paper done although he said he had tried. He called on the professor humbly, contritely, and the professor said, "I'll tell you what I'll do, Mr. Maxcey. I'll give you an oral examination in lieu of the paper."

"Yassuh," Maxcey said, frightened. I don't think he thought the professor was going to look at his teeth. I don't think he knew what was coming next at all.

"Mr. Maxcey, name the endocrine glands."

"The endocrine glands?"

"Yes. Just name them."

"Well, suh, There's the thah-roid," Maxcey said dreamily.

"That's right."

"And there's the para-thahroid."

"That's good. Go on."

"And there's the tabloid . . . and there's the hemorrhoid. . . ." Maxcey sat there, the professor said, clutching his little finger and glaring at it. We had told him there were five endocrines.

The professor stared at him a second to see if Maxcey was kidding him, but Maxcey never kidded anybody. Then, as Maxcey said later, the professor "like to ruptured himself laughin'" and he said, "Mr. Maxcey, I'm going to give you an A."

Maxcey came loping into the house, cuffed the heads of all the bridge players, and shouted, "Where's mah jug? I got mahseff an A!" That evening he drank nearly a gallon of some white stuff we called "sheep-dip" that came off a farm near Jackson. He was the first man I ever saw drink from a jug with one hand, throwing it gracefully over his elbow. Someone had given him "asteroid" as the fifth endocrine and at midnight he was prowling up and down the corridors, the jug dangling from one finger, interrupting studiers, waking sleepers, shouting, "Son, you know the names of the endocrine glands?" and he would tick them all off. The House Committee fined him five dollars because A's weren't as rare as all that, but he didn't care. The Speech professor told the story and eventually it went all over the campus.

After I had gotten through first-year Greek, my own work went well enough. I moved into the fraternity house, a brand-new Elizabethan pile, and my roommate and I decided to study every day. But to keep from looking as if we did, we studied at that idle time, from five until seven. While the rest of the brothers were playing bridge, taking showers, or listening to records, we had our door locked and we hit the books. Nobody caught us at it. Since we had to study only a couple of evenings a week in addition, we acquired the welcome reputation of intelligent bums because we were always ready to drop the books and go to a movie or a speakeasy.

I am not aware that I had, as some people do in college, a ripsnorting intellectual awakening, although several of my professors tried to jog me into one. My first class in the university was in English. On the first day, the instructor, a fresh-cheeked, lame young man, came in without a word to us, wrote "Great is Diana of the Ephesians" on the blackboard, and said, "Write for twenty minutes about that." None of us thought it silly. It cowed and appalled us all. The longer I thought about it, the madder I got. At last I wrote this on my paper and handed it in, "It's a hell of a note to expect freshmen to comment on the Pauline Epistles." I don't know what the instructor thought but he took me out of freshman English and put me into a sophomore class where I was immediately asked to describe a man doing physical work to the point of exhaustion but I can't recall the professor who assigned that one.

Only two or three of my teachers stand out in my mind. One is an old man, erect, with his open hands away from his sides, reciting Goethe's *Faust* from memory, as tears ran down his face. Some of the class giggled. Now that I am older, I know he didn't give a damn whether anyone giggled or not, but I was terribly afraid he was going to be hurt then and I poked the guy in front of me and told him to shut up. After that I got up my German before any other subject, and I have never believed that his tears were pedagogical.

Another was a tough little Scot from Aberdeen and Cambridge, all tweed and flying hair like the British. I say tough because I became his student assistant in my senior year and one night I saw him drink two bottles of horrible bootleg whisky and walk away. This was astonishing because he was no bigger than Jimmy Wilde, the flyweight champ, but he dominated his classes and he did it by contempt. He would ask wide-eyed students from Kalamazoo or Grand Rapids about Maillol, Braque, or Paul Klee, and when their tongues clave to the roofs of their mouths, he would sniff and go on about Rimbaud or Eliot—who was very new then and his special property. I asked him why he put these hard questions when it was so obvious that no one knew the answers. "They must hear the names sometime, mustn't they?" he said. My acquaintance with him was no protection. Once in a paper about Huxley's *Antic Hay*, I said that I didn't believe people like Gumbril, Lypiatt, or Coleman had ever existed. He wrote in the margin, "You just haven't been around enough." I knew that but it stung me to have it pointed out when I was trying as hard as I could.

Later he was fired. Only grave moral turpitude was grounds for firing a full professor, and the story was that he had been found in bed with the leading lady of an itinerant drama group. It didn't occur to me at the time but this is an inherently unlikely story. Who does the finding (a student, a dean, a uniformed policeman?) and how do they know when to time it? I am inclined to believe that he was as contemptuous of his colleagues as he was of us and they used the actress only as a lever. A few years afterward he died of yellow jaundice on Staten Island, oddly enough.

My roommate and I took a course in Fine Arts. The label didn't mean what it implied. It was, like all such courses, a history of painting, architecture, and sculpture. The professor was a thick bald man with a face like a mandrill. He wore a neat serge suit, and he moved and spoke with a briskness we all thought inartistic. When he threw slides of Sant' Ambrogio or Azay-le-Rideau on the screen, I had the impression that he was discussing valuable pieces of real estate which we could buy at a good price if we were sharp about it. He had reduced his course to a twenty-page outline, price a quarter at any of the bookstores. When it came to the final exam, my roommate and I decided to ignore the questions, learn his outline, and give it back to him.

Through two hot June days, lolling in our shorts, we conned that damned outline over like a poem until we knew it cold. (I have never been able to shuck some of the facts. They remain in my memory as cold and unfruitful as pebbles. The water for the aqueduct at Nîmes comes from the springs above Uzès. The "eye" in the Pantheon at Rome is 24'9" across.) On the day of the final we wrote out the whole outline. We were the first ones to finish. As we turned in our blue books, he picked them up and thumbed through them. When he saw what we had done, he said, "If you have made one mistake, I'll flunk you." We hadn't, though, and he had to give us A's. Everyone said he had been a guard in the Metropolitan Museum.

From *A Frieze of Girls* (New York: McGraw-Hill, 1964).
Reprinted with an introduction by Charles Baxter
(Ann Arbor: University of Michigan Press, 2004).

Peggy Goodin

☩

from Take Care of My Little Girl

Two days later the Queens had an afternoon luncheon. A girl named Dallas, short for Dorothy Alice, was put in charge. Dallas had short blond hair, a long nose, very black eyebrows, and a Hollywood bra. She was interested in becoming a fashion writer and now and then she wrote columns for the *Daily* playfully signed Alice Bluegown and Miss Muffet and Helen of Troy. She was fond of men (the Phi Delts had elected her Desert Island Date) but she was infallible about women. Since Dallas had become a Queen, the Queens had become truly swish. They affected ascots, ballet shoes, tailored boys' shirts, and wrinkled trench coats. They were more like Dallas than Dallas was, with the possible exception of Ingrid Bergman. Since some things were useless from the beginning, it was only right that Dallas should have a look at any new material she'd be expected to take in hand. . . .

During pledging everybody had yellow cornflowers to hold and grape-juice to drink. Liz was deeply impressed with the words. The Queens stood for High Ideals and Eternal Sisterhood and they told the pledges they must begin to Feel Their Responsibility. The pledges said "Yea," and "Amen"; their shoulders drooped but the weight was sweet.

At the end of it there were fifteen ladies-in-waiting, possessed of silver pledge-pins.

Nominally the new pledges were "little sisters"; the theory was that each Queen ought to be a big sister to someone smaller and weaker, thereby offering the benefit of advice and occasionally allowing her stockings to be borrowed. In practice the choice became one of alphabetical allotment, entailing no particular trouble for anyone.

Upstairs in a room with two double-bunk beds and a gingham-covered bulletin board full of dance programs Liz sat talking, knee to knee, with Sister Dallas. "You've got it on wrong," Dallas told her. "Hook your thumb in the notch between your collarbones and spread your fingers. Put the pin where your third finger falls . . . like this. It's an easy way to tell. Sorry you'll be living with Casey, not that we aren't crazy about Casey . . . she's literary, or did you know? . . . but she won't be much help to you. How tall *are* you? Well, anyway, you have individuality. Stand up a minute. Now sideways. Ever tried these? Stick 'em inside and let's see. Don't be silly, some of our best girls do. Maybe you need something less pointed, but the idea's sound.

"Actually you're rather Vogue . . . it's a matter of starkness. There's so much you can do with it when it's unadorned. Why don't you wear your hair straight with a streak in front? You could bring out your eyes with gold suede. Your ears aren't pierced, I suppose . . . I use a hot needle and just wiggle the thread around inside for ten days. Painless. You can get a little tight if you're sensitive. I'll probably be doing two or three.

"You're not engaged or anything, are you? We could use it . . . gives you status. Your style definitely isn't jeune fille. You'll probably appeal to Phi Psi's, not Beta's. I'll take you along to the Jug to meet Sam. That's Sam on the floor. God, he falls off whenever the window's open. Cute, isn't he? Very Eastern, hates it out here, simply loathes it.

"What kind of men do you like?"

Liz didn't know, and her horizons had been stretched too far to hazard a guess. "What kinds are there?"

Dallas reached for a Pall Mall. "How true. But you'll be better off if you limit yourself, at least in the beginning. I'd suggest you pass up letter-men for activities-men. They're smoother. As I said, you're not jeune fille."

"I've gone steady," Liz ventured.

"Oh, I wouldn't worry about *sex*," said Dallas. "You can handle that. Unless, of course . . ." She looked at Liz. "Use discretion. Don't go after more than one pin in the same House. You know how men gossip."

"Did you bring your clothes?" Casey asked, coming in. "The closet's ready."

Liz explained. Dallas was clearly delighted. "If you have a charge at Clausson's we'll drop in and buy all new ones."

"Come, come, little fly," said Casey. "Crawl out of the web and follow me."

Liz moved in the next night. Rooming with Casey was a mixed honor. Casey had short red hair, a square expressive face, and a squat body, too broad for her height. She worked on the *Daily* and she wrote short stories which the campus literary magazine assured her were chock-full of lyrical passages. In her spare time she dabbled in sculpture. Casey was not cordial to more than three or four Queens. Among other things, she said, she preferred tropical fish. No one quite understood why she stayed with the Queens. In a word, she felt martyred. After all, it was something of a compliment to be misunderstood by the Queens; and for an artist, Casey had been told, misunderstanding was inevitable. As a square peg in a round hole, she was conscious of both public and private distinction.

Spiritually it was a Spartan existence, but the meals were excellent.

Her room was on the third floor. It had two beds, two chests of draw-ers, and, in the center of the room, two desks pushed together. On the walls were a Miró print (Person Throwing a Stone at a Bird) and water colors painted by friends. A Webster turntable sat on the floor beside a stack of records . . . Stravinsky, Bartók, Schoenberg, and *Six Songs For Democracy*. To the collection Liz added some early jazz and Marlene Dietrich.

"Junk, I suppose," said Casey pleasantly. "Especially Marlene. Who's Bessie Smith?"

Liz sat down on one of the delinquent suitcases, newly arrived. "A blues singer who recorded in the '20's. She's dead now. Bled to death outside of a hospital in Mississippi because it was a hospital for white people. Which side of the closet do you want me to take?"

"Put it anywhere." Casey swung open the door and kicked a laundry bag into the corner. "You sound promising, but we probably won't get along. Lots of people don't like me."

"How'd you get to be a Queen?" Liz grinned.

Casey raised one bushy red eyebrow as high as it would go and then dropped it. "The same way you did."

It was a chilling thought. Liz began to hang up clothes.

"Maybe you'd better pile that on the bed. There's a cocoa party in the kitchen."

"Aren't you coming along?"

"I usually pay my fifty-cent fine," said Casey, "and go out for coffee."

From *Take Care of My Little Girl* (New York: E. P. Dutton, 1950).

Ted Solotaroff

✣

from *First Loves: A Memoir*

There was also college life, which I'd decided to try for a while. At an interdorm dance, I found a small, sweet-faced girl with a shy dignity who liked my patter, and soon we were dating. Greta Stein was the daughter of German Jewish refugees, which gave a certain gravity to the relationship, if only in my eyes. In her own, she was a happily conventional Michigan coed whose strong, foreseeing parents had trained her to look forward, not back. She wore Peter Pan collars, bobby socks, penny loafers, and a frequent smile.

The fastest way into a culture is a romantic attachment and Greta was a Jewish Miss Midwest. I hung on the way she pronounced *forest* and *water*, spoke eagerly of the "Frosh hop," knew the names of all the trees and plants in the Arboretum. Soon I was spending three evenings a week in the lounge of Stockwell, where decorous necking was permitted and, after we had become "serious," Sunday afternoons in the Arboretum where we went to grind against each other. Taking Greta to the homecoming dance, visiting her once again prosperous parents in Detroit, who showed me where her stability came from—I was "happy as a clam," as she would say.

There was also the easy, democratic fellowship of Adams House, its touch football team that I played on, the nightly study breaks when our circle of mostly brainy upperclassmen strolled over to the Union for the intense midwestern milkshakes you ate with a spoon. Best of all, on alternate Saturdays, were the home football games. By noon, a great maize-and-blue wave of expectation picked you up in its crest and carried you with the other hundred thousand celebrants to the great bowl of a stadium. Being freshmen, Greta and I sat in the end zone where the band assembled before the game and then, led by its unique prancing marshal, sent forth the rousing "Hail to the Victors" and, under our roar, quick stepped down the field like some huge, precise, joyous machine.

Then came the game itself, in which the heroes we had been reading about all week in the *Daily* performed like the national champions they had been the year before. I gave myself up entirely to the pageant, the contest, the intently peering or cheering communion. Michigan football, with its legendary Jewish quarterback, Benny Friedman, had initially led me to dream of coming here, and on Saturday afternoons the twelve-year-old me met up with the reader of *The Iliad* to root together for Chuck Ortman, the powerfully armed tailback; Al Wistert, the pillar of the offensive and defensive lines; "Killer" Kempthorn and Dan Dworsky, the havoc-making linebackers.

This was still the Bronze Age, so to speak, of college football, when men played both offense and defense and, substitutions being sharply limited, were on the field most of the game. Without face masks, they were as accessible to the eye and imagination as baseball players. Compared to the much more specialized, regimented, and complex game that was soon to come with the T-formation and unlimited substitution, single-wing college football of the late forties was more personal, more physical, and hence more classical in the Greek sense. It was what remained of the warrior society of Homer in which individual ability, stamina, and resourcefulness counted for more than strategy and team management.

The awesomeness of the players, the intensity of my feeling for them, came home to me one afternoon in November. I had gone out for the freshman basketball team and, to my surprise, was still there after the first two cuts. I had developed painful calluses on the balls of my feet, and one of the coaches sent me over to the training room to have them treated. It was the Friday before the Ohio State game that would decide the Big Ten championship, and when I entered the training area there they were—Ortman and Kempthorn, Wistert and Dworsky, along with the rest of the starting team and the few key substitutes—each sitting or lying in the buff on a training table with a white sheet around his middle, waiting for a rubdown. They were transfixing—sheer, heroic male beauty and force in their young prime, Achilles and Patroclus, Ajax and Ulysses, come again, at ease before battle. My eyes must have been as wide as a girl's, for one of the players rose from his elbows and gave me a What're-*you*-doing-here look.

I quickly turned away. I had been in plenty of locker rooms and envied this torso, those arms, that dick, but now, for the first time, the dart of ravishment had entered my heart. "This is what it must feel like to be queer," I thought.

The sentiment was to recur during the basketball season, as I watched the Hollywood-handsome Pete Elliot turn from quarterback to point guard. I attended the games as a civilian, having quit the freshman team before the final cut that would probably have landed on my neck anyway. Coming back exhausted to the dorm each afternoon, bearing the bruises of the picks and hacks and floor burns that serious basketball produced, I could barely focus on Thucydides, my latest discovery. Playing college basketball even at the freshman level had been one of my abiding fantasies, an accomplishment that would redeem my mediocre high school performance. But I was not that person anymore, I wanted to perform now with my mind. . . .

The other influence that pulled me into the arts was that of the newly formed Art Theater Club in Ann Arbor. As with the Lido Beach circle, I was brought into it by Murray Gitlin, whose major may have been in psychology but whose heart was in performance, whether as an actor or a dancer. Along with his deep, classy elocution, he had a leonine head of hair, and together they produced a dramatic contrast to his chubby body and warm, soft temperament. He had that ready presentation of himself, the range of slightly exaggerated expressions, an emotive makeup, that went with being an actor. He tried out for the first production of the club, T. S. Eliot's *Murder in the Cathedral*, and was given the role of one of the hostile barons. I began to tag along to rehearsals. After all, almost all the leading European writers wrote for the stage, which was why they had a theater of ideas and we had Broadway.

This comment came from Strowan Robertson, the director of the Art Theater Club. Strowan was the Stanislavsky of Ann Arbor, an attractive, sandy-haired fellow with a nimble mind and a rakish slouch. In his late twenties, he came from Canada but sported a relaxed version of the Oxbridge manner. He seemed to speak in mostly soft labial puffs. But the puffs usually had a dart in them that sped to his point and made it stick in one's mind. He taught in the speech department, where the drama courses and productions were confined, as he liked to say, and he had recently founded the Art Theater Club to give himself and the local talent a much livelier repertory and a more professional stage.

After a few weeks I stopped feeling that I had just jumped down from the cabbage truck and took my place in the group as Murray's roommate and a green but promising rookie. We usually met at a table at the League, the women's activity center on campus, favored by the intellectual crowd over the macho Union, where I had hung out the previous year. There seemed to be two Universities of Michigan, culturally speaking: the cosmopolitan, contemporary one and the provincial, traditional one, the first attached to the great marketplace of ideas, the second to the Big Ten.

Everything about Strowan smacked of the big-time literary world. He didn't drop names and titles so much as float them among us, as he might our own, usually bearing an idea, a judgment, a provocative detail. Brecht was a bitter clown who happened to be a genius; *The Brothers Karamazov* was a novel of ideas that moved like an express train. That Strowan would launch his theater with a play by T. S. Eliot proved to me both his prowess and audacity. Eliot, like Joyce, was a sacrosanct writer, to be admired from the distance of his difficulty. Strowan brushed off the Eliot aura as though it were so much dust obscuring his visage. That he decided to put on the play in a church rather than a theater was another example of his brio, the last thing one looked for in those deadly earnest literary times. It was also an example of his ability to impose himself, a trait that I resented and was still too insecure to adopt but was beginning to see made the difference between the true artist and the merely talented.

Murder in the Cathedral was a big hit and the Art Theater Club was off and running. Strowan's table at the League or at the company's local pub became a charmed place, located somewhere between Ann Arbor and Greenwich Village. Len Rosenbaum, who would later have a stage and film career under the name of Mark Lenard, had been brought from New York to play most of the male leads. He was a big, handsome guy who radiated sexuality—a kind of Jewish Marlon Brando. Another prominent male actor was Dana Alcar, also large and imposing, who ended up in Hollywood. And there was Nancy Connable, who had what Strowan called a glamorous intelligence. She came from a politically prominent family and lived in a large lakefront house outside Ann Arbor that impressed me almost as much as she did. I imagined, imagined intensely, that she must be having an affair with Strowan or Len or Dana. One Sunday afternoon that fall, I found myself at her house with some of the other members of the company. I sat there drinking Scotch for the first time, listening to a conversation so languid and knowing and polished that it might have been piped in from the banned copy of *Memoirs of Hecate County*, which someone in the group had lent me. I realized how small-time I still was, even how paltry my romance with Lynn was in this atmosphere of midwestern *luxe, calme,* and *volupté.* . . .

Dylan Thomas came to read in Ann Arbor one March day in 1950. A hard wind was blowing that afternoon as I walked over to Rackham

Auditorium with my new friend, Saul Gottlieb, a twenty-eight-year-old freshman who had published a story and a poem in *Penguin New Writing*, a leading literary magazine of the war years. "He's sent his wind on ahead of him," remarked Saul, who had heard Thomas read at the Ninety-second Street Y in New York. "He's going to turn Rackham into Fern Hill."

"Fern Hill?"

"That's one of his major poems. You're in for an experience."

Little did I realize. Were it not for Oscar Williams's *Little Treasury of Modern Poetry*, I would hardly have known who Dylan Thomas was. Each night, my classwork done, I would read it into the early morning, consulting the little oval portraits in back to help me connect at least that much with the difficult poems, to thrill all the more to the dynamite ones. Modern poetry had such a glamour then that I would pore over those portraits as reverently as I had once done with the team picture of the Brooklyn Dodgers, looking for portents and clues of significance between the face and the name, humanizing the gods and goddesses.

So I was all the more taken aback when, after the introduction, a roly-poly clownlike figure wove to the podium of the opulent new auditorium, grasped it hard, and began to peer around as though trying to figure out where he was. The halo of frizzy gray curls, the puffy face that had once been angelic, announced that he was indeed Dylan Thomas, wearing a suit that looked like he had slept in it. Taking a full moment to look around and get his bearings, he said something like "I do not usually read my poems in Radio City Musical Hall. But then again, we are all pigs here, so I'll have a go at the trough."

The words were in keeping with his appearance and completely at variance with the most distinguished voice I had ever heard. And having gotten his displeasure, or whatever it was, off his chest, he let the voice take over or rather joined it in passionate wedlock to the poem he began to read. A year before, Frank Huntley, my advanced-exposition teacher, had walked into class one day and, to change the atmosphere, had read some poems—Blake's "Tyger," Yeats's "The Second Coming," e. e. cummings's "Buffalo Bill"—poems I had never heard of before and that probably made me an English major once and for all. Now, Dylan Thomas took that experience of the power of poetry to the next level. Hearing phrases like "the synagogue of the ear of corn" or "the heydays of his eyes," or lines like "The force that through the green fuse drives the flower / Drives my green age," or poems like "In My Craft and Sullen Art" was like a reveille to my spirit. My courses were teaching me that literature was texts to analyze; Thomas's imperial voice and cosmic language and mountainous range of feeling declared that literature was a natural religion that in the right hands hallowed the world. Nor was this true only of his own poems, which put Pan back in pantheism. In the cathedral of that intonation and diction, other poems became objects of worship: not only those by Yeats and Hardy but Henry Reed and even a poem of John Betjeman, which he transformed from light verse to delicate art.

After the reading, the audience was invited to go backstage to meet Thomas. It wasn't like a reception; it was more like a tryout for the team with a vaunted new coach. He sat astraddle a folding chair and we sat around him on the floor. Perhaps it was arranged this way to keep him away from the booze a while longer. The questions came from the star graduate students and younger faculty, but I was burning to ask one too, not only to touch the force field of this living presence of Literature but also to find out something.

"How conscious are you of other poets, like the ones you read today, when you're writing?"

He gave me an appreciative smile and some words that are still deposited in my account of memorable moments. "I try not to be conscious of anyone when I'm writing," he said, "least of all, myself."

I was so taken with the second part of his answer (it was just what Eliot said—literature was an escape from your personality) that I failed to grasp and heed the first.

From *First Loves: A Memoir* (New York: Seven Stories Press, 2003).

Joyce Carol Oates

from All the Good People I've Left Behind

What is that music? Fern, her eyes watering from the smoke, examines record albums; she doesn't know if she is merely hiding from the party or whether she is genuinely interested in what she has been hearing. When they first arrived some very bizarre music was playing—sitar music, evidently: someone named Kartick Kumar, from India—and now it's ballads, folk songs, lovely melancholy haunting sounds. "False-Hearted Lover," "We Are Crossing Jordan River," "All the Good People I've Left Behind," Woody Guthrie's "Ranger's Command." Odetta. Pete Seeger. (Only a few months later Fern will hear Joan Baez singing "Silver Dagger" and "House of the Rising Sun" and "Wildwood Flower," and she will realize that she first heard Joan Baez at the Hechts' that evening: and her eyes will fill with sentimental tears: and for the next decade she will associate Joan Baez's clear, deceptively "fragile" voice with the complex of emotions surrounding her first pregnancy at the age of twenty-three.)

Jerry Hecht barges forward to welcome Maxine; he kisses her on the cheek, then again on the ear. She laughs and pushes him away. Ted, watching, manages to smile since he knows it is all meant in jest, it is merely a gesture of affection. (Perhaps an affectation.) He lights a cigarette, having misplaced the one he was smoking—has someone else taken it?—or did he drop it?—and wonders if anyone notices his strained unconvincing smile. Or hears his forced laughter.

He can't help it—he experiences pain when he sees Maxine so obviously enjoying herself with another person—with another man. The pain is not metaphorical, it is physically and spiritually real: a kind of spasm in his chest, as if the muscles about his heart contracted suddenly.

He turns away and joins Alex, who is standing next to that tall redhead in the floor-length dress (it is made of some rough pretentious fabric and appears to have been hand-painted: peacocks and tendrils and simple, stylized, cream-colored blossoms); the two of them are listening, or trying to listen, to a rangy, nervous young man with a somewhat blemished skin—Hammersly—Ted can't remember his first name though Maxine introduced them only a few days ago, at the Pretzel Bell—Robert?—Ron?—Rod?—a drop-out from the graduate program in English who is rumored to be (or who presents himself as being) a genius of some sort. He is telling Alex and the red-head about his plans for an "enormous encyclopedia" of a novel. Engagingly ugly, wearing glasses with frames that resemble Ted's, he gestures broadly with both hands and speaks in a high-pitched, rather combative voice of the need for literature to become less and less human—more and more stylized—designed to mock the merely emotional, the merely personal. He will retreat from active life, he declares, and spend the next ten years on an immense "clockwork" novel: he will take with him dozens of books, history and science and philosophy, and the wilder sort of mysticism, and perhaps comic books as well, and he will work slowly, very slowly, with grim cold infinite patience, and thread together fragments from all these books along a continuum of his own creation (but it will be a mockery, of course: a mock-narration), and when the novel is completed it will be—ah, they're smiling, are they?—they doubt him?—when it's completed it will be proclaimed as a masterpiece, an epic, a work comparable to *Ulysses*.

"Comparable to what?" the red-headed girl says, cupping her hand to her ear.

"To *Ulysses*! *Ulysses*!" Hammersly shouts.

"Why not *Finnegans Wake*, while you're at it?" Alex says.

Hammersly waves them aside, dismissing them.

(Ted, whose area of specialization is David Hume—whose dissertation topic is Hume's "positivism" and his refutation of Spinoza—has not read *Ulysses* or *Finnegans Wake* and he suspects that Alex, a biochemist, has not read them either; but he is impressed with his friend's remark. He feels, in fact, a small thrill of something close to childish glee—a sense of triumph at Hammersly's apparent anger. Hours later, safely home and in bed with Maxine, he will confess to her that the reason he dislikes parties is because they seem to bring out in him perplexingly infantile emotions: he loathes himself at such times. If he cannot be mature and civilized and intelligent, if he cannot be equal to his own high intelligence, he truly loathes himself. It is no one's fault but his own, however—no one's fault but his own. And he will ask her in a soft, guilty voice if she still loves him, and she will answer, sleepily, that of course she loves him: loves him very much.)

"Isn't he a pompous bastard?" Alex asks, flushed with victory.

Ted agrees but the red-headed girl holds herself apart, her gaze moving across the room. She is a strikingly beautiful girl of about twenty-one or twenty-two who reminds Ted of his own wife, though she is much thinner than Maxine. He is about to say something to her when she sights a friend and bounds away, calling out happily, and Alex and Ted are left together, side by side. (Oddly, they often find themselves in this position at parties, as if they are observers, witnesses, not really participants. When they first met, a few years ago, it was at a party no less foolish and hectic than this one; they found themselves on the periphery of a group loudly discussing the University of Michigan's football team and its prospects for the coming season, and turned to each other, at the same moment, with the same expression of mild contempt.)

"Should we—"

"Maybe we should—"

"—want to hunt up Maxine, and I'll get Fern—?"

Married students' housing is east of the University, in a series of dormitory-like buildings covered in brown siding. From the outside the buildings look almost attractive, but they are thin-walled, and the lack of privacy is disturbing to Fern. An only child, a chronically "high-strung" girl, she finds it difficult to adjust to the proximity of her neighbors. Quarrels and boisterous laughter and the shouts of children and the sounds of televisions and phonographs and even, occasionally, the sounds of love-making; noisy plumbing, doors slamming, car motors being started early in the morning—it is all disturbing and sometimes depressing.

"I can't live here," she told Alex when they first moved in. She wept in his arms often, that first year. "I can't stand it here."

"Honey, please, what are you saying?" Alex asked, in anguish. "Don't you love me? Don't you love me? Don't you love me?"

Newly married, very much in love, they often misunderstood each other. They tripped over each other's words, half-deliberately; it was not uncommon for them both to burst into tears. (Maxine and Ted discussed this charming peculiarity in their friends' marriage, at length. Ted thought it silly and demeaning, and Maxine pretended to think it unnecessary, though in fact she regarded the Enrights with compassionate envy. "You're so *fortunate*, you don't know how *fortunate*, really," she told Fern a half-dozen times.)

Over the months, however, both Fern and Alex have become adjusted to life in the married students' quarters. Like the other tenants they publicly denounce it, of course, and want to leave as soon as possible, but Alex is able to sleep here as well as he's ever slept anywhere, and Fern has become halfway fond of their cramped apartment. It is their first home, after all. She believes—correctly, as it turns out—that she and Alex will never be quite so happy again.

Now Maxine is admiring the way she has decorated the kitchen: autumn colors of green and gold and dark orange. Those copper pans?—a wedding gift, yes. From Alex's sister. The Corning Ware casserole dish—a gift from her grandmother. Fern is pleased with Maxine's admiration though they have had this conversation before, and Maxine's enthusiasm, her cheerful busyness, are a little distracting in such close quarters. (In the living room Alex and Ted are talking animatedly; Fern wishes Maxine would join them. She doesn't like to be helped putting food on the table, Maxine's presence makes her nervous, but she has somehow slipped into the custom of allowing Maxine to help since it seems in a way important to Maxine. Important, too, are their exchanges of confidence at such times. It was in the Enrights' kitchen some months ago that Maxine told Fern how much she loathed—her word, loathed—Ted's parents, and it was while Fern was helping Maxine make dinner for a gathering of couples, last spring, that Maxine told Fern how envious certain other people were of them: not only of Alex and Ted, but of the Enrights and the Mandels as friends. *Friends.* "Around here where people are always stabbing one another in the back," Maxine said passionately, "it's something of an oddity, I suppose." Fern had been rather surprised: did people stab one another in the back often?—had she been missing a great deal? Tonight she tells Maxine about the outcome of the pregnancy test and finds herself trembling with the audacity of what she is saying. Maxine's pupils seem to darken. She immediately embraces Fern. "How wonderful! Oh how wonderful for you! For you and Alex!" Maxine whispers.)

Spaghetti with meat sauce, and Italian sausage, and mushrooms. Toasted garlic bread. Green salad with oil and vinegar and chickpeas. Chianti. Grated romano cheese. From the other room the urgent, well-rehearsed voices of the Kingston Trio—"Woke up this mornin' feelin' mighty mean, Thinkin' 'bout my good gal in New Orleans"—a record from Fern's undergraduate days at Western Michigan. Alex's and Ted's on-going argument, which their wives have come to fondly mock, about immortality—free will and determinism—the function of reason—the meaning of "instinct." And life: what *is* life?—consciousness?—reality itself?

They finish two bottles of red wine and open another. Everyone is talkative tonight, even Fern. Easily and effortlessly they move from solemn philosophical topics to a discussion of movies (both Alex and Ted agree that the greatest living actor is Marlon Brando: they vie with each other, doing imitations of Brando in "On the Waterfront" and in "Viva Zapata!" Maxine has earned their grudging regard by being the only one of the four to have seen Brando's first movie, "The Men," many years before). After movies they discuss music, and books, and suddenly they are exchanging bits of gossip about their friends in graduate school—someone is about to quit in disgrace, someone else has already received an offer from an excellent university in the East, still another is having serious difficulties with his dissertation. Ted and Alex swing back onto the topic of philosophy again. What *is* the truth? There must be an absolute truth, of course, a final, imperishable standard against which finite truths are measured. Otherwise—

Otherwise what? Chaos?

"But we may have to learn to live with chaos," Ted says cheerfully.

"You!" Maxine mocks. "Why, you get upset if I hang your shirts on the wrong side of the closet! And you should see him fly into a rage," she says to Fern, "if I happen to use his towel—just drying my hands, you know, not even thinking about what I'm doing. Chaos indeed!"

Alex laughs politely, but it's clear that he is primarily interested in talking with Ted. And Ted loves to talk, of course. Whenever possible he leads the discussion back to his area of specialization—David Hume's refutation of someone and someone's subsequent refutation of him. (The history of philosophy seems, to Fern and Maxine, a ceaseless drama involving innumerable small triumphs and small defeats, one great man supplanting another, reigning for a time, and being in turn supplanted by someone else. Such a lot of fuss over so little!) Ted speaks brilliantly and passionately of the need to relentlessly examine one's intellectual assumptions. What *is* reason, after all? Is it possible to be truly rational, or is it possible that all thoughts are conditioned by emotions, however hidden? Can there be anything approaching an impersonal thought? A "thought" not determined by its human subject? . . . Maxine enters the discussion, stating, not for the first time, that one must be a "complete" human being and that Ted's philosophical heroes seem to have left the human element entirely out of account, even when they were pretending to include it; Fern, cleverly repeating something her philosophy professor said a few years back, points out that most philosophical systems can't really be refuted but at the same time are totally unconvincing. Alex disagrees. He disagrees heatedly. There are certain things that are incontestable, like the evidence of one's senses, one's own intrapsychic experience, if that experience is accepted as an end in itself and not referred to the so-called "objective" world. "My own experience is incontestable," Alex says. "And whatever operates within the dimension of my experience is real enough: it's as much of truth as we're required to know."

If Alex believes fiercely, Ted disbelieves; if Ted believes, Alex disbelieves. They love to talk—to hammer things out. Occasionally all four of them burst into laughter. The Kingston Trio is replaced by a mournful singer of Portuguese ballads, the third bottle of chianti is emptied, Fern's eyelids begin to droop. Free will and determinism? Are the terms merely words, without meaning? Sometimes Ted insists they are, sometimes he is willing to listen—politely, patiently—to his friends' opinions on the subject. There have been nights when free will has won out; other nights when determinism, fatality, the dreaded "block universe" has won. Of course they are all free—within limits. Of course they are all conditioned—aren't they? Economically, biologically? In terms of the environment? But they *feel* free. And if they feel free what else matters? Even Ted is forced to agree reluctantly with Alex on the issue of intrapsychic experience. ("However deluded that experience really is," Ted cannot resist adding.)

From *All the Good People I've Left Behind*
(Princeton: The Ontario Review, Inc., 1979).

Marge Piercy

ℚ

from Braided Lives

Mornings we load our trays with desiccated eggs, toast, a pat of unidentifiable jelly, bitter coffee. Too sleepy to talk we bolt our food. Julie, who has a single room down the hall and does not eat breakfast, joins us for coffee. Then we hasten together out to the muddy path that runs above the women's athletic field. Clatter and clank of dishes, women pouring from every door to join the clotted processional downhill and up again. The wind at the brink blows the last wisps of sleep away, leaving us cranky and raw from late studying.

I trot wagging my tail to offer my themes to Professor Bishop. Long face running well up into his scarce hair, long liver-spotted hands whose deft red sarcasms dot my papers, he is the dyspeptic angel who guards the gate to my paradise of words. To seduce his wearily malicious surfeit of freshman prose, I tell him tales of my childhood. He assigns a theme on privilege: I write on Father. He assigns a theme on freedom: I write of Mother. "Amusing." "Astringent." The circus of my upbringing stands open for your delectation, Mr. Bishop, although my clowns turn somersaults in terror of your scorn, not at all sure why we are funny.

Slimy grappling in zoology lab. The diagrams in the manual are precise, but my frog holds only eggs. We are handed live frogs to pith their brains. My partner jabs nervously. Blood oozes on the frog's spotted back as it screams, kicking long and distorted like a saint from El Greco, in my partner's clumsy fist. Taut with fury I take the frog to drive in the needle, my hand wet with slime and blood. Proud of my successful brutality, I look up to see Donna charging out the door, the lanky lab assistant fluttering behind. "It's the waste," she says later. "Killing them and nobody learned a thing. Better to stab those hateful premed students." She is intransigent even in petty hatred, intense where I am mottled and curious.

I struggle through the central lobby in the liberal arts building known as the Fishbowl. Hot and disheveled I subside into a front seat in a wedge-shaped auditorium to gaze on my idol, Professor Donaldson. I had intended to take ancient or medieval history, ending up in American only because at registration I heard two students gossiping about what a pinko Donaldson is. His classes are standing room only, full to the legal limit of 440 and beyond with those formally or informally auditing.

He starts talking almost before he is in the door. He uses his jacket sleeve to erase what he scrawled earlier, occupying space he requires again. Slim, agile, he is over six feet tall but does not seem so because he droops, his head like a prize dahlia the stem cannot hold upright. I suspect he has grown his full auburn beard to look older than his students. Who could have expected the Pilgrim Fathers to have politics or the Revolutionary War to sound like a real revolution in Bolivia? Since last Wednesday he has broken his glasses. They are held at the hinge with tape I find endearing.

Saturday morning after looking up his address, I drag Donna off to gaze upon what turns out to be a Tudor-style red brick apartment house on North State Street altogether too bland and normal to suit my fantasies. The seventh time around the block, Donna who has never seen Donaldson but is willing to share my infatuation companionably, at last complains. But we are rewarded. He comes out with a woman wearing a trench coat much like his. Chestnut hair in a long single braid. They climb into his blue VW bug and drive off.

"At least you know he likes women," Donna says. "Can we go home?"

"She didn't look much older than me. She looks like a student."

"Twenty-two maybe. Gorgeous boots. Good tweed skirt. Money, I'd say." Donna has humored me but on the way back she begins to charge interest. "This is ridiculous. You're comfortable in these crushes. Running across town to spy on him. You could meet him if you wanted to. Just march up to him and preempt his attention."

"I couldn't," I mumble. "Why should he notice me? He has a thousand students at least."

"Wear your new black turtleneck."

"A third of his students have tits, Donna. I'm sure he's seen them before."

"You're defeatist, Stu. You can't drift along this way, having nice safe crushes on men from a distance of two hundred feet."

Why not? I'm not bored. I'm happy. When I explain this, she becomes more annoyed. "You talk about wanting to experience everything, but it's all rhetoric. You're scared."

The subtext of her argument is that I must prove myself normal, heterosexual. The reason for my resistance is half incompetence—I have not the tiniest notion how to begin—and half satisfaction. I have someone to love: Donna. I just want to read my books and listen to our music and run around town like a puppy set loose, taking in all the free concerts and cheap plays I can gobble and talk and talk and talk to her.

We do talk. "Defense" is the dirtiest word we know. We condemn racism and militarism and our parents; we make dramas of what we would say to McCarthy. We seek a fluid openness in which to think means to speak and results in being understood—immediately; in which to conceive of an action is to be more than halfway toward doing. We try. Our white room burns. Outside the air feels laxer.

We share a booth in the sweetshop across from the dorms. Our coats are buttoned to the neck because we are dressed only in skirts. Our blouses and underwear are churning clean in the house laundry room. A foul supper left us hungry. "So why sit and starve?" I demanded. Now with the rough lining of my jacket chafing my nipples tender and a newer dare on the table, I am torn between the excitement of our games and the fear of how fast they escalate.

"We need a teapot." She motions toward the metal pot that just served us. "You struck out as a child. I just blundered into trouble. I must learn to act."

"But if they catch us tonight?" Our booth is open to the counter where the scrawny proprietor leans. Donna has toward her slim body a cool functional pride I can admire but not imitate.

"That's a weak shitless reason." She empties the pot into her cup and crams it into her open purse. As she rises and heads for the cashier, I stuff the ashtray, butts and straw ends and all in my pocket, and hurry after. Damp with sweat my fingers fumble the coins.

In the wet street we grin at each other. "What a nice teapot, my dear," I lilt. "Has it been long in your family?" I turn out my pocket and shake the mass of butts and ashes into a puddle as she hops on a low wall and balancing struts past me. It electrifies me how what I say to her does not return to me thoroughly chewed as with Howie but leaps into action.

The snow swirls in the courtyard, large cotton candy flakes Julie plays at trying to catch at our open casement window. On the ledge where I so often curl or sprawl, she is sitting, one leg in plaid wool slacks drawn up, one with the booted foot flat on the floor. "You think we could have missed them?" she asks in her deep cooing voice.

"She'd be up here by now."

Julie's short fawn-colored hair was done yesterday in stiff loopy curls and she keeps fingering it shyly but obsessively. "Perhaps he's taking her to supper."

"He's got no money. Besides, she *said* she'd come back." Last night Donna went out with an art student. Now we wait for our first look at this Lennie. "He's ugly in an attractive way," Donna told me. "He's subversive-looking. He grew up in a slum and he's *brilliant!*" Sophomore from Brooklyn, he's here like us on scholarship. I wonder if his being Jewish shows my influence.

"I don't know why we're making such a to-do about it," Julie murmurs sourly. "She finds a new one every three weeks." Julie comes from Bloomfield Hills, a wealthy suburb of Detroit I had never heard of until I came to college and discovered that was one of the few areas around Detroit you were allowed to be from. Julie's parents bought her culture along with horseback riding and skiing lessons, but she took to books and music too seriously to please them. She finds us vulgar but intelligent. I find her a lonely snob with vulnerable patches. She is tall and pear-shaped, blushes easily and hates herself for it. Now a cry bursts from her, her charm bracelet jangling. "Come here!"

I jump up, grazing my head on the upper bunk. Donna in her blue coat is walking twined around a boy just a little taller. Curly red hair thick as a fox brush and a luxuriant red beard halo his face in tangles. Jostling at the casement we wave madly. "Hey, Donna!" echoes through the court till she looks up grinning and waves and Lennie turns where she is pointing and waves too, his beard jogging as he calls out something.

Julie brings her hand to her mouth, palm out. "It's too much," she giggles. "He looks like a madman! Van Gogh crossed with a rabbi!" She laughs till her eyes are wet.

"Julie, so help me if you don't stop giggling I'll push you in the closet! Admire him for her!"

She shakes my hand off, subsiding. "You want me to tell her he's handsome?"

"Say . . . he looks interesting."

Donna rushes in, flinging her coat at her desk chair. "People! What a wonderful afternoon!" Her fine hair clings to her scrubbed-looking cheeks. Her eyes squint up to blue slits of joy.

"What did you do?" I ask.

"We walked. Up- and downhill, walking in the beautiful clean sweet snow. Making tracks." She kicks off her shoes soaked dark. "What do you think of him? Isn't he wonderful? Isn't he wild-looking?"

"He looks interesting," Julie says primly, glancing at me.

"I'd love to meet him," I say. "Did he kiss you?"

"Hundreds of times. All up and down every hill." Her laugh barks, high and lively with delight. "His beard is soft, like cat's fur!"

Julie checks her slender gold watch. "Well, I must be off to Le Cercle Français. . . . Shall I see you at supper?"

As soon as the door closes behind her, Donna throws her arms around me in a violent shy hug, drawing back before I can respond and hopping past her chair. "He's marvelous, Stu. He knows everything! He's like you—quick and a little dogmatic and all warm and soft inside."

"You like him, Donna? This one you really like?"

"I love him."

"I'm glad. See, things are working out better already. This is the sort of man you want—somebody you can talk to." I pace the room, flapping my arms with excitement and truly I am not jealous. My love for her is at once humble, white hot and nonpossessive. I want the world for both of us. I want her to sail out on daily adventures of learning and doing and feeling and sail back into harbor with me at night to share and discuss.

She is staring in the mirror, bleak, cynical. "What am I doing with someone so wonderful? I'll just fuck up. Fat chance I could do anything right. I don't deserve him. . . ."

I must give you a sense of its bounty, this nurtured plot of well-used Arboretum. A dirt road branches through the wooded hills from the entrances: a back door for hobos by the burning dump, a formal entrance for Sunday drivers where fraternity row and rangy rooming houses begin to give way to wide-lawned residences that parents nod at from their cars, substance approving of substance—the route that winds down from a view of the river coiling like a scythe through the countryside and the two sentinel hospitals, University and the Veterans Administration, on opposite banks stolid in the distance. But the entrance worn by lovers is below the dorms, the route between ravine and cemetery that funnels into that first wide place that alone has a common name, the plateau; the other hills, ravine of rocks and green-eyed creek, submarine cove of waist-high ferns, hollow of slithering willows pocket dark, have names only for those who have lain and printed themselves on that earth.

In the afternoons of spring and fall botany classes troop through behind their hearty instructors, taking notes and flushing couples from the thickets. Trees grow lofty here. Rumor has it the hills are accretions of old condoms, and perhaps the cast sperm has quickened the soil. At night we grope hand in hand while nymphs sigh in the tall and spooky trees and the flesh of lovers stuns from the dark like gardenias. No, you cannot visit this place. You cannot enter merely by walking downhill. You have to be so young you're still scared by dark stairs. You have to believe sex is wicked and splendid magic. You have to be desperate and needy to taste the flavor of these trees and bushes, playground of drifters, runners, botany field trips, fraternity beer parties, edgy delinquents with switchblades hot and shiny in their pockets, sunbathers, picnickers with babies and fried chicken but always and ever by sun and by moon and by rain under the cover of the leaves and the overarching branches, the lovers rustle.

We stand at the forking of the road at the foot of a steep rocky hill. He pulls me up. I scramble after clutching at roots. We climb to a shallow bowl of Scotch pines. The shaggy poles rise straight with patches of russet wood showing through the bark. The sun slants through the high branches to make bright patches on the floor, thick and soft with blanched needles. He circles the rim with his head jutting forward. "Great site for a fort. It commands the road." He stares at me and something tightens in his face. "Completely alone. If you yelled, no one would hear." Tentatively he puts his hands on my throat, then hard. "Aren't you afraid?"

I smile. "No."

"You trust me." He turns away, kicking at the needles. "I wonder how much? Even here we've been preceded."

Ashes beneath the needles. "At least a season old."

He nudges the old ashes. "This is our hearth."

"Maybe we could build a little fire and cook supper here sometimes."

"Right. Get those flat stones from the hillside." He plunges over the rim and I follow, crashing through the thickets. The first stone I try to dislodge is embedded too deep but the second gives as I haul, sending a leggy thing scurrying. He is setting two level stones side by side. Sweat breaks out along my back, my hands are bruised, but the ring grows. Finally he fits the last stone in.

He sprawls, and after a last survey, I join him. Labor has made the place ours. "Bet we could build a shack," he says. "Why not? Two crazy poets gone back to nature. Once a month we trot out, me with a grandfather beard down to the waist and you in nothing but your long black hair, and order a few supplies. 'Deliver them to the front gate of the Arb, please.'"

I rest my head on his arm. Interwoven branches. Slashes of late afternoon sky. "We could gather berries and nuts. Plant a little garden."

He draws me closer. "Can't you see us all ragged and fierce and hairy? There'd be rumors—wild hermits, live in trees and throw rocks at strangers. We'd set traps for rabbits. Somebody'd catch sight of us running along all shaggy like Bigfoot. . . ."

Gently I brush the needles from his hair. When his eyes gloat on me with that dark somber shining, I am beautiful. The ground prickles, scented with resin. Above branches rub and dip. No footsteps to set us misbuttoning, only the chatter of a squirrel, the pulse of bird wings. Weight my body rounds to. This time before he enters, he touches me, fumbling with powerful effect. It had never occurred to me that he could touch me, for that seemed to me to belong to those distant pleasurable games everyone seems to agree are more dangerous than drag racing. Then he moves in me alive and warm as if he turned and leapt. I close my eyes and our bodies swell huge. Deep and elongated we grow rushing backward like fast trains. Half afraid of the hot lick of urgency I clutch him, the scratchy flame that catches and fades, catches and fades in my cupped distorted upward-striving body.

Then I am freed falling backward while the star streaks, hovers burning and finally explodes and the streamers flare through my thighs and breasts and arms, the sparks hang and die one by one. It feels right, it feels familiar, it feels ancient.

When he has come and slides out of me, condom dragging, I say, "Mike, I came. I did. I really did."

"I knew we'd break through soon. What's it like for you?"

I loll in my muscles, warm as bathwater. Effort to talk. The completeness of pleasure separates us. "Heat . . . urgency."

"For me too." He settles curled against me. "Must be the same."

"Stupid we can't know. I'd like to crawl into your fingers and look out through your eyes."

"You haven't read Plato but he puts it nicely. We were round animals once, but the gods got jealous and split us. So we're all trying to find our other proper half."

"Mike . . . the way you touched me first? I liked that."

"Oh." He is silent. "The guys told me to try that when I said you weren't coming."

I sit up, clutching at my scattered clothes. *"What guys?"*

"The guys in the dorm."

"How could you discuss me with them?"

He grins. "They're envious because I'm getting laid regular. My stock has shot up. You're telling me you don't talk about sex with Donna or Julie?"

"But not what we do."

He shrugs. "Actually it may have been Lennie's idea. It's easy, once you get the knack of it."

I sit still clutching my sweater. All over town he has been discussing my body and its habits. I want to crawl into the earth. I sit on, trying to plane down my shame roughly so I can fit past. I will brazen it out with all of them. What else can I do? . . .

My first civil rights action is meek. Eighteen of us gather in the blowing sleet to picket a local restaurant. Donna, Lennie and I march arm in arm. Donaldson is involved, which prompts Donna to try to awake my old crush on him, but I love her and no one else. My love for Donna is a small furry muff my buhbe gave me when I was five, ragged but still eloquent of another time and country, wherein my hands sought, to find only each other, but nonetheless were warmer.

In 1955 we are only cautiously radicals "of sorts," a professor in the zoology department having been fired after the last House Un-American Activities Committee incursion into Michigan for being "an avowed Marxist." I go regularly to a study group where we look earnestly into each other's eyes. Even to discuss civil rights or social change feels dangerous. The FBI may burst in the door; one of us may be an agent. A student in the Labor Youth League (membership of four) found out his girlfriend had been scared by the FBI into providing lists of everyone who attended his frequent parties. All of us know stories of teachers who lost their jobs because they once signed a petition for the starving children of Ethiopia or the bombed villages of Spain, thus revealing themselves Premature Anti-Fascists. The FBI agents visit the morgue of the school newspaper to read old editorials in case whoever they are investigating once wrote something critical of The American Way of Life. Ideas feel incredibly potent in this thick atmosphere. Passing along a copy of Gunnar Myrdal's An American Dilemma or E. P. Thompson's History of the English Working Class feels like a brave political act.

We are PAF: the Political Alternatives Forum. Even that bland label has to most ears a harshly subversive sound and I cannot pull Donna or Lennie in with me. Lennie doesn't trust me—I am the evil bitch who wounded his poet. Donna claims to find the discussion dull, though she comes with me occasionally. "All those men and only two women!" Alberta Mann is the other woman, Donaldson's girlfriend. Donaldson is our faculty sponsor, so we can be a recognized student group to stage our little protests, show an occasional film (*Battleship Potemkin, The Grapes of Wrath, Open City*), bring in a progressive folk-singer, that is when we can get approval. We have to pass through two deans and a vice-president to sponsor Pete Seeger. We also hold forums on H-bomb testing, abolition of dormitory hours for women, the U.S. Marine invasion of Guatemala. At those timid meetings I live for a few moments in a world larger than that bounded by dormitory and classroom.

From *Braided Lives* (New York: Summit Books, 1982).

Tom Hayden

⚑

from Reunion: A Memoir

The Conversion: Ann Arbor, 1957-61

At Ann Arbor, there was North Quad, South Quad (where I lived), East Quad, and West Quad. Nearly thirteen hundred young men were cramped into my sterile quad, arbitrarily assigned to roommates, whether we preferred each other's company or not. An eleven P.M. curfew was imposed. The cafeteria food was processed and served with, it seemed, as little flavor or nutritional value as possible. After freshman year, students moved out and began to discover that the surrounding community was just as curiously lacking in adequate student services. Off-campus housing was hard to find; parking was scarce; even the libraries lacked enough seats.

The barracks culture, with its twin lacks of privacy and community and its sink-or-swim message, extended to the academic sector as well. Lecture classes typically involved a distant professor speaking from notes, three times weekly, to a jammed crowd of three hundred or more students. Smaller classes usually were led by teaching assistants (TAs), young graduate students who earned part-time income by teaching seminars where one could learn what was intended to be taught in the larger lectures. While many of these TAs were stimulating, they had no training as teachers (neither did the senior faculty). Instead, they were serving as apprentices to full professors, usually helping on research and writing projects for their bosses while trying to eke out their own doctoral thesis.

It soon became obvious to most freshmen that we were unwanted orphans in the educational hierarchy, an amorphous mass of bodies that might someday become academic sorcerer's apprentices. While their dollars subsidized the research-oriented university, our parents remained blissfully content that their children were obtaining the presumed status and educational benefits of the UM degree. Not surprisingly, about 40 percent of undergraduates never finished their four-year programs in this impersonal atmosphere, a dropout rate that remains the same today.

As in high school, I managed to find a creative handful of professors and classes. I briefly explored the fraternities, but found them absorbed in mindless partying and status comparisons. In a short time, I involved myself with the institution that would become my own fraternity, the *Michigan Daily.*

Located just behind the administration building in a dignified, ivy-covered, two-story, red-brick building, the *Daily* was the most important student institution on the campus and perhaps the most respected university paper in the United States (competing each year with the *Harvard Crimson* and a few others for national awards). It attracted not only would-be journalists but, more important, many thoughtful student activists who wanted to challenge the university to live up to its educational ideals. The paper was professional; reporters and editors worked every day from noon until late at night. It rolled off the presses on the first floor at about three A.M. and circulated six days a week among tens of thousands of university readers. It was intensely competitive, with reporters rising from rookie status to important news "beats," then to desk-editor positions, until finally the outgoing senior editors proposed their successors to a university board of control. When I walked across its massive, churchlike stone floors, I was impressed, even in awe of the place. An older friend from Royal Oak, Joanie Katz, introduced me around and made sure that I was provided interesting assignments. Within a year I was spending more of my time at the *Daily* than in class-rooms, eating take-out while editing copy there late at night, even falling asleep on the desks.

Through the *Daily*, I formed a picture of the university and the world. I met and wrote about Governor G. Mennen "Soapy" Williams, the liberal Democrat who later served in the Kennedy administration. I covered regents' meetings, where I watched conservative corporate leaders in action for the first time. I followed the dismissal of an allegedly Marxist professor and learned the history of the McCarthy period. I wrote about racial discrimination in the fraternity system and learned what it was to be attacked by outraged alumni. I covered a minor riot against dormitory food and crusaded successfully to prevent the arbitrary expulsion of the two ringleaders. Along the way, I was fortunate to find supportive professors in political science, philosophy, and journalism, who intellectually complemented my work on the paper. I formed an idealistic conception of the university as a "community of scholars" and, in a stream of editorials, measured it critically against the impersonal bureaucratic atmosphere.

I rose in the *Daily*'s ranks, drawing the concerned interest of administrators, the respect of some of the faculty, and a growing following among many students. My parents were pleased at the prospect of my becoming a professional journalist, and I imagined myself as a future foreign correspondent. But as in high school, my drive for success was tempered by a disquiet about the world around me. I rejected, for example, the campus honorary societies that automatically incorporated rising *Daily* editors along with fraternity and student government leaders in their exclusive ranks. After my freshman year, I took an apartment with a student named Tom Lamm (whose brother later became governor of Colorado), who resembled the James Dean character in *Rebel Without a Cause*, even down to the white T-shirt and red jacket he routinely wore to classes. We immersed ourselves in philosophy, kept our distance from the fraternity culture, rode motorcycles, and individually hitchhiked to all corners of America during vacation breaks. Gradually, I began going out with women who had the same searching qualities. All the while I managed getting good grades and promotions at the *Daily*, but that part of me still exploring the emotional and intellectual wilderness remained very strong.

There was yet another network of students who were attracting my curiosity, and I, without knowing it, was attracting theirs. They were the first core of student activists exploring a new politics on the threshold of the sixties. By 1959, the first signs of national campus activism were visible to a careful eye. In 1957, students in Berkeley formed a reform-minded campus political party called SLATE, the first of its kind. In 1958, ten thousand students joined a school-desegregation march in Washington, D.C., an event that startled me as I chose pictures and designed a front-page layout of the event for the *Daily*.

To the extent there were any organized student groups in the late fifties, however, they were small, fragmented, lineal descendants of left-wing groups that had last flourished in the thirties and flickered out by the McCarthy period. Whether socialist, communist, or anarchist in their political roots, they tended to be confined to students who were from Jewish, immigrant, New York backgrounds. One such group which had seen better days was the Student League for Industrial Democracy (SLID), an offshoot of the New York–based League for Industrial Democracy (LID), which in turn was an educational arm of the once-proud, now-musty trade unions like the International Ladies' Garment Workers' Union. The venerable SLID was formed in 1905, making it the first student organization in America and four years the senior of the National Association for the

Advancement of Colored People (NAACP). In its robust years, its top ranks included such future leaders as Jack London, Walter Lippmann, Upton Sinclair, and John Dewey. But in recent times it had been virtually dormant, reflecting the exhaustion of the American Left by the fifties.

In 1959, however, the improbable was about to happen. In the unlikely setting of Ann Arbor, a visionary young man named Robert Alan Haber was planning to take over the New York–based SLID and convert it into Students for a Democratic Society (SDS). His apartment, above a hangout called the Cottage Inn, was just behind the *Daily* building. Looking then as he would twenty-five years later, Al Haber was bald, smooth-skinned, bespectacled, of average height, trim in build. I judged him to be ten years older than I. It was never clear if he was enrolled as a student or graduate student or whether he was just dropping in on lecture courses. However, when I visited his one-room apartment, I was amazed that every wall, from floor to ceiling, was filled with books. They covered every subject, especially politics, history, and philosophy. Al built himself an amazingly large desk in the center. His bed was against the wall, and there were a few plants and a cat, which sat on Al's lap and licked itself. I had never seen anything like this apartment. Al was writing what he called a "tome." Like his other vagaries, it wasn't clear if he was writing an academic thesis, a book, or an open-ended notebook. He would only identify the chapter headings as "Art," "Science," "History," and the like.

But Al's eccentricities and nondescript appearance created a certain charisma. When he spoke, I felt an intense, intellectual focus, even when I didn't understand what he was talking about. Al's father, William Haber, was a senior university professor and official, a major figure in the Jewish community, and a prominent national Democrat whose deep ties went back to his own youthful, New Deal idealism thirty years before. Picking up the threads of his father's political past, Al wanted to weave them into a new fabric for the students of his time. Somehow intuition told him that a new student movement was around the corner. His practical instincts (he was also a carpenter) told him that he must attract and mold a nucleus of followers.

The main two he recruited, who would form SDS with him, were also rooted in a radical history, though they were much younger than Al. Sharon Jeffrey, a sophomore who looked like a cheerleader with her blond hair, blue eyes, and quick smiles, was the daughter of Mildred Jeffrey, a top leader of the United Auto Workers, a close associate of Walter and Victor Reuther since the industrial strikes and sit-ins of the thirties, and a powerful woman in the Democratic party. Sharon was a born organizer with great talent. She also became Al's girlfriend. Bob Ross was a small and muscular native of the Bronx, raised one block from Yankee Stadium, who still spent his summers as a New York lifeguard. According to family lore, his grandparents met at a gathering of Russian revolutionaries on the Lower East Side—but on entering the university in Ann Arbor, his modes of disaffection tended toward jazz and the beat poets. Haber revived the young Ross's political interest, and Ross quickly proved to be precocious, articulate, and well versed in leftist doctrines.

Haber wanted to recruit me into his small conspiracy, but I was absorbed with work at the *Daily*. I liked him well enough, but he was too involved in what I considered theoretical abstractions at the time. The only campus group that drew my active interest was called Americans for World Responsibility, the creation of two graduate students, Al and Judy Guskin, who began a lobbying campaign for an international peace corps. It was before that group that I gave my first public speech, twenty double-spaced pages that took me forty-five minutes to read.

Haber's plan, already in the works, was to recruit a new cadre of student activists from around the country to the LID and gain the blessing of the LID elders for a revival of the student organization, now to be named SDS. In keeping with its tax-exempt educational character, Haber proposed holding a conference on "civil rights in the North" in Ann Arbor in the spring of 1960.

Haber's intuition was prophetic. On February 1, 1960, the historic events of the decade unexpectedly began. Four unknown black students staged a sit-in at a segregated lunch counter in Greensboro, North Carolina, and started what was soon called "the movement." From that point until the August 1963 march on Washington, there commenced an era of unmatched idealism in America. The student civil rights movement took the moral leadership, showing how values could be translated into direct action. Students across the country became agents for social change on a larger scale than ever before. A new, more hopeful, presidency was in the making. In this brief moment of time, the sixties generation entered its age of innocence, overflowing with hope.

It was the moment Al Haber had waited for. In Ann Arbor, he, Jeffrey, and Ross joined the picket lines that began to form at the local Kresge chain store to create support and pressure on behalf of the students trying to desegregate lunch counters in the South. Their plans for the May civil rights conference blossomed. I watched the picket lines as a reporter and wrote supportive editorials. The marchers, a few students like Ross and Jeffrey combined with a number of longtime off-campus liberals and radicals, were singing old labor songs I didn't recognize. The singing was spirited; the songs were suddenly relevant. I felt an affinity with them for the first time, but still I remained an aspiring *Daily* writer, not yet thinking of myself as an activist. I enjoyed expressing myself in words, but I was not comfortable carrying a picket sign.

My attitude imperceptibly changed as spring 1960 wore on. As thousands of southern students were arrested, and many beaten, my respect and identification with their courage and conviction deepened. The SDS civil rights conference was a surprising success. Sharon's mother arranged a ten-thousand-dollar UAW grant that could employ Haber as a full-time organizer. The presidential primary campaign of John Kennedy, which invoked a return to government activism after eight quiet years, was also fanning the early fire of my political passion.

But that spring I primarily focused on the grueling competition to become the *Daily* editor in chief for the coming 1960–61 year. The paper was proudly autonomous within the university community, but ultimately it was controlled by a board that reflected administration, faculty, and private interests. So far as I knew, the board had never interfered with the paper's internal freedom, but this year was different. My fledgling activism, frequent criticisms of the university, and partisan coverage of the civil rights movement were worrying the campus administration. Privately, they were not sure they wanted a strident advocate controlling the editorial pulpit—neither were some of the outgoing senior editors, who held more conservative political views than mine. I felt as if I were on trial without quite knowing the accusations or how to defend myself. I wanted the job badly.

Weeks of impasse followed, while I waited nervously. The question broadened from my qualifications to whether the judgment of the outgoing editors—who had decided to recommend me—would be respected or overturned by the board. Finally, in a late-night meeting, the board named me the new editor. Much relieved, I committed the paper to greater editorial coverage of the new movement of students "seeking a voice in the decisions affecting our lives." I was beginning to think of myself as an oracle for this student awakening.

From *Reunion: A Memoir* (New York: Random House, 1988).

Ruth Reichl

⚤

from *Tender at the Bone: Growing Up at the Table*

Most freshmen arrived in Ann Arbor with their parents in tow. I watched enviously as they moved desks into the dorm and went off for farewell celebrations. My mother was still in Europe, trying to finish her book, and it never occurred to Dad that I might like company on my first trip to college. Anyway, had he asked I'm sure I would have told him to stay home.

But when I climbed down from the bus in front of the Student Union I realized that there were 30,000 students at the University of Michigan and I did not know one. I picked up my bag and headed in the direction of Couzens Hall, praying that my roommate would be there.

She was not; all I found was a note saying she had gone home to Detroit and to take whichever bed I wanted. I snooped through the things she had left behind, but they weren't very telling: I now knew she was small and thin and that her name was Serafina.

When Serafina finally showed up two days later I realized it was probably a good thing my mother hadn't brought me to college after all. Mom wasn't thrilled about the University of Michigan, and I was going to have to prepare her for my roommate. Serafina was beautiful, with big liquid brown eyes framed by straight, short, shiny black hair. She was smart and funny with an offbeat sense of humor. And her skin, even in winter, was the color of a perfect tan.

But Mom never gave me a chance to prepare her. One day in early October I walked in from English 101 and Serafina said, "Your mother just called. She's flying straight from Paris and she'll be here tomorrow. She said she wanted to meet my parents."

"Uh-oh," I said. Serafina's parents were the most generous people I had ever met. They had been in America a long time but they still spoke with a Caribbean lilt, caressing every word before releasing it. When they talked of Guyana it was as if they had just come to Detroit for a visit and would be returning any time. I tried to imagine my mother in their modest apartment but I couldn't picture her there, surrounded by the smell of curry and coconuts.

But Mom didn't ask to go to their apartment. She came barging into the dormitory with a big smile that fell apart when she saw Serafina. She struggled for control, gathered her face together, and held out her hand. "Serafina?" she said hesitantly.

Later she apologized to me. "I just can't help it. I guess I'm a prejudiced person. It never occurred to me that your roommate would be Negro."

"Oh, she's not," I said fervently, parroting what Serafina herself had told me. "Her family is from Guyana. They are of mixed French and Indian blood. They are not Negro." And to prove it I gave her some of the coconut bread that Serafina's mother had sent.

"That's a relief," said Mom, helping herself to a piece.

From *Tender at the Bone: Growing Up at the Table*
(New York: Random House, 1998).

An Awful Lot Was Happening

When you come down to particulars everything's more
    complicated.
Fervent gestures in the South U restaurant, even the Greeks
behind the counter listen. Burned draft cards,
lamb's blood poured over files at the downtown draft board
—acts of resistance, moral values begun.

Saint Augustine in *De Trinitate* didn't see memory structured
by public events. A great moment in my life—not purple clouds
which excited my longings in Nichols Arboretum;
instead, the rumor cancer spread through Lyndon Johnson's
    brain.
Saint Augustine in his *Enchiridion ad Laurentium* didn't see

her dress and bra across the only chair in my small room
at One Thousand Four Olivia. I couldn't comprehend
whether more words might mean more, my greed, untrained,
not yet certain of its justifications.
And there was war. And from the bluffs above the Huron River

rain of starlight above Ann Arbor's lights, three, four
bell chimes ringing in the Tower. It wasn't Rome.
She dizzied me with excessive desires and thoughts.
What I wanted from all my talk of beauty, she said, was power,
and because of it, she said, I'd cause much suffering.

Although I never bragged misery—maybe once. I was serious.
What was I supposed to do when I heard you could be beaten or
    worse
in the neighborhood in Detroit between Linwood and Dexter,
the color of your eyes wrong. These are facts.
Professor Fuller's response that no one taught them to be quiet.

Glass from the bank's large plated windows all over the street.
I telephoned—line busy; tried again a few minutes later
—no answer. Where is she?—the verge of tears.
Swinburnian dactyls merely went through my ears. Advocated
concision, spatial range, temporal disposition of simple language.

And didn't the spokesman for the Black Action Movement
also receive a number over three hundred in the draft lottery
and attend graduate school? —I came back.
Three years later, every space turned inside out.
January, noon, beams of light across you shake out. Confused,

whirling joy when you slid off me. I leaned
again to embrace you. Uniform Commercial Code on the table.
On the dresser, a cup of coffee, tulips in a vase.
How to explain to myself how much I love you.
In the Law Quadrangle—my peer. He commanded Marines

in the Anhoa Basin. What did I know—what hookworms are
    like.
What it's like to shoot a Viet Cong, popped from a hole, in the
    eye.
A piece of metal in your kidney. It's too easy
to be sheep, he concludes, softly. Or too difficult,
I add, softly. He stares at me and whispers something.

When I answered I intended to maintain freedom my brother
    was riled.
What, or who, collides in you beside whose body I sleep?
No work at Tool & Die, Motors, Transmission, or Tractor
while the price of American crude rises another dollar.
There really wasn't enough work anywhere. And there was war

God the spirit of holy tongues couldn't release me from,
or from my dumbness. Pressured—delirious—
from too much inductive thinking, I waited for
the image in whose presence the heart opens and opens
and lived to sleep well; of necessity assessed earth's profit

in green and red May twilight. —You came toward me
in your black skirt, white blouse rolled at the sleeves.
Anticipation of your eyes, your loose hair!
My elementary needs—to cohere, to control.
An awful lot was happening and I wanted more.

From *Curriculum Vitae* (Pittsburgh: University of Pittsburgh Press, 1988).

Wendy Wasserstein

✿

from *The Heidi Chronicles*

They all sit down. HEIDI *moves her chair and sits slightly outside the circle, behind* FRAN.

JILL: I'd like to call to order this meeting of the Huron Street Ann Arbor Consciousness-raising Rap Group. Heidi, Becky, since you're new, I want you to know that everything here is very free, very easy. I've been a member of the group for about five months now. I'm a mother of four daughters, and when I first came I was, as Fran would say, "a fuckin' Hostess cupcake." Everybody in my life—my husband, Bill, my daughters, my friends—could lean on perfect Jill. The only problem was, there was one person I had completely forgotten to take care of.

BECKY: Who was that?

JILL: Jill.

BECKY: I feel that way sometimes.

SUSAN: We all feel that way sometimes.

BECKY: You do?

FRAN: No. We grow up on fuckin' "Father Knows Best" and we think we have rights! You think Jane Wyatt demanded clitoral satisfaction from Robert Young? No fuckin' way.

SUSAN: I love you, Fran.

JILL: I love you too, Fran.

FRAN *primps:* Maybe I should dress for combat more often.

SUSAN: Fran, sometimes I think you let your defensiveness overwhelm your tremendous vulnerability.

JILL: Becky, Heidi, you should know that Fran is a gifted physicist, and a lesbian, and we support her choice to sleep with women.

BECKY: Sure.

FRAN: Do you support my choice, Heidi?

HEIDI: I'm just visiting.

FRAN: I have to say right now that I don't feel comfortable with a "just visiting" in the room. I need to be able to come here and reach out to you as my sisters. Okay, Heidi-ho?

HEIDI: Okay.

FRAN: Just don't judge us. Christ, we spend our lives having men judge us. All right, let the good times roll!

SUSAN: I'll start. This week I think I made a little headway, but I'm also afraid I fell back a few paces.

JILL: What did you decide to do about the *Law Review?*

SUSAN: I accepted the position.

JILL: Good.

SUSAN: Becky, I was seriously considering beginning a law journal devoted solely to women's legal issues. But after some pretty heavy deliberation, I've decided to work within the male-establishment power base to change the system. *Gives a power salute.*

JILL: Susan, I'm so proud of you for making a choice.

SUSAN: Do you know my mother would have married me because I have this position?

FRAN: What are you bullshitting about? You're going to work from "within the male-establishment power base." And I'm going to date fuckin' Tricia Nixon. Susan, either you shave your legs or you don't.

SUSAN: I love you, Fran.

FRAN: I scare the shit out of you, Susan.

BECKY: Why are you yelling at her?

SUSAN: Becky, Fran is one of the most honest people I've ever met. She's a great friend.

BECKY: Well, she sounds kinda like Bobby.

JILL: Who's Bobby?

BECKY: Well, Bobby's my boyfriend. Well, we kinda live together. Well, my father and mother split up last year. My father is in the film department here, and last year he made this documentary called *Flower Children of Ypsilanti.* It won a whole bunch of awards and stuff.

HEIDI: Is your father Ed Groves? That's a great documentary.

BECKY: You saw it?

HEIDI: I'm a graduate student. That means I go to a lot of movies.

BECKY: Well, remember that blonde girl with all the rope bracelets who wanted to go to San Francisco so she could sleep with Donovan? She's my father's other wife.

FRAN: Fuckin' mellow yellow.

SUSAN: That's illegal.

BECKY: They're not really married. She just kinda wears his ring. Anyway, when he left, my mom flipped out. So she went to Esalen in California. I think she's talking to a tree or something. She was only going for a week, but it's been six months. So I asked Bobby to move in, at least until I finished high school, but it's kinda not working. But I don't know.

JILL: You don't know what?

BECKY: I mean, I try to be super nice to him. I make all his meals, and I never disagree with him. But then he just gets angry or stoned. So when I need to think things through, I lock the bathroom door and cry. But I try not to make any sound. Now you're all going to hate me, right?

FRAN *goes over to* BECKY: Lamb, no one here is ever going to hate you.

JILL: Becky, do you want to stay with me and my family for a while?

FRAN: I love you, Jill.

SUSAN: I love you, Jill.

BECKY: But I thought you had to learn to take care of Jill.

JILL: Women like us have to learn to give to those who appreciate it, in-stead of to those who expect it.

FRAN: And those cocksucker assholes have been expecting it for cen-turies.

BECKY: I think you're all fantastic. You are the best women I have ever met. I am *so* glad I came. *Embraces them all.*

FRAN: Thank you, Becky. All—right! Now I would like to hear from our "visitor" what she thinks of our rap group so far.

HEIDI: I thought you don't want to be judged.

FRAN: I'm asking you to share. Not to judge.

HEIDI: I think Jill is very generous and I think the girl with the rope bracelets would have been much happier with Donovan.

JILL *laughs:* Heidi, where do you go to school?

HEIDI: New Haven.

FRAN: Becky, "New Haven" means "Yale" in Eastern egalitarian circles.

HEIDI: I'm in the Art History Graduate Program. My interest is in im-ages of women from the Renaissance Madonna to the present.

FRAN: A feminist interpretation?

HEIDI: Humanist.

FRAN: Heidi, either you shave your legs or you don't.

HEIDI: I'm afraid I think body hair is in the realm of the personal.

FRAN: What *is* your problem, woman?

HEIDI: I don't really want to share that with you. I'm stingy that way.

SUSAN: My friend Heidi is obsessed with an asshole.

HEIDI: Susie, that's personal.

JILL: "Personal" has kept us apart for so many years. "Personal" means I know what I'm doing is wrong, but I have so little faith in myself, I'm going to keep it a secret and go right on doing it.

BECKY: Heidi, can I rub your back? Sometimes that helps my mother.

JILL: We shouldn't force her. Maybe Heidi isn't at the same place we are.

HEIDI: I *am* at the same place you are.

FRAN: How are you at the same place we are?

HEIDI: I think all people deserve to fulfill their potential.

FRAN: Yeah. Except for you.

HEIDI: What?

FRAN: Heidi, every woman in this room has been taught that the desires and dreams of her husband, her son, or her boss are much more important than her own. And the only way to turn that around is for us, right here, to try to make what *we* want, what *we* desire to be, as vital as it would undoubtedly be to any man. And then we can go out there and really make a difference!

SUSAN: I'm so happy I'm living at this time.

FRAN: Heidi, nothing's going to change until we really start talking to each other.

HEIDI *looks at all of them and sits down. She grabs Susan's hand:* Okay, Fran. I met a guy three years ago at a Eugene McCarthy mixer.

FRAN: Jesus. "Neat and clean for Eugene."

HEIDI: Anyway, we've been seeing each other off and on ever since. He dates a lot of other women, and, uh, I get to see him maybe once every few weeks. He's a teaching fellow at the law school. *Catches herself.* Becky, "the law school" means "Yale Law School." I'm an Eastern egalitarian asshole from Chicago.

JILL: So, big deal.

HEIDI: Thanks.

SUSAN: The point is that Heidi will drop anything—work, a date, even a chance to see me—just to be around this creep.

HEIDI: He is a creep. But he's a charismatic creep.

FRAN: I fuckin' hate charisma.

HEIDI: When I need him, he's aloof. But if I decide to get better and leave him, he's unbelievably attentive.

BECKY: Your asshole sounds just like my asshole.

HEIDI: But you see, Becky, the problem isn't really him. The problem is me. I could make a better choice. I have an old friend, Peter, who I know would be a much better choice. But I keep allowing this guy to account for so much of what I think of myself. I allow him to make

Wendy Wasserstein ⟨⟩ *149*

me feel valuable. And the bottom line is, I know that's wrong. I would tell any friend of mine that's wrong. You either shave your legs or you don't.

FRAN: I like your friend, Susan. She has a way to go, but she's one smart repressed lady.

HEIDI: Becky, I hope our daughters never feel like us. I hope all our daughters feel so fucking worthwhile. Do you promise we can accomplish that much, Fran? Huh? Do you promise? Do you promise?

FRAN *gets up and embraces* HEIDI: I take it back. I love you, Heidi.

JILL: I love you, Heidi.

BECKY: I love you, Heidi.

SUSAN: This really has a feeling of completion for me. Full circle. Heidi and I grew up together. We were *girl*friends. But I wanted her to be able to meet my *women* friends, because you are all *so* important to me. And, Becky, that includes you. You are very important to me now. *They are all embracing.*

JILL: I think we're all just terrific! And I swear that neither snow nor sleet nor Aphrodite's tits could keep me from getting my ass here.

FRAN *slaps Jill's hands:* All—right, Jill!

BECKY *slaps Jill's hands:* All—right, Jill!

HEIDI & SUSAN *slap Jill's hands:* All—right, Jill!

JILL: All—right, Heidi!

BECKY: All—right, Heidi!

FRAN: All—right, Heidi! *Turns to slap Jill's hand again.* All—right, Jill!

JILL *moves away and changes the subject:* Why don't we all sing a favorite camp song of mine and of my children. Okay? Okay. We all get into a circle and join hands. And it goes like this . . .

They take hands.

JILL, *instructing:*

> Friends, friends, friends,
> We will always be . . .

They repeat the refrain and begin awkwardly to sway.

ALL:

> Friends, friends, friends,
> We will always be . . .

JILL:

Whether in hail or in dark stormy weather

ALL:

Whether in hail or in dark stormy weather

JILL:

Camp Truckahoe will keep us together!

ALL:

Camp Truckahoe will . . .

FRAN *breaks out of the circle:* Fuck this shit! *Puts Aretha back on.*

ALL *sing along, dancing:*
R-E-S-P-E-C-T,
Find out what it means to me.
Sock it to me, a little respect,

FRAN *leads the women in making a power salute on "a little respect" each time it is sung.*

Sock it to me, a little respect,

Scene ends with their arms up and the women proclaiming—

ALL: A little respect!

From *The Heidi Chronicles and Other Plays* (San Diego: Harcourt Brace Jovanovich, Publishers, 1990).

Elwood Reid

༕

from *If I Don't Six*

I save Michigan for last.

At Michigan everybody wears maize and blue and hates Ohio State and Michigan State. There are cars everywhere and the air tastes like aluminum.

As soon as I hit town, one of the recruiting coordinators drives me to the stadium and walks me down this long tunnel out onto the frozen field. A small patch of razor-sharp green turf has been cleared of snow. Everything goes quiet except for the rattle of empty flagpoles.

Then my recruiter, Coach Gibson, trots out from the tunnel, stops me on the fifty-yard line and asks if I can hear one hundred thousand people cheering.

I can't, but I nod and smile anyways and say something stupid like, "A hundred thousand?"

Then he takes me to the locker room. A painting of a large black eye set inside a maize and blue triangle covers the entire back wall. Gibson points at the eye and gives me this speech about the Eye of Michigan; how every player who has ever played before me will be watching over everything I do. Above the eye are the words: ACCEPT WITHOUT PRIDE, RELINQUISH WITHOUT STRUGGLE.

I recognize the quote from somewhere and finally it hits me. "Marcus Aurelius," I say, pointing at the words.

Gibson looks at me as if I've just spoken in church.

"It's from *Meditations*," I say.

"Who in the hell is Marcus Aurelius?" Gibson sputters.

"Emperor of Rome and Stoic," I say.

"Son, I can tell you, without a doubt, that Coach Roe sent us out to face the Trojans of USC in the Rose Bowl with that quote. I don't know about any Greek emperor, all I know is that we kicked some Trojan butt that day."

I nod and let it go at that.

He calms down and points out this board that hangs over the locker room doorway that says GO BLUE.

"Every player touches the sign before he takes the field," he says, pointing at the door. "Go ahead . . . I want you to touch it."

I know he's not going to leave me alone until I do, so I raise up both hands and place them flat on the brass letters, pat them once or twice.

Gibson, "Did you feel it?"

"Yeah," I say, still thinking about empty flagpoles and the cold bronze of General Patton.

Afterward Gibson takes me to see Coach Roe.

Coach Roe is a tall silver-haired guy with one of those movie star chins and cold unblinking eyes. There are stories about him yelling and screaming at recruits. I've watched him on television kicking grass at refs, tossing his headset to the ground in disgust, snapping clipboards and even smacking players in the facemask when they fuck up. For football. For victory.

Before I go into Roe's office, Gibson says, "Just look him in the eyes and shake his hand like a man—a good firm one."

I turn to go but he stops me, his wide face solemn and swollen. "One more thing—remember the Eyes of Michigan are on you."

My hands shake as I knock lightly on the door and hear a voice on the other side telling me to come in.

I push open the door and see Coach Roe standing over his trophy case staring into the glass at his own reflection. He grins at me and points at a chair.

"Mr. Riley," he says. "Somebody told me you were a ballplayer."

My throat goes dry.

"That's what you're here for, isn't it?"

My voice cracks. "I hope so."

Roe grins again and sits down behind his desk, balls his hands into fists and places them on his credenza. Then he launches into this speech: "Last boy I took from Cleveland started smoking cigarettes and bird-dogging women. Hit like a goddamn girl even though he was supposed to be Mr. Blue-Chip All-American. But he wasn't good enough to wear the maize and blue."

"What happened?" I ask.

"He quit. Shit his pants and moved back to Cleveland with some nice Polish girl and got himself a job with the UPS."

I wait, let him size me up.

"Now, I ain't saying every mother-loving ballplayer from Cleveland is soft," he says. "Being a Wolverine isn't something I can teach you. You got to be mean and stubborn as a mule, hell-bent on kicking some ass. What I'm looking for, Riley, is just a few guys who are willing to spill blood and guts, guys who want to win so bad they'd tackle their mothers and sack their sisters. What I want to know, Riley, is if you want it that bad. Because if you don't, I can assure you that there's some other flat-ass hungry kid who does."

I'm usually not big on the rah-rah stuff, all that win-one-for-the-Gipper crap, but watching Coach Roe I feel the blood go up into my ears as he pounds out the words on his desk. And before I know it my hands start to sweat and I feel like hitting somebody.

"Yes," I say, jumping out of my chair and sticking my hand out for him to shake. He lets it hang there, just grinning at me as the veins in his neck retreat back into the flab. I feel stupid and he knows it.

"Good," he says. "Now sit down and let's talk about what Michigan has to offer."

My heart's still banging away, but I sit and feign interest as he sells me on Michigan, how it's a top ten academic institution, best facilities, great place to live and study, etc. But I'm not listening, instead I want to hear more of the speech, see Roe's veins flare out again, because he's got something I can't quite place. Coach Gil never had it or if he did our team's piss-poor performance couldn't dredge it out of him. Even my wrestling coach, who motivated us with long stares of disapproval, doesn't have what Coach Roe seems to have. I know that if he asks I'm going to say yes.

This starts me to thinking about how playing for any coach is pretty masochistic stuff. For starters, all coaches take it on faith that you're a shitbird until proven otherwise. You hate them and love them. Praise is rarely offered, instead a good tackle or touchdown run is met with a nod or sometimes nothing at all. The effect of this, despite every rational thought, is to try harder. You want to get that smile or arm-swinging praise out of the coach, just to see it. So when a coach finally breaks down and offers a "Way to go, Riley" or "Nice job" you don't care anymore. You are a tree in winter, one hard bastard, a rock of hatred. That's when you become a sickdog motherfucker. A baby killer. Nobody likes you. You don't even like yourself, only what your body can do to another player. Practicing is like putting out the sun and you like it. That's the fucked-up thing about it—you like it. Other guys take the lack of praise personally and walk around all gloom and doom. They never learn to eat it and to hate. Put it this way, Mean Joe Green didn't have daffodils in his heart. He was one black angry dude. He lived to swing around the end on a full rush, busting forearm into facemask, spitting at his opponents and hating everything about them, even the way they laced up their cleats.

I know right away that Coach Roe's a master of this bullshit, a maker of men who hates the way machines do: cold and indiscriminately. The funny thing is that it doesn't prevent me from wanting to play for him. Suddenly all that crap about books and being smart doesn't seem to matter so much and I begin to admit to myself that I have wanted this all along—that here my size and ability to hit are not only wanted but respected.

So I listen to his crap about Michigan, Center of Athletic Excellence, Champions of the West and so on, thinking that playing for him would be like Coach Gil times ten.

I leave his office high on purpose and full of dreams.

Coach Gibson meets up with me in the hallway and starts yammering about how many kids have already signed with Michigan and how long it would take me to earn a starting position. He explains the red shirt policy, training table and how many frosh make the travel team.

At lunch he keeps up about the tradition at Michigan listing all of the pro players who have played for the maize and blue and who look good for the draft this year. So far nobody has mentioned the full ride.

"Am I going to see Coach Roe again?" I ask.

Gibson stops midchew and sputters, "Hell, yes, son." Then he looks at me as if I'm retarded.

"Who else are you recruiting at my position?" I ask.

"Well, we've got a verbal from this big son-of-a-buck from Pennsylvania."

"What's his name?"

"Frank Himes—you guys ought to get along—that is if you commit."

I look down into my plate of fries, worried that no one's mentioned the full ride yet. "When am I going to . . ."

He cuts me off with a stupid story about the Rose Bowl.

After dinner Gibson takes me to see Coach Roe again.

This time he's dressed in a tight-fitting suit, his fingers wrapped in bowl rings, eyes still as pond water. A woman with black hair and liver-spotted hands sits next to him, staring at the room full of oversize bodies.

He motions for me to sit next to him.

"My wife," he says, pointing at liver spot woman.

Wife nods and goes back to staring. Waiters and busboys rush up to Coach Roe asking for autographs on linen and menus. I watch the way they look right through his wife.

Coach Roe pushes his plate away. "Coach Gibson says you're getting a little anxious."

I nod.

He turns to his wife. "The kid likes Michigan."

All I can do is smile.

"You and me are going to have a talk tomorrow morning," he says. "Iron this thing out."

Then he sends me off with a little pat on the back, the sort you might give to a child.

From *If I Don't Six* (New York: Doubleday, 1998).

Part Four

☙

Spirit of Place

Nancy Willard

♔

from Sister Water

If you stand for hours by the window in the dayroom at Hopecrest, you can stare at the parking lot and grounds that stretch half a mile west to Drummond Avenue. But if you walk down the corridor of second floor east, past Dr. Davidson's closed door till you reach the window at the very end, you can see the Huron River. The choice is yours.

If you have a hawk's eyes, you can travel upriver to Delhi and Dexter. The fishing is good there, and if you go in the fall you can refresh yourself at the Dexter cider mill. Summer and spring, canoes glide under the viaducts, about half a mile south of Barton Pond.

Paddle slowly across Barton Pond toward the dam and you'll see blue herons reading the water for sunfish, red-winged blackbirds glinting in the cattail marshes, and carp lolling like fat little islands, their fins rising above pickerel weed in the shallows. You can stop here all day, watching for muskrats, turtles, and dragonflies. You'll miss the grand houses of Barton Hills, the country club where the small boats dock, and the golf course. The choice is yours.

Or you can let the current carry you past Riverside Park toward Fuller Park. If you trust the river, it will carry you all the way to Lake Erie.

But maybe you don't want to travel that far. You say, Fuller Park is far enough. You can stop at Pawquacha Hoot 'n Scoot, operated by Thomas Bearheart, who sells bait to the fishermen and cold drinks to the swimmers and picnickers. For fifteen cents you can buy a postcard showing the great horned owl of Michigan in 3-D. There is a bait store out back, famous for its copper fishhooks hand-forged by Thomas Bearheart's cousin in Drowning Bear, Wisconsin.

But mainly people come to read the notices tacked on the walls inside. Rumor has it that the people who put them there are all relatives of Thomas Bearheart, and they have been here, in one guise or another, almost as long as the river; generations of Pawquachas have lived and died on it. Fishermen, scavengers, divers, dowsers. Water is their occupation. The people who specialize in pool and fountain installations are as skillful as beavers at making structures that water must pass over or through. Some notices promise to find "the well that's right for you." Others advertise "Lost articles found" or "Expert divers available" or "Salvage for sale cheap." Those who dive at night are so sensitive to the light that their skin darkens at sunrise and pales when the sun goes down.

Others, nimble as squirrels, will shingle your roof or fix your TV antenna.

Only one phone number is given: Thomas Bearheart's. If you call Thomas Bearheart and state your problem, he will dispatch someone to do the job. There are those who say that Thomas Bearheart's relatives don't fix things, they only exchange old problems for new ones. A woman on Devonshire, for whom a river man installed a new drain, complained it was badly clogged with moccasin flowers and water hyacinths. A plunger couldn't begin to unclog it; the roots were endless. A man on Spring Valley Road had his television set repaired by one of the river women, and shortly thereafter a strange shadow swam across the screen and blocked out half the picture. It looked like a little-mouth bass, and in spite of the expensive efforts of the Sears, Roebuck service department, it stayed for a month.

Folks who wouldn't dream of answering one of the notices on the walls of Pawquacha Hoot 'n Scoot will not hesitate to buy crab apple jam from Thomas Bearheart's relatives on Saturday morning at the Farmers' Market. Or black cherry jam or rosehip jelly, or hickory nut bread, or their special sumac relish, which they call shandygaff. A few passengers on the Lake Shore Limited rushing toward Chicago claim to have seen marvelous gardens in the wildest stretches of the river at twilight. Once a man came to the market with nothing to sell but three small black masks. He claimed he'd traded a dozen ears of sweet corn for them, and the masks were good and fearless; he knew the raccoons personally. No one had the courage to buy them. It is known that the Pawquachas live by secret tides in their blood, as distinctive for each of them as the whorl of their fingerprints, and under certain conditions a deep instinct turns them into animals of the river. When they meet danger, they will almost certainly change, as a chameleon changes, if they see it in time. They will also change when the moon unsettles the delicate balance in their blood. By means of this simple defense, they have survived the loss of their land, their religion, their government—everything except the river, which has kept them alive.

What sells fastest is their wild rice, and Thomas Bearheart's relatives will not tell where it grows or who harvests it. If you are seized with a desire to find the source, change yourself into a trout and take the long way, following one of the underground streams into Lake Michigan. If you cross the lake and keep a northerly course, you will find yourself knocking at the Door Peninsula. "Door" is short for Door of the Dead— Porte des Morts, as the French sailors called it. The ships that sank here may be rolling across the floor of Lake Huron by this time. Everything is connected, and the water people know this.

Or you can take the shortcut and paddle to one of the passages in the Huron River, which reflects this world so clearly you can see into the next one. When wild flags blossom along the river's edge in this world, snow whitens the banks in that one. And when trout and sunfish sleep under a skin of ice here, the swamps there hum with bees and cicadas, kingbirds and vireos and warblers. Walk against the current. Follow one of the streams that spill into the river till you find the spring at the bottom. You have found a doorway into the spirit world. Be careful. It is not safe to pass through that doorway without a guide.

But maybe you don't want to travel that far. You say, Ann Arbor is far enough. Stand still in the stream. Listen. Thomas Bearheart's cousin picks up her hammer. Can you hear it ringing as she forges copper fishhooks in Drowning Bear, Wisconsin? Put your ear to the water as if it were a train track and listen for travelers rushing toward you, invisible as the dead and noisy as a pack of dogs.

From *Sister Water* (New York: Alfred A. Knopf, 1993).

Nancy Willard

⟨ϸ⟩

from Things Invisible To See

In any quiet town you can find a street, a field, a stand of trees, which breaks into the dreams of its citizens years after the dreamers have left home for good. For generations of dreamers in Ann Arbor the Island has beckoned, flickered, faded, and risen again. Yet Island Park is surely not different from other parks in other cities lucky enough to be divided by one of those lazy brown rivers that join shanties and brickyards to golf courses and boat houses. In summer the water is too shallow for a row-boat, but canoes from the livery on Barton Pond thread their way past black willow and wild cherry and crab apple, among islands large enough to offer standing room only to one adult human and five muskrats, or four otters and half a dozen mallards. There are picnic tables on the right bank, where the new road runs, and tall grass along the left bank, where the old road sleeps, and a bridge between them, big enough for one car to pass over. Once, whole families of Negroes who lived by the tracks that followed the river could be seen on that bridge, fishing for carp or crayfish.

A footbridge joins the right bank to the only island that could support a population larger than one adult human and five muskrats or four otters and half a dozen mallards. On the Island—for so it is called, as if no other island were worthy of the name—stands a modest Greek temple with a roof like the lid of a fancy tureen and a colonnade running all around. Is it a circular temple proper to the worship of Hermes in winged cap and winged sandals, sacred to crossroads, the messenger of the dead? Is it sacred to the genius of this place?

No. The temple is sacred to two toilets, hidden at opposite ends behind appropriately marked doors. From far off, the graffiti on the doors do not show and the rough plaster walls might pass for Carrara marble. On a spring morning, when the black willow is leafing and the wild cherry beginning to bloom, if you are taking the Wolverine to Detroit or Battle Creek, you might look out of the train window and think you are passing the temple of love on the sacred island of Cythera, as Watteau painted it. And long after you've forgotten where you are going and why you are going there, the temple will appear to you in dreams, and you will wonder if your soul lived here before it put on its burden of flesh.

On this cloudy day the temple hung over the river like a ghostly sepulcher. Snow added its cubits to the stature of the roof, the trees, the picnic tables spread as if with that hidden fabric called "the silence cloth" by housewives who keep it under the finer damask one, to absorb the clatter of dishes and silver. Snow softened the bare limbs of the bushes.

Under its roof of ice, the river sent up bubbles: the telegraphed laments of the fish.

A single twig was now a thing of great beauty: a wand, a power, a glory. A sign.

Ben turned down Catherine Street and passed the open arcade where tomorrow morning at eight the manager of the Farmers' Market would walk up and down ringing a bell, to signify that the stalls were now open for business. During the winter only a few farmers huddled over small stoves behind their counters. Tomorrow the smell of kerosene would hang over the kale, dug out of snow fresh that morning, and over the cartons of eggs which had to be kept in the back of the trucks to prevent them from freezing.

Beyond the market rose a block of storefronts that belonged indisputably to the Negroes. There was a barbershop, a hardware store, a harness shop—in fine weather the bridles were hung around the doorway for show—and a secondhand store, which as long as anyone on the block could remember had displayed in its window a huddle of green glazed jars and liniment bottles filled with colored water. Sometimes they appeared in a row on the sidewalk. Nobody ever took them. They gave you the feeling they might cry out and the owner would hear them.

Behind the shops—and no white person had ever seen what lay behind the shops—was a graveyard for those who did not or could not get themselves properly buried in the Ebenezer Baptist cemetery. The graves looked like beds for penitents: a long slab of concrete studded with buttons, shells, beads, or nails. An iron pole joined headstone to footstone; in warm weather it held pots of geraniums and marigolds, night shade and devil's claw. There were names but no inscriptions. In the headstone of Pharoah Dawson was embedded the headlight of the Cadillac that carried him to a fiery death. From the stone of Sister Harriet Doyle rose an open hand, in whose palm gleamed a mirror, like a tiny frozen pond.

Nothing was broken, kicked over, or disturbed. Perhaps the faces on the little clay pots that grinned on the graves protected them. From deep sockets their eyes, made of mirrors or balls of white clay, seemed to glow, and though their teeth were no more than kernels of corn, a guilty visitor might see his own death grinning there. The Barbershop Cemetery, people said, was a mighty powerful place, and people went there for reasons that had nothing to do with honoring the dead.

The paved road gave way to brick and dipped sharply to the left, toward the river and the stone fortress that was the train station, a granite vision of Byzantium: towers, arches, porches, windows curved like giant keyholes, iced and glittering. Today, behind stained glass hidden by snow, the stationmaster knelt at the hearth and laid a fire. A handful of passengers stood waiting hopefully, listening for trains, postponing the moment when they must rush out to the cold platform where baggage carts waited like large, sad animals, their wheels frozen and clogged with snow.

From *Things Invisible to See* (New York: Alfred A. Knopf, 1984).

Max Apple

from Roommates

In the summer before my freshman year, I went to Ann Arbor for three days of orientation. I took the Greyhound bus. I promised Gootie that I would eat everything.

I stayed in a dormitory room and thought I smelled pork everywhere. I took tests in math and Spanish and English, but my anxiety was about the dining room, not the classroom.

I roomed on the third floor with a group of other Michigan boys. They were accustomed to cafeterias. For my first dinner I squeezed into a crowded elevator and then followed everyone to the dining hall. I tried to decide which of the hulking eighteen-year-olds around me I'd trade my pork to.

I walked through the line, imitating those ahead of me. I picked a salad, avoided the Jell-O, which I knew contained boiled animal hooves. When it came to the main course I froze. A woman in a hairnet finally pushed a plate at me—potatoes with a little pool of gravy in the middle and meat.

I went to a table by myself, but in seconds the other seats filled up. The boys' dormitory was jammed with freshmen-to-be, and I was determined to be one of them. I chewed the tiny green salad with gusto. Then I lifted my fork to the gray-brown gravy and mixed it throughout the potatoes. I listened to the conversation around me, hoping someone would name the main course, but they were talking about Plato.

When the other eaters were almost finished I finally had the courage to ask.

"Meatloaf," one said.

"Hamloaf," said another. They bussed their trays.

"Whatever it is," the meatloaf man said, "it sucks."

I waited until my tablemates left the room, then I carried my tray to the garbage. I hadn't even touched a drop of gravy.

In my three days of orientation I ate only breakfast cereals. I came home pale and hungry.

"That's it," Gootie said. "He can't go to college."

I'd never seen her happier. I was ready to agree. I was so worried about what I could eat that I did badly on all my exams. The counselor assigned to me told me he didn't know how I'd gotten a scholarship. He advised me to go to Grand Rapids Junior College and take remedial English.

"You're going to Ann Arbor," my mother said, "and you'll eat like everyone else, and you'll be smart. What do tests know?"

Gootie plugged for junior college. "You can go there," she said, "and come home for lunch."

"It's only a two-year college," I reminded her.

"You can learn plenty in two years," she said.

I was leaning toward staying home, but as I struggled to decide my father reminded me of what happened when he took me to my first big league game.

I was ten, and we went to see the Tigers play the Red Sox. We left home at six A.M. so we'd be in Detroit early enough to watch all of batting practice.

It was a five-hour drive to Detroit. I was too excited to sleep the night before. For breakfast I had only thin cocoa. I carried my glove, hoping for a foul ball and my Scripto pencil for autographs just in case I ran into Al Kaline or Ted Williams in the parking lot. At a rest stop in central Michigan I left my lunch on a picnic bench. I wanted to go to my first big league game without the burden of a half-pound tuna sandwich on yellow challah. I wanted my hands free for pop fouls, in my lap I wanted only a scorecard.

By the time we got to the ball park it was the fast of Yom Kippur on the backseat. My father circled Briggs Stadium, looking for a parking place. "There it is," he said. Weak and dizzy, I looked up to see the dark green stadium surrounded by a rotting ghetto. A row of solemn black men held placards stating *Parking* $1.00 and pointed to their backyards.

My stomach ached. My fingers were hardly strong enough to unlock the door. "You've got to eat something," my father said. He turned away from the stadium toward a bleak business district.

We couldn't go too far or we'd miss out on the parking and the batting practice. My father stopped at a kosher-style deli.

I was so hungry that I left my baseball glove in the car. The waiter told me that the hot dogs were kosher, but I also noticed every variety of swine on his menu.

I ordered a Coke. My father, almost in tears, begged me to eat so I could enjoy the game.

"Tell him to eat, please," he asked the waiter.

The waiter gave me a "Let the little bastard starve" look and returned to the kitchen.

Then a middle-aged waitress came through the swinging varnished doors. "Honey," she said, "come with me."

She pulled my head off the counter and took me into the kitchen. She let me watch while she put two kosher hot dogs into a thick plastic bag and then boiled them in that bag.

She produced a packaged rye bread and pointed out the vegetable shortening. She brought out a side dish of vegetarian baked beans and sat next to me while I ate. She even gave me some hard candy for dessert.

"Those hot dogs were kosher," my father said of that incident, "but you almost spoiled it for yourself by being so stubborn. That was just a double-header. This time it's your education. You'll have plenty of chances to keep kosher, you can do it for the rest of your life, but if you don't go to college now, you'll never go."

He walked me outside to his Dodge truck, which he kept in a cement block garage across the street from our house. He unlocked the cab and opened the glove compartment. He took out the pair of tiny yellow mittens that I had prized when I was about five.

"My work gloves," I said.

"Every time I get a new truck, I toss 'em into the glove compartment. They remind me," he said, "that I don't want you to be a truck driver."

In September my parents drove me to Ann Arbor. They helped me unload my belongings in South Quad, and then, for the first time in my life, they took me out to dinner.

My mother had done some research. She asked my sisters and the parents of children who she knew had gone to Michigan. She wanted the name of the best restaurant in town.

I wondered why my father wore his light blue suit and a tie and my mother her best flowered dress. I thought it was to impress the other parents. They didn't tell me until I was in the car that our destination was the Sugar Bowl.

By the time we got there about eight, the restaurant, on Main Street in downtown Ann Arbor, was empty. I later learned it usually was. The Sugar Bowl was a huge high-ceilinged place with plaster columns and walls of two-tone green. A Greek family owned it, and they all worked there. The menu came in a padded red cover. It felt like a textbook.

"Everyone says this is the best," my mother said, as Demetra, our waitress, ushered us to an eight-person booth. All the booths were that size or larger. My feet barely touched the ground. I felt as if I were on an island.

I had, of course, been in restaurants—the coffee shop variety—but I'd never had to face a menu. I had ordered only orange juice or ice cream or a Coke. Now the pressure was on.

My parents tried to pretend it was an everyday event, just an American mom and dad taking their college boy out to dinner. My mother was cheerful; she chatted about her cousin Mamie, who told her about the Sugar Bowl. Mamie had been there during the Depression.

Demetra's English was not great. "Welcome, scholars," she said. We had to repeat every order, and I think she wrote them on the pad in Greek.

"He'll have a steak," my mother said, "the best one you've got."

They worked at being casual. My father talked about the Michigan football team, about the beautiful dormitory my sister Bailey had lived in. He reminded me to give him a copy of the combination to my bike lock. We killed time while in the dark kitchen of the Sugar Bowl, my steak sizzled.

The only full restaurant meals I could recall were at the synagogue. Every year, as a fund-raising event, a speaker came from New York. Women from the sisterhood cooked. We ate on rented tables in the social hall and sat on folding chairs donated by the Alt Mortuary.

It was expensive, maybe twenty or thirty dollars a plate, but my mother wanted me to go to these events. I went during the heyday of my sisters' debating career. Although I didn't take debate, my mother still had hopes that the example of those pitchmen and moralists whom the synagogue paid two hundred dollars and up would someday inspire me to great oratory.

Demetra arrived with my dinner beneath a steel cover. She laid the meat in front of me, surrounded by steaming mashed potatoes and green beans boiled to a pallor. I had heard of T-bones, and now I saw one. I recognized the *T* surrounded by fat and gristle, caught a glimpse of the dark marrow.

"It looks delicious," my mother said as she sipped her orange juice.

My father raised his coffee cup. "*L'chaim*," he said.

Their bravery put a lump in my throat. My father's grandmother left Pennsylvania in the 1880s to return to Poland because she didn't trust the kosher food in America. Gootie's step-grandmother lived in Brooklyn beyond the age of one hundred without ever tasting canned food.

Our family history was studded with such culinary denial. In our house, fast days were big events—not only Yom Kippur. Rocky fasted for the destruction of the Temple and in sympathy with Queen Esther. Gootie, a libertine like me, checked cabbage and broccoli for weevils. She sifted through dry lentils individually, and she put marks with a file on the silverware so she could tell meat from milk cutlery even in the dark.

I caught my mother staring at the steak. That T-bone was not meat, it was a border. She and my father and all my ancestors sat on one side of the table—the steak and I on the other. Demetra, who had been in Ann Arbor for only three months, sat in a booth across from us, missing Greece and waiting to see if we'd want dessert.

It was already eight-twenty. My father had a four-hour drive home and then on Monday a grueling 250-mile round trip in the truck to buy scrap from his best customer, the Kysor Heater Company.

"Don't let it get cold," my mother said. I thought she might reach across the table and cut the steak into chunks for me as if I were a three-year-old, but she didn't. She looked away from me at the plaster of paris frieze on the wall where Greek heroes with lidded eyes reminded other diners of classical dignity.

I cut, I bit, I chewed. My mother held her breath. I swallowed. I thought they would both applaud. After the first bite I ate everything on one side of the long bone. It was a love feast. I did it for them, they did it for me.

They drove home satisfied that I would not starve in college. In the dormitory I unpacked my clothes and didn't vomit.

My roommate, a muscular sophomore from Detroit, had lived in the dormitory the year before. He had friends and spent the evening in one of the lounges playing bridge. About midnight he returned.

"What did you do?" he asked.

"My parents took me out for a steak dinner."

"Lucky you," he said.

From *Roommates: My Grandfather's Story* (New York: Warner Books, 1994).

Charles Baxter

෯

Hybrid City

When he was still in high school, my son and I went canoeing on the Huron River one afternoon in early July. The sun was out but produced no effect of swelter. The river had its pleasant airborne vegetative smell, like wet leaves pouring into the bathtub. We started at the Argo Pond canoe livery and paddled up as far as the dam, then headed back.

Our trip turned into a little allegory of Ann Arbor. First there was the slightly pastoral effect of the river in those sections where greenery still persisted and trash hadn't piled up. But nearby us on the water were other rowboats and canoes: young couples, probably lovers, passing languidly here and there, and then a noisy canoe piloted by a bearded guy arguing vehemently with another bearded guy in the bow about translations of Vallejo. Only in Ann Arbor! The two men were so loudly argumentative that my son and I could hear every word. I doubt that this quarrelsome pair even saw the water beneath them or the trees to the side. And then, of course, on both riverbanks, partially obscured by foliage in the service of landscape architecture, we saw the massive, solemn, and comically gargantuan mansions owned by the captains of industry, medicine, and the law.

The trouble with writing about Ann Arbor is that it is a city with no essence. About Detroit, where I worked for fifteen years, you think: *cars,* and *manufacturing,* and you call it: *Motown,* and the nickname pretty much sums it up. In Buffalo, where I lived for four years prior to my time in Detroit, the city's past and its mortal industrial remains were visible everywhere; even the windshield wiper factory on Main Street had a gloom-struck, sullen appearance, like an industrialized House of Usher. But Ann Arbor is a hybrid city of subcultural communities that have been genetically spliced together by the forces of history, and, no, the University of Michigan does *not* entirely account for its peculiar forms of diversity, or the intensity about peoples' feelings for it, pro and con.

Ann Arbor—where I lived for thirty years, where I passed what will be most of my adult life—is typically a place for people to reside when they're on their way somewhere else, and it is therefore a locale for change and conversions. It has a life-is-elsewhere, just-passing-through, *temporary* quality, like California. Natives are few. Students arrive with their parents, are educated, fall in love, then graduate, often leaving by themselves, without parental help. They're altered, most of them, and generally go on with their lives in other, more permanent, settings. For many of them, Ann Arbor takes on an enchanted stage-backdrop aura that I hoped to turn to slightly droll effect when I wrote *The Feast of Love*. Such passers-through tend to love the place and insist on thinking of it, projectively, as eternally youthful, The Homeland of Promise.

The centers of the Homeland of Promise are the Arboretum in late spring and Michigan Stadium in early fall. They are pits of procreative and recreational energy. It is entirely appropriate that lovers should have once traditionally snuck into the Big House to have sex on the fifty yard line, and that graduation ceremonies are held, year after year, in that same spot.

The last semester I lived in Ann Arbor, I took the bus to work, and I walked whenever and wherever I could. I often made my way on paths through the Pioneer High School woods, down Seventh, east on Pauline, past Allmendinger Park, onto Main, where I headed north past the South Main Market and Overture Audio. Walking in Ann Arbor makes anyone look like a loser or an undergraduate, and sometimes gangs of teenage boys, heading to or away from Pioneer, shouted insults at me. When I didn't walk, I rode my bicycle. All this was an antidote for some cultural malevolence I was trying to undo personally and quixotically. In some private part of my mind, I was protesting my and everyone else's reliance on gasoline, our lethal addiction to it. Standing at the bus stop, eyeing the motorists, I would think: *there certainly are a lot of luxury cars in this town.* You can get a good look at the range of Ann Arborites if you're stranded at a bus stop, waiting for the Number Fifteen, in a snowstorm.

From a bus stop, our fellow Washtenaw County citizens look intelligent and preoccupied and well-meaning and busy and a bit smug.

Behind you at the bus stop is someone reading a book in French (snow is falling into the book), and when the bus itself arrives, it is full of mutterers. What a town of talkers! Often it's brilliant muttering, tenurable in its eloquence. Ann Arbor has many inhabitants who give lectures for a living, but, take my word for it, giving lectures does not improve one's character. Quite the opposite. The lecturer ends up having a high opinion of his opinions, because, during the day, others are busy taking notes on every stated pronouncement. For every lecturer there has to be a listener. The habit of lecturing sometimes locates itself where it does not belong, in domestic life, at dinner parties, where the cuisine, or the paintings, or wonderful little restaurants in Provence, get the lecture-treatment. I was once invited to a dinner party in Ann Arbor where the host stopped all our civilized conversations, calling them "chitchat," and asked us all, going around the table, to talk, one by one, about our careers.

All the same, I loved Ann Arbor for the presence of friends, and for the city's nurturing environment: our son was conceived and born there, grew up there, went to high school and left home from there. In his way, he was a prototypical Ann Arborite: he arrived, he was raised and educated, he attended the Michigan Theater from time to time, and he left. I found my adult life in Ann Arbor; I found my way there, my living and my vocation.

The city's flaws were mine, as well; no fault of the city is alien to me. Living close to the stadium, hearing the cheers in the distance like the sound of surf landing on sand during those autumnal Saturday afternoons, I thought I recognized the recreational arrogance that the rest of Michigan identifies as *the* characteristic of Our Very Wonderful Town. The spiritual practices of humility—the highest disciplines of the soul—are not, it has to be said, held in great esteem in Ann Arbor.

There is a Babbitry of the small town booster, and then the Babbitry of great academic achievers, the anointed ones who are still somehow stranded in this modest-looking Midwestern city, exiled from Byzantium. How did that happen? Poor souls, they have to *think* their way even to the dinner table, where, over the roast beef, they can't stop being prideful and brilliant and assertive and opinionated about every feature of life. It can stimulate you and it can wear you down. Here on my desk is a request from a former student for a recommendation, "to help me escape this horrible, loathsome town. (AA's got this oh-so transparent skein holding it together made of money and entitlement and ego like no other place I've lived, and I'll never feel I belong, never, because I can't and don't want to.)" This is a cry of the soul that, in one form or another, I have heard many times.

What about those who come to be changed and somehow *don't* find what they need? They leave Ann Arbor feeling peevish, cast-down, disappointed, uncured—like someone who might have come to one of our hospitals and for whom there was no diagnosis or treatment. "Ann Arbor?" another friend says, when I ask him his opinion about it. "Michigan's largest adult daycare center."

And yet. Everyone has a mental scrapbook. Here I am, walking through the Arb with a friend and his large dog—we make our way down to the river and watch a freight train pass by; and here I am with other friends in a restaurant on State Street, laughing; and here, out on Scio Church Road, is the little church cemetery with its headstones carved in German; and over here is the most beautiful cottonwood tree I've ever seen, by the side of the river at the Hudson Mills Metropark picnic area; here are dozens of friends and colleagues, and, given the slightly burnishing effect of memory, they are all smiling; here are the wonderful schools, mainstream and alternative; and the hospitals where I was cured of my physical maladies; here, on the window ledge of the barbershop on Liberty—no longer there—is a tiny Z-gauge train set chugging on a tiny oval track; over here is a bar—also no longer in existence, replaced by a bank—at the corner of Liberty and Stadium, filled with men and women dressed in their summer softball uniforms; here is a pond in Greenview Park in the winter, frozen over, and I am one of the skaters; the Hopwood Room, with its large table of literary publications; here is a homeless shelter, and over there is the German translation of *The Book of Mormon*—*Das Buch Mormon*—that I found lodged in a tree in the Pioneer High School Woods; and now Frank Zappa is about to take the stage in Hill Auditorium, and I am in the balcony, waiting; another concert, and it's Evgeny Kissen; and now I am in the living room in our house on Woodland Drive, listening to the tornado siren at the corner of Greenview and Glen Leven, a loud voice telling everyone to take shelter; all the Krogers have been shut down, following a strike by the workers; Senator Philip Hart is giving a speech, and then he dies, and my heart is broken—where will we find another senator like him?—; I am walking across campus and someone is playing the music of Erik Satie on the carillon; an ice storm brings down branches on Granger, and all through Burns Park, where all traffic is blocked; I am looking out through the window in front of me, trying to think of my next sentence.

And now we are boarding the Amtrak train for Chicago, and as we settle in, the train starts up with a bit of a lurch. It's fall, and for several miles, as we leave Ann Arbor behind, we pass alongside the river whose riverbank trees are turning color. They fall; they are preparing for winter. Everything comes back to the river. We who have lived there are like its water: passing through, passing away.

From *Ann Arbor (W)Rites: A Community Memoir*, edited by
Nicholas Delbanco (Ann Arbor: Ann Arbor District Library, 2004).

Charles Baxter

ஃ

from The Feast of Love

On the first floor near the foot of the stairs, we have placed on the wall an antique mirror so old that it can't reflect anything anymore. Its surface, worn down to nubbled grainy gray stubs, has lost one of its dimensions. Like me, it's glimmerless. You can't see *into* it now, just past it. Depth has been replaced by texture. This mirror gives back nothing and makes no productive claim upon anyone. The mirror has been so completely worn away that you have to learn to live with what it refuses to do. That's its beauty.

I have put on jeans, a shirt, shoes. I will take a walk. I glide past the nonmirroring mirror, unseen, thinking myself a vampire who soaks up essences other than blood. I go outside to Woodland Drive and saunter to the end of the block onto a large vacant lot. Here I am, a mere neighbor, somnambulating, harmless, no longer a menace to myself or to anyone else, and, stage by stage, feeling calmer now that I am outside.

As all the neighbors know, no house will ever be built on the ground where I am standing because of subsurface problems with water drainage. In the flatlands of Michigan the water stays put. The storm sewers have proven to be inadequate, with the result that this property, at the base of the hill on which our street was laid, always floods following thunderstorms and stays wet for weeks. The neighborhood kids love it. After rains they shriek their way to the puddles.

Above me in the clear night sky, the moon, Earth's mad companion, is belting out show tunes. A Rodgers and Hart medley, this is, including "Where or When." The moon has a good baritone voice. No: someone from down the block has an audio system on. Apparently I am still quite sleepy and disoriented. The moon, it seems, is not singing after all.

I turn away from the vacant lot and head east along its edge, taking the sidewalk that leads to the path into what is called Pioneer Woods. These woods border the houses on my street. I know the path by heart. I have taken walks on this path almost every day for the last twenty years. Our dog, Tasha, walks through here as mechanically as I do except when she sees a squirrel. In the moonlight the path that I am following has the appearance of the tunnel that Beauty walks through to get to the Beast, and though I cannot see what lies at the other end of the tunnel, I do not need to see it. I could walk it blind.

On the path now, urged leftward toward a stand of maples, I hear the sound of droplets falling through the leaves. It can't be raining. There are still stars visible intermittently overhead. No: here are the gypsy moths, still in their caterpillar form, chewing at the maple and serviceberry leaves, devouring our neighborhood forest leaf by leaf. Night gives them no rest. The woods have been infested with them, and during the day the sun shines through these trees as if spring were here, bare stunned nubs of gnawed and nibbled leaves casting almost no shade on the ground, where the altered soil chemistry, thanks to the caterpillars' leavings, has killed most of the seedlings, leaving only disagreeably enlarged thorny and deep-rooted thistles, horror-movie phantasm vegetation with deep root systems. The trees are coated, studded, with caterpillars, their bare trunks hairy and squirming. I can barely see them but can hear their every scrape and crawl.

The city has sprayed this forest with *Bacillus thuringiensis*, two words I love to say to myself, and the bacillus has killed some of these pests; their bodies lie on the path, where my seemingly adhesive shoes pick them up. I can feel them under my soles in the dark as I walk, squirming semiliquid life. Squish, squoosh. And in my night confusion it is as if I can hear the leaves being gnawed, the forest being eaten alive, shred by shred. I cannot bear it. They are not mild, these moths. Their appetites are blindingly voracious, obsessive. An acquaintance has told me that the Navahos refer to someone with an emotional illness as "moth crazy."

On the other side of the woods I come out onto the edge of a street, Stadium Boulevard, and walk down a slope toward the corner, where a stoplight is blinking red in two directions. I turn east and head toward the University of Michigan football stadium, the largest college football stadium in the country. The greater part of it was excavated below ground; only a small part of its steel and concrete structure is visible from here, the corner of Stadium and Main, just east of Pioneer High School. Cars pass occasionally on the street, their drivers hunched over, occasionally glancing at me in a fearful or predatory manner. Two teenagers out here are skateboarding in the dark, clattering over the pavement, doing their risky and amazing ankle-busting curb jumping. They grunt and holler.

Both white, they have fashioned Rasta-wear for themselves, dreads and oversized unbuttoned vests over bare skin. I check my watch. It is 1:30. I stop to make sure that no patrol cars are passing and then make my way through the turnstiles. The university has planned to build an enormous iron fence around this place, but it's not here yet. I am trespassing now and subject to arrest. After entering the tunneled walkway of Gate 19, I find myself at the south end zone, in the kingdom of football.

Inside the stadium, I feel the hushed moonlight on my back and sit down on a metal bench. The August meteor shower now seems to be part of this show. I am two thirds of the way up. These seats are too high for visibility and too coldly metallic for comfort, but the place is so massive that it makes most individual judgments irrelevant. Like any coliseum, it defeats privacy and solitude through sheer size. Carved out of the earth, sized for hordes and giants, bloody injuries and shouting, and so massive that no glance can take it all in, the stadium can be considered the staging ground for epic events, and not just football: in 1964, President Lyndon Baines Johnson announced his Great Society program here.

On every home-game Saturday in the fall, blimps and biplanes pulling advertising banners putter in semicircles overhead. Starting about three hours before kickoff, our street begins to be clogged with parked cars and RVs driven by midwesterners in various states of happy pre-inebriation, and when I rake the leaves in my back yard I hear the tidal clamor of the crowd in the distance, half a mile away. The crowd at the game is loudly traditional and antiphonal: one side of the stadium roars GO and the other side roars BLUE. The sounds rise to the sky, also blue, but nonpartisan.

The moonlight reflects off the rows of stands. I look down at the field, now, at 1:45 in the morning. A midsummer night's dream is being enacted down there.

This old moon wanes! She lingers my desires and those of a solitary naked couple, barely visible down there right now on the fifty-yard line, making love, on this midsummer night.

They are making soft distant audibles. . . .

So they load him into the nearest car, which happens to be David's, and David and Diana and Chloé prepare to take Oscar—*Oscar's body*—to the University Hospital, where Margaret has just, as it happens, finished work and is headed in the opposite direction, back to me.

But they have all forgotten about the football traffic after the game. Every street in Ann Arbor is snarled with cars. This is a small city, and it takes a long time to empty of traffic. The stadium holds over one hundred thousand human souls. When David honks and waves his arms frantically, the drivers ahead of him and to the side honk happily in return and wave their arms and make the V-for-victory sign, or, using the same gestures that David has used, hold their fists in the air, unless they're Ohio State fans, in which case they sit and glance around sullenly, hands clutching the wheel. No matter how much he honks, no one moves aside, no one lets him proceed with the body of Oscar to the hospital. There is no space to move. In both directions the traffic has halted, like blood in a blocked artery. He cannot shout. What good would shouting do, in this crowd of happy shouters? They're all shouting. He's one of many. He can't get out of the car because that would accomplish nothing: the cars in front of him are stuck as well. His sedan with its occupants moves by slow increments toward the hospital.

What's worse is that the cars to the right and left of him have stopped in the same traffic jam he's in, and their happy inebriated passengers witness Chloé bending over on the seat and breathing into Oscar's mouth. They misunderstand what they are observing. They think it's passion. They think it's the feast of love in the back seat. Apparently they don't see her clamping his nostrils shut, as she breathes her breath into his lungs, because they give her smirks and grins and smiles, honking in great amorous collaboration at what they take to be Chloé's celebrational mouth-to-mouth. Go for it, girl! Go Blue! And they don't stop giving her the high sign until she turns her face away from Oscar's. Then she fixes her eyes on them, and she screams, but the scream is swallowed up in the tumult. She then brings her mouth back to his, to keep him alive.

It all takes a long time.

And still he isn't alive when they arrive at the hospital, and nothing that is done to him there can bring him back. He has had (we learn these helpful terms later) hypertrophic cardiomyopathy, the medical slang for which is "hocum." Goddamn these doctors anyway, with their jargon, their jauntiness, damn them all except for Margaret, who is my beloved exception. Ventricular fibrillation dropped him down. Eventually he was declared dead, Oscar was. An autopsy showed an abnormally enlarged murmured heart, from the track and the basketball and the genetic code, though I refuse to give up the metaphor and think it enlarged itself from his love of Chloé. Margaret explained all this to me in her calm, horizon-greeting African Zen style, using terms like *commotio cordis*. Against the terrors and sorrows of death, only the multisyllabic Latinate adjectives and nouns for protection, the know-how, and then the prayers, for those who have them.

There I was, caged. I sat in the front seat next to David, with Chloé bending over Oscar in the back, trying to breathe her life into him. All around us people, these fans, these monkeys, hollered. They whooped. They celebrated. On their faces were all the manifestations of *glee*. Being of a difficult and combative nature, I wanted to kill them early in their lives.

I sat in the car, containing myself but wild with sanctioned fury, and then I thought of whom I would sue.

Oscar and Chloé, these two kids, who had served me coffee day after day out at the mall—I had taken a liking to them. I enjoyed the spectacle of how they felt about each other. I thought it was rather inspiring, actually, those two orphans, with nothing, really, to their names. They weren't middle class in any of the tiresome customary ways, and they didn't have two nickels to rub together. You could tell from the fatigue lines under their eyes that they'd been around a few blocks. Sometimes, seeing them working together at Jitters, I thought: David should marry me. We could have that. Except, possessing money, we would have it easier, we would do it with a little more style and a little less emotion.

And now, in the backseat, Oscar looked, to all appearances, no longer living, no longer even dying. His dying had been successfully accomplished. Watching Chloé trying to keep him alive, putting her lips to his, I started to cry. I *never* do that.

I'm a lawyer. I reached for the car phone. I called the emergency number. I explained the situation. The dispatcher told me that no ambulance would be able to move faster in this traffic than we were able to do. No helicopter would be able to land where we were located, the congestion being what it was. Such a maneuver, I was informed, would be unsafe. It would be faster if we just continued to drive.

So we stayed in the car.

I'm a lawyer. I think about responsibility. And in my ire, I thought: I'll sue the university, for staging the game; I'll sue the city of Ann Arbor, for having clearly inadequate plans for controlling and siphoning off the traffic. Within Ann Arbor, I'll sue the police department and individuals within that department, standing at intersections and misdirecting the cars, buses, trucks, and vans; and then I will organize a suit against the city manager, for permitting the congested and overfilled parking lots to block proper egress from the city; and the zoning board, for the proximity of the buildings. I'll sue the architects, for the design of those buildings. I'll institute proceedings against the automobile manufacturers, for the size and shape of these vehicles. I'll sue the athletic department, no, I've already done that; I'll sue the advertisers who have supported these games; and I'll sue the Wolverine Fan Club; I'll sue each and every one of the businesses lining this street, for being located there and for blocking our way. I'll sue the driver of the car in front of us and I'll sue his drunken girlfriend—I already have their license plate number committed to memory—and the two passengers in the back, waving at us while David gives them the finger and then leans on the horn, they'll all be penniless by the time I'm finished with them and sorry that they were ever within living proximity to me. In my wrath I'll sue the drivers and passengers in front of *them*. I'll sue the manufacturer of the football that Oscar caught, that proximate cause, I'll drag the officers of that company into court and pull their names through the mud, so that even their children will refuse ever to speak to them. I'll sue the makers of the clothes Oscar wore, including his shoes (he may have slipped! he may have lost traction! he may have fallen because of the shoes!); I'll find out what he ate while he watched the game, and I'll sue the brewers of the dangerous beer he drank and the makers of the arteriosclerotic snack food he consumed; I'll sue the tattoo artist who tattooed the skull and crossbones onto Oscar's back (Chloé told me about it) with the word "Die" underneath it, goddamn it, I'll sue them for *prophecy*; I'll sue Oscar's father, the Bat, for not taking care of him, for not preventing this eventuality, and for generally endangering Oscar and Chloé's welfare; I'll sue the doctors, I will take their fat-cat medical school asses to court and nail those asses to the wall, for *whatever* they give him, for *whatever* they do, in their wisdom and knowledge, oh, let them try anything, fuck them all, for I shall see to it that their efforts could be construed as unprofessional, mistaken, foolish, and wrong. I'll sue the doctors and the drug manufacturers for not bringing him back to life; I'll sue Jesus, who is acquainted with Chloé and who once met her at a party, for not being here, when we needed Him; and I'll sue God, who passes out misfortune with equanimity.

Such were my thoughts as we motored, inch by inch, toward the university hospitals.

Oscar had been a young man, physically beautiful, and in wonderful condition except for his now-defunct heart. After they were done with

the electrical defibrillation, the intubation, the epinephrine, the lido-
caine and the procainamide, and the chest compressions, they harvested
him. They sold him off for parts, down to the skin and bones. He helped
save the lives of others, et cetera, et cetera.

From *The Feast of Love* (New York: Pantheon Books, 2000).

Pete Waldmeir

❦

Michigan's Great Victory Makes Football
Worthwhile, 1969

ANN ARBOR–Don Canham stood at the entrance to the tunnel which leads from the Michigan Stadium floor to the dressing rooms, one eye on the clock and the other on the field, where the Wolverines were up-setting No. 1–ranked Ohio State 24–12.

"Fifty-six seconds," Canham grinned. "Fifty-six seconds left in the greatest college football game of all time.

"This, gentlemen, is what it's all about. Not the money. Not the sea-son ticket sales. This excitement.

"The greatest college football crowd in history watching the greatest college game in 100 years."

With that, Canham turned on his heel and darted up the tunnel, striding confident in the fact that Michigan had pulled the upset of the season—if not the decade—in beating Ohio State before 103,588, as Canham said, the largest college football crowd in history.

Not the Rose Bowl or any other major stadium can match that atten-dance record. Few games, for that matter, ever have matched the excite-ment generated by the upset.

Calling this upset "the greatest game in the history of college foot-ball" may be a little thick to swallow, but it has to rank with the finest Michigan victories of all time—with Fritz Crisler's 55–0 clobbering of Michigan State in 1947 and at least on a par with the 1950 "Snow Bowl" at Columbus, where Crisler's team upset the Buckeyes 9–3 in a blizzard and went on to the Rose Bowl.

This time the bowl date was all wrapped up. But there was more than a holiday trip at stake for the Wolverines.

It was a matter of pride.

"Sure, we knew we had the Rose Bowl trip wrapped up," chortled Michigan Coach Bo Schembechler, "but we didn't want to go out there as the second-best team in our conference.

"We wanted to win—to beat the No. 1 team in the nation, to beat

Ohio State—and go out there as just what we are, co-champions of the Big Ten.

"How did we do it? I'll tell you how. We did it because we knew that it wasn't going to be a slaughter. We knew that we could contain certain phases of their game and make certain phases of ours work.

"We knew we couldn't make the mistakes that other teams made. We couldn't let them get the drop on us. We had to stay close and hope for some kind of a break."

Schembechler has set a bit of a record of his own. Once a player and later an assistant under Woody Hayes, the 39-year-old Schembechler is the first Michigan coach since Fielding H. Yost did it in 1901 to take his football team to the Rose Bowl. And now, instead of going out as No. 2, he's making it as a co-champion with his old boss.

Schembechler attributed the upset to heady play.

Defensive coach Frank Maloney, a former Michigan player, gave still another explanation.

"Look at Ohio State's offensive," Maloney pointed out. "They got one touchdown from that great offensive team. They got the other because of a great punt return.

"We said 100 yards—give their fullback, Jim Otis, 100 yards and be happy. Our plan was to cut off the running by the Ohio quarterback, Rex Kern."

The plan didn't work to perfection, but it was good enough. Otis picked up 144 yards rushing and one short touchdown. But Kern, who runs better than he passes (in the tradition of the OSU quarterbacks, except Joe Sparma), made only 53 yards on the ground.

Maloney pointed to the other factor which aided the Michigan cause.

"Bo told these kids," he said, "that if we could get in front of Ohio State and come to the dressing room leading at the half, we could beat them. Teams that rely on the punishing fullback like Otis and on the running game in general don't play catch-up football very well.

"Kern is just an ordinary passer, you know."

Vindication fairly dripped from the Michigan team Saturday. Last year's whipping by the Buckeyes was well-remembered.

You'll recall that in that one, Woody Hayes went for a two-point conversion in the game's last minute to bury Michigan 50–14, at Columbus.

Well, this afternoon when Woody was behind throughout the second half and scrambling to extend a 22-game winning streak and retain a hope for establishing the Big Ten record for triumphs, the chilled Michigan crowd got its kicks.

"Goodbye, Woody; Goodbye, Woody," they sang, as much for the regional television cameras as for their own pleasure.

While they sang, Woody marched sleeveless up and down the sidelines. Last week as Ohio State whipped Purdue to clinch its share of Michigan's Big Ten football championship, Woody pulled a Red Auerbach. When he got far enough ahead, he broke a long-standing tradition and pulled on a quilted jacket for the first time in modern history.

If Woody had the jacket with him Saturday afternoon, he might have been tempted to pull it over his head. . . .

Woody's greed was evidenced early in the game when, with fourth down at the Michigan two-yard line the first time Ohio State had the ball on offense, he shunned a sure field goal and went for a touchdown—and missed.

That could be forgiven. After all, even champions gamble and lose sometimes. So the next time Ohio got the ball it scored. But the third time—the third time is when all turned around.

Michigan had accomplished the impossible. Michigan had scored on a 56-yard drive with sound football and went ahead, 7–6. Then Woody went ahead 12–7, and his placekicker made the point for a 13–7 advantage.

But wait. . . Michigan was detected offside.

There was a quick huddle on the Ohio State sidelines and Woody decreed that Ohio take the penalty, nullify the sure one-point conversion and go for two points.

Kern disdained the run from 1½ yards out and elected to pass. He was buried by Pryor and Keller and that was the end of the Buckeyes' scoring.

Last Saturday, after Michigan had pulverized Iowa, Moorhead had outlined Michigan's strategy for Ohio.

"It's just another game," said Moorhead. "Just an ordinary game. We'll take it to them, run what we run best, don't panic, and win." And that, ladies and gentlemen, is exactly what happened.

Last night, Moorhead hurried to shower and dress, then joined his father at his fraternity house for dinner and a little television watching.

"Suppose you might call it scouting," Moorhead explained.

The TV fare: USC and UCLA in the other game to decide who spends New Year's Day in Pasadena.

Detroit News, November 23, 1969.

Bob Ufer

Burying Woody Hayes

Editor's note: I have been warned on numerous occasions that every Michigan football fan will expect to see the following poem, by superfan Bob Ufer, in this anthology. So here it is.

It was November 22, 1969 that Ohio State came to bury
   Michigan all dressed in maize and blue.
The words were said, the prayers were read, and everybody cried.
But when they closed the coffin there was someone else inside.
Oh, they came to bury Michigan, but Michigan wasn't dead.
And when the game was over it was someone else instead.
22 Michigan Wolverines put on the gloves of grey
And as "Revelli" played The Victors
They laid Woody Hayes away.

Donald Hall

♌

Kicking the Leaves

1

Kicking the leaves, October, as we walk home together
from the game, in Ann Arbor,
on a day the color of soot, rain in the air;
I kick at the leaves of maples,
reds of seventy different shades, yellow
like old paper; and poplar leaves, fragile and pale;
and elm leaves, flags of a doomed race.
I kick at the leaves, making a sound I remember
as the leaves swirl upward from my boot,
and flutter; and I remember
Octobers walking to school in Connecticut,
wearing corduroy knickers that swished
with a sound like leaves; and a Sunday buying
a cup of cider at a roadside stand
on a dirt road in New Hampshire; and kicking the leaves,
autumn 1955 in Massachusetts, knowing
my father would die when the leaves were gone.

2

Each fall in New Hampshire, on the farm
where my mother grew up, a girl in the country,
my grandfather and grandmother
finished the autumn work, taking the last vegetables in
from the cold fields, canning, storing roots and apples
in the cellar under the kitchen. Then my grandfather
raked leaves against the house
as the final chore of autumn.
One November I drove up from college to see them.
We pulled big rakes, as we did when we hayed in summer,
pulling the leaves against the granite foundations

185

around the house, on every side of the house,
and then, to keep them in place, we cut spruce boughs
and laid them across the leaves,
green on red, until the house
was tucked up, ready for snow
that would freeze the leaves in tight, like a stiff skirt.
Then we puffed through the shed door,
taking off boots and overcoats, slapping our hands,
and sat in the kitchen, rocking, and drank
black coffee my grandmother made,
three of us sitting together, silent, in gray November.

3

One Saturday when I was little, before the war,
my father came home at noon from his half day at the office
and wore his Bates sweater, black on red,
with the crossed hockey sticks on it, and raked beside me
in the back yard, and tumbled in the leaves with me,
laughing, and carried me, laughing, my hair full of leaves,
to the kitchen window
where my mother could see us, and smile, and motion
to set me down, afraid I would fall and be hurt.

4

Kicking the leaves today, as we walk home together
from the game, among crowds of people
with their bright pennants, as many and bright as leaves,
my daughter's hair is the red-yellow color
of birch leaves, and she is tall like a birch,
growing up, fifteen, growing older; and my son
flamboyant as maple, twenty,
visits from college, and walks ahead of us, his step
springing, impatient to travel
the woods of the earth. Now I watch them
from a pile of leaves beside this clapboard house
in Ann Arbor, across from the school
where they learned to read,
as their shapes grow small with distance, waving,
and I know that I
diminish, not them, as I go first

into the leaves, taking
the way they will follow, Octobers and years from now.

5

This year the poems came back, when the leaves fell.
Kicking the leaves, I heard the leaves tell stories,
remembering, and therefore looking ahead, and building
the house of dying. I looked up into the maples
and found them, the vowels of bright desire.
I thought they had gone forever
while the bird sang *I love you, I love you*
and shook its black head
from side to side, and its red eye with no lid,
through years of winter, cold
as the taste of chickenwire, the music of cinderblock.

6

Kicking the leaves, I uncover the lids of graves.
My grandfather died at seventy-seven, in March
when the sap was running; and I remember my father
twenty years ago,
coughing himself to death at fifty-two in the house
in the suburbs. Oh, how we flung
leaves in the air! How they tumbled and fluttered around us,
like slowly cascading water, when we walked together
in Hamden, before the war, when Johnson's Pond
had not surrendered to houses, the two of us
hand in hand, and in the wet air the smell of leaves
burning;
and in six years I will be fifty-two.

7

Now I fall, now I leap and fall
to feel the leaves crush under my body, to feel my body
buoyant in the ocean of leaves, the night of them,
night heaving with death and leaves, rocking like the ocean.
Oh, this delicious falling into the arms of leaves,
into the soft laps of leaves!
Face down, I swim into the leaves, feathery,
breathing the acrid odor of maple, swooping

in long glides to the bottom of October—
where the farm lies curled against winter, and soup steams
its breath of onion and carrot
onto damp curtains and windows; and past the windows
I see the tall bare maple trunks and branches, the oak
with its few brown weathery remnant leaves,
and the spruce trees, holding their green.
Now I leap and fall, exultant, recovering
from death, on account of death, in accord with the dead,
the smell and taste of leaves again,
and the pleasure, the only long pleasure, of taking a place
in the story of leaves.

From *Old and New Poems* (1978; New York: Ticknor and Fields, 1990).

Richard Goodman

⚑

Homage to Cazzie Russell

This is not a story about watching a great basketball player. This is a story about beauty.

In 1963, when I was a freshman at the University of Michigan, the school hadn't had a good basketball team in years. And *never* a great one. Not that anyone even knew that. The last time Michigan had won a Big Ten title in basketball had been in 1948. When you said "basketball" in conjunction with "Michigan," in 1963, you said it with derision, as you would when speaking about a third world airline. The mockery was particularly caustic since the football teams were always so mighty. The Michigan basketball team consistently finished near the bottom of the Big Ten, if not precisely at the bottom. No one went to the games.

The present basketball stadium, the one you see on television if you follow college basketball and watch Michigan play, didn't exist in 1963. Instead, we had a ratty, ill-lit gymnasium with the kind of pullout bleacher seats you find in a high school. It didn't matter much, since they were usually empty. One of the coaches at the time put it this way, "The basketball spirit in this school is so low, you can go to a game and get a seat five minutes before game time." If you tried that at a football game—not that you could, since seats were assigned—you'd be run out of the stadium on a rail. When he was asked about how to increase attendance, the coach said, "We've even thought of asking the pigeons."

I don't remember why I went to that first basketball game. Probably because someone told me that the team was actually *good* that year. The *basketball* team? I asked. The main reason they were good, this friend went on to say, was a guy from Chicago, a guy from a school called Carver High, a guy named Cazzie Russell. Cazzie? What a funny name. Short for . . . what? Out of curiosity, I went. I remember I sat in the first or second row. I wasn't expecting much, but it was better than studying. I could always leave.

Onto the floor he walked. Cazzie Russell. He was tall—six feet five and one half inches tall. He was broad-shouldered, lanky and muscular.

His hands were large, anyone could see that right away. His aspect had a sweetness to it—he had a wonderful smile, but he wasn't a huge smiler on the court. He had sculpted, Mayan features, classical, and his skin was the color of peat. He discarded his warm-up suit, took a basketball, and was all business. And passion. He wore number 33. I watched him shoot his practice shots from distances I felt were unreasonable, perhaps illegal. All that's changed now, but back then . . . back then. Sometimes we're lucky enough to see something marvelous before its time.

He played guard. It's quite common now, even in college basketball, to have a guard that tall. But not then. He was magnificently tall at that position. I couldn't ever look at him without thinking that. Michigan's other guard, Bob Cantrell, *was* small, 5'8". He looked fairly ridiculous next to Cazzie. I remember two more names: Oliver Darden, who played forward, was 6'7". And Bill Buntin, a lumbering, often overweight, often-brilliant center, who was around 6'10". I don't have a mental picture of the other forward who played thirty-five years ago. Gone.

As soon as Cazzie took the ball, I knew in that way we know all things that will change our lives, I was seeing something wonderful. Just the way he held the ball when he dribbled was a revelation. He cradled the ball as if it were something precious. He exquisitely enveloped the ball with his palm; it seemed as if the ball, for a millisecond, refused to leave; it looked, at the apex of the bounce, as if it wanted to remain in Cazzie's palm, his embrace was so tender. With each dribble—what a lackluster word for what Cazzie did—you felt *envious* of the basketball, because it was being caressed and urged with such affection.

Cazzie didn't move like Michael Jordan. He didn't start and stop with such shocking suddenness as Michael. He was fluid. It was as if you could follow his game with a continuous, winding line, like Picasso drawing in air, with no interruptions. He was liquid. Even within the chaos of nine other big bodies, he was uninterrupted grace. Cazzie shot the ball, of course. That was what we all waited for—the slow giant leap into the air; the ball cradled by those two magnificent hands; the barely discernible release. And, at the apex of his jump, the ball again seemed to hesitate, unwilling to forsake the warmth, the understanding of Cazzie's hands. But leave those hands it did. It sailed toward the net, in an arc as doubtless and instinctual as a hawk's soar, and we all knew, halfway there, that there would be the gentlest, barest shiver of net as the ball whistled through, and nothing more.

He was beautiful. What he *did* was beautiful. Not simply accomplished or skillful or graceful. *Beautiful.* I had never seen anyone play basketball like that. I had never seen anyone do *anything* like that. That a young black man from Chicago, from the inner city, could do these things was new to me. So you can see how sheltered I was. Back then, well, the white world and the black world just didn't mix that often. Not to mention—yes, to mention!—I had gone to an exclusive (ha!) boarding school for five years. We had a few black students, but their parents were wealthy, and we had no sense of what was really out there. I was ignorant of so many things. In that ill-lit place, I saw firsthand that I didn't have to open a book to find beauty. I saw that I didn't really understand the scope of beauty. It was *there,* on the basketball court.

You may know who he is, Cazzie Russell. You may know he played thirteen years in the NBA, including some wonderful years as a sixth man with the New York Knicks when they were champions. You may even know that he's a basketball coach now, at Savannah College of Art and Design. If you do, can you forget all that for an instant? Can you put yourself inside a freshman's head (remember, you'll get your identity back) who knew very little about basketball and who had never heard of Cazzie Russell and who, as Rod Serling might have said, "would, on what seemed a rather ordinary Saturday afternoon in early December in the quaint college town of Ann Arbor, Michigan, find himself in a world he never dreamed existed."

Oh, all of us shouted and screamed! The place, once more of a monastery than a stadium, rocked and rolled with communal exuberance. I came back. Again and again. I came back to confirm what I had seen. I came back to see a god. I was inebriated, smiling, short breathed. *This was living!* Nobody had told me. Certainly nobody at my uptight, white, ersatz-British boarding school. No, they hadn't told me that gorgeousness was waiting out there for me. They hadn't told me that a man on a basketball court would uplift my heart and soul! They hadn't told me this was what college would be like!

Yes, I came back. I came back like the spiritual alcoholic I was, dying for more, dying to see Cazzie Russell play again—and score. God, he scored! Twenty-five, thirty, forty points a game! He may have been incredibly graceful, but he was also highly intense. He always wanted the ball, had to have it. He would implore with his hands and face when he didn't have it. But most of all, he wanted his team to win. You saw it, you felt the crisis of his urgency. In later games, I saw him near to tears when his team couldn't rise to the occasion. He exhorted, and he demanded. His teammates tried to respond, and, more often than not, they did. When they couldn't, Cazzie's face became a twisted agony, like a child's who has been told he has to stay at home the day of the circus. No one received sterner criticism than he did from himself, though. When Cazzie made a mistake, he rebuked himself publicly and severely. It was hard to watch.

Michigan didn't win the National Championship any of the years Cazzie played. His second playing year, I think, Michigan went to the finals. I was somewhere where I couldn't watch it on television. I think on the road. But I could picture Cazzie, his huge heart nearly breaking, exhorting, trying, working his miracles—then in tears, the game ending, seeing that Michigan would lose. No, they didn't win the NCAA Championship, but they did win the Big Ten title, something they hadn't done in fifteen years. And they beat some wonderful teams. What a ride we all had! A ride on the broad big shoulders of Cazzie Russell. What a soft, flawless shooter! To this day—even after the mighty Chris Webber—he still holds the career scoring average at Michigan, 27.1 points.

The other players? Oliver Darden was a laconic forward who always did his job, rebounded well, and on occasions was brilliant as a comet. Bill Buntin, the center, was a star in his own right. Without Buntin—Cazzie or no Cazzie—Michigan would never have done so well. He was big, strong and fearless. His aspect was so dreadful at times that, like the Mikado, you were afraid to look at him directly. We loved Buntin, too, and he did wonderful things. There were times when he didn't play his best, and our hearts sank when that happened, because we knew so well how amazing he could be and how important his full measure was to the team.

Yes, the team was wonderful, but I came again and again to see Cazzie Russell. I went every chance I got. To see grace, personified. Not just basketball grace—Renaissance grace, Homer grace, bird-soaring grace. I may have been a clunky college student, but I was bright enough to realize I was in the presence of perfection. Maybe I couldn't express it—I didn't have the emotional vocabulary or the confidence yet—but inside me I knew. Deep within me I knew Cazzie was truth and beauty. Years later, I was watching a Woody Allen film, and it all came back to me. In the film, (I forget which one), Allen is married to a pretentious woman who works in academia. They go to a party given by her friends, and Allen disappears. His wife finds him in a room watching the New York Knicks play on TV. He's rapt with the game. Could Cazzie have been playing that day? Possibly.

"Why do you watch that?" his wife asks derisively. "It's just a basketball game." Allen snorts in his inimitable Woody way. "Why? Why? Because it's perfection," he tells her, without even looking her way.

The schools don't teach you that.

Or maybe they do.

from *Ascent* (Winter 2003).

Dudley Randall

♎

Winter Campus, Ann Arbor

April took flesh in clear September air
when one girl paused upon the colonnade,
turned, and for a heartbeat hovered there
while yellow elm leaves drifted past her hair.

Here, now, the same soft youngness is conveyed
as these bareheaded throngs stream to and fro
with footfalls noiseless in the sudden snow,
a hum like bees pulsating on and on
while treble voices tremble in the air
and rime with chiming of the carillon.

From *Michigan: A State Anthology*, edited by David D. Anderson
(Detroit: Gale Research Company, 1983).

☧

from The Port Huron Statement of the Students for a Democratic Society, 1962

The Students

In the last few years, thousands of American students demonstrated that they at least felt the urgency of the times. They moved actively and directly against racial injustices, the threat of war, violations of individual rights of conscience and, less frequently, against economic manipulation. They succeeded in restoring a small measure of controversy to the campuses after the stillness of the McCarthy period. They succeeded, too, in gaining some concessions from the people and institutions they opposed, especially in the fight against racial bigotry.

The significance of these scattered movements lies not in their success or failure in gaining objectives—at least not yet. Nor does the significance lie in the intellectual "competence" or "maturity" of the students involved—as some pedantic elders allege. The significance is in the fact the students are breaking the crust of apathy and overcoming the inner alienation that remain the defining characteristics of American college life.

If student movements for change are rarities still on the campus scene, what is commonplace there? The real campus, the familiar campus, is a place of private people, engaged in their notorious "inner emigration." It is a place of commitment to business-as-usual, getting ahead, playing it cool. It is a place of mass affirmation of the Twist, but mass reluctance toward the controversial public stance. Rules are accepted as "inevitable," bureaucracy as "just circumstances," irrelevance as "scholarship," selflessness as "martyrdom," politics as "just another way to make people, and an unprofitable one, too."

Almost no students value activity as a citizen. Passive in public, they are hardly more idealistic in arranging their private lives: Gallup concludes they will settle for "low success, and won't risk high failure." There is not much willingness to take risks (not even in business), no setting of dangerous goals, no real conception of personal identity except one manufactured in the image of others, no real urge for personal fulfillment except to be almost as successful as the very successful people. Attention is being paid to social status (the quality of shirt collars, meeting people, getting wives or husbands, making solid contacts for later on); much too is paid to academic status (grades, honors, the med school rat-race). But neglected generally is real intellectual status, the personal cultivation of the mind.

"Students don't even give a damn about the apathy," one has said. Apathy toward apathy begets a privately constructed universe, a place of systematic study schedules, two nights each week for beer, a girl or two, and early marriage; a framework infused with personality, warmth, and under control, no matter how unsatisfying otherwise.

Under these conditions university life loses all relevance to some. Four hundred thousand of our classmates leave college every year.

But apathy is not simply an attitude; it is a product of social institutions, and of the structure and organization of higher education itself. The extracurricular life is ordered according to in loco parentis theory, which ratifies the Administration as the moral guardian of the young. The accompanying "let's pretend" theory of student extracurricular affairs validates student government as a training center for those who want to spend their lives in political pretense, and discourages initiative from more articulate, honest, and sensitive students. The bounds and style of controversy are delimited before controversy begins. The university "prepares" the student for "citizenship" through perpetual rehearsals and, usually, through emasculation of what creative spirit there is in the individual.

The academic life contains reinforcing counterparts to the way in which extracurricular life is organized. The academic world is founded in a teacher-student relation analogous to the parent-child relation which characterizes in loco parentis. Further, academia includes a radical separation of student from the material of study. That which is studied, the social reality, is "objectified" to sterility, dividing the student from life—just as he is restrained in active involvement by the deans controlling student government. The specialization of function and knowledge, admittedly necessary to our complex technological and social structure, has produced an exaggerated compartmentalization of study and understanding. This has contributed to: an overly parochial view, by faculty, of the role of its research and scholarship; a discontinuous and truncated understanding, by students, of the surrounding social order; a loss of personal attachment, by nearly all, to the worth of study as a humanistic enterprise.

There is, finally, the cumbersome academic bureaucracy extending throughout the academic as well as extracurricular structures, contributing to the sense of outer complexity and inner powerlessness that transforms so many students from honest searching to ratification of convention and, worse, to a numbness to present and future catastrophes. The size and financing systems of the university enhance the permanent trusteeship of the administrative bureaucracy, their power leading to a shift to the value standards of business and administrative mentality within the university. Huge foundations and other private financial interests shape under-financed colleges and universities, not only making them more commercial, but less disposed to diagnose society critically, less open to dissent. Many social and physical scientists, neglecting the liberating heritage of higher learning, develop "human relations" or "morale-producing" techniques for the corporate economy, while others exercise their intellectual skills to accelerate the arms race.

Tragically, the university could serve as a significant source of social criticism and an initiator of new modes and molders of attitudes. But the actual intellectual effect of the college experience is hardly distinguishable from that of any other communications channel—say, a television set—passing on the stock truths of the day. Students leave college somewhat more "tolerant" than when they arrived, but basically unchallenged in their values and political orientations. With administrators ordering the institutions, and faculty the curriculum, the student learns by his isolation to accept elite rule within the university, which prepares him to accept later forms of minority control. The real function of the educational system—as opposed to its more rhetorical function of "searching for truth"—is to impart the key information and styles that will help the student get by, modestly but comfortably, in the big society beyond.

The Society Beyond

Look beyond the campus, to America itself. That student life is more intellectual, and perhaps more comfortable, does not obscure the fact that the fundamental qualities of life on the campus reflect the habits of society at large. The fraternity president is seen at the junior manager levels; the sorority queen has gone to Grosse Pointe: the serious poet burns for a place, any place, or work; the once-serious and never serious poets work at the advertising agencies. The desperation of people threatened by forces about which they know little and of which they can say less; the cheerful emptiness of people "giving up" all hope of changing things; the faceless ones polled by Gallup who listed "international affairs" fourteenth on their list of "problems" but who also expected thermonuclear war in the next few years: in these and other forms, Americans are in withdrawal from public life, from any collective effort at directing their own affairs.

Some regard this national doldrums as a sign of healthy approval of the established order—but is it approval by consent or manipulated acquiescence? Others declare that the people are withdrawn because compelling issues are fast disappearing—perhaps there are fewer breadlines in America, but is Jim Crow gone, is there enough work and work more fulfilling, is world war a diminishing threat, and what of the revolutionary new peoples? Still others think the national quietude is a necessary consequence of the need for elites to resolve complex and specialized problems of modern industrial society—but, then, why should business elites help decide foreign policy, and who controls the elites anyway, and are they solving mankind's problems? Others, finally, shrug knowingly and announce that full democracy never worked anywhere in the past—but why lump qualitatively different civilizations together, and how can a social order work well if its best thinkers are skeptics, and is man really doomed forever to the domination of today?

There are no convincing apologies for the contemporary malaise. While the world tumbles toward the final war, while men in other nations are trying desperately to alter events, while the very future qua future is uncertain—America is without community, impulse, without the inner momentum necessary for an age when societies cannot successfully perpetuate themselves by their military weapons, when democracy must be viable because of its quality of life, not its quantity of rockets.

The apathy here is, first subjective—the felt powerlessness of ordinary people, the resignation before the enormity of events. But subjective apathy is encouraged by the objective American situation—the actual structural separation of people from power, from relevant knowledge, from pinnacles of decision-making. Just as the university influences the student way of life, so do major social institutions create the circumstances in which the isolated citizen will try hopelessly to understand his world and himself.

The very isolation of the individual—from power and community and ability to aspire—means the rise of a democracy without publics. With the great mass of people structurally remote and psychologically hesitant with respect to democratic institutions, those institutions themselves attenuate and become, in the fashion of the vicious circle, progressively less accessible to those few who aspire to serious participation in social affairs. The vital democratic connection between community and leadership, between the mass and the several elites, has been so wrenched and perverted that disastrous policies go unchallenged time and again.

From *Port Huron Statement of the Students for a Democratic Society*, 1962.
<http://coursesa.matrix.msu.edu/ hst306/documents/huron.html>

Sven Birkerts

⚓

from My Sky Blue Trades: Growing Up Counter
in a Contrary Time

Still riding the momentum of transition, I hiked up the street to Borders, which had moved during the time of my absence from its old location into a massive new space almost directly across the street. I found Tom Borders in the little warren of upstairs offices. He remembered, of course, that I had left town to make my way as a writer, but he did not prod me to find out why I was back. Instead, he gazed out into the middle distance, as if to consult the family plan for world domination, and then, settling on something, looked over and offered me a job. It was that simple. I would start in a few days' time. I would be presiding over the remainders area in what was called the "mezzanine.". . .

But the real shift came early one January afternoon when Tom Borders signaled me to his office as I was coming in from lunch. Louis was already there, watching me with an expression that gave nothing away.

We all got on well. I'd worked for the brothers in their first store. We'd gone out for beers once or twice after unpacking big shipments or doing inventory. We joked easily with each other. But there was no small talk on this occasion. Tom came right out with it: Did I want a better job? They still had the lease on the old store across the street. They'd hired two book dealers to manage the other store—the Charing Cross Book Shop—selling used and rare books. But things had not been working out. Tom slowly rubbed his jaw, as he did whenever things got serious. He and Louis wanted to give the business one more chance—they had started with used books and wanted to keep the connection. One new person had already been hired. Would I consider being his partner?

"Co-manager," said Louis. He was smiling now, reading my reaction. "It would be more money."

"But"—Tom was coming in right behind him—"you'd be working your ass off."

Tom and Louis walked me across the street that evening. They unlocked the door of the old shop but left off the overhead lights. There was a light on in back. I heard the creak of a nail being pried from a board. Moving forward, I saw a stocky man in a T-shirt. He was holding a crowbar and addressing himself to a wall of empty shelves. There were books piled everywhere.

"Gene—"

The man waited, gave one last yank on the bar, then turned. Beard. Red face. Glasses.

"Gene, this is your new partner."

And that was it. Tom and Louis stayed just long enough to set up a meeting for the next day and then left. Gene regarded me for a moment with ill-concealed skepticism and then turned back to his demolition. I moved around slowly behind his back, inspecting the piles of books, eyeballing the sections, taking in the dimensions of the place with a freshly proprietary eye. I knew every dent and crevice from having worked here before, but now it all looked unfamiliar.

"So you like books—" Gene talked without turning around. I caught the irony in his tone and tried to respond in kind.

"I do."

"Here, hold this, would you?" I caught the end of a teetering board. "What's your specialty?"

I hesitated. "Fiction, I guess. Modern stuff."

At this Gene laughed. "Modern fiction—" He looked briefly in my direction. "You know, they don't even offer courses on that in English universities. That's something you're supposed to get up on your own."

I snickered, as if this were self-evidently preposterous.

Gene inspected the structure of the next area of shelving, then—abruptly—turned. "What else?"

I was caught off guard. "What else what?"

"What else do you know?" Now I heard an edge in his tone. I surveyed my attainments and came up with nothing. Finally, looking at Gene, then past him, I shrugged.

"How about you?"

Gene didn't miss a beat here. "I'm ABD in Renaissance lit," he said. "I'm just taking a break."

"Oh." I didn't know what ABD meant and was suddenly afraid to ask.

We stayed there a while longer, Gene tearing out sections of shelving, stacking boards neatly against the wall, while I perched on a stack of green geological survey volumes and smoked. In the short time I sat there, I got the first inklings of his erudition. Gene loved the Latin poets—Propertius, especially—and tried to read them in Latin. He was a student of radical thought, from Marx to Raymond Williams; adored jazz, Indian raga, Italian opera, the chamber music of Haydn. Anything, of course, having to do with the Renaissance: the works of Frances Yates, E. R. Curtius, R. R. Bolgar; Dante, but not just *Inferno* . . . I stopped listening, felt the suck of imploding ignorance, and wondered if I could still back out without losing face completely.

But I didn't. I went to the meeting the next day and paid very close attention as Tom and Louis explained the operation from start to finish. They were, they said, willing to inject a certain amount of fresh capital. Our first task, aside from making the sorts of cosmetic alterations that Gene had already begun, was to build stock. We were to advertise for books, buy libraries, go to estate sales and book fairs. They believed that Ann Arbor could support a high-quality used- and rare-book shop. There was, both brothers kept affirming, work to be done.

I loved books, and though I was not a scholar, I had imagined myself to be fairly well read. Needless to say, my self-image, already somewhat shaky, suffered a serious decline when I began to spend time with Gene. Which I started to do that very day. Indeed, for the next six months or so, I saw more of Gene than any other person, including Marcie. We were on a mission, chained together. We were going to make this store work. Gene took the lead, set the agenda, and I followed. Something about his certainty, his energetic clarity, compelled me. He had a vision of Charing Cross as a circulation center, a hub, a daily "must go" for all members of the town's sizable intellectual community. Interesting, affordable books, good taste, an environment that would make people want to come in and, once in, to linger. As a man in need of a vision, I was easily sold.

I campaigned hard for Gene's approval. After I had recovered from the shock of the first meeting, my crisis of intellectual inferiority, I decided that I wanted to learn things, to know. I would take in everything I could from Gene. Once he sensed this, Gene changed. The more I deferred—asking questions, pushing for minutiae, nodding interestedly— the warmer my partner became. Together we hammered, nailed, varnished, stacked, and sorted. And then, armed with the store checkbook and a generous allowance, we traveled around the area in the store's pickup truck, going to book sales, buying libraries from retiring professors or their widows, all the while talking. Mostly, of course, it was Gene talking. My role was to audit, to keep the line of questioning alive. And that I was good at.

We were both in flight, using this unusual opportunity to redirect ourselves. I was a would-be writer who hadn't written for most of a year, who was just beginning to put his life together after an emotional catastrophe. Gene was a brilliant, willful perfectionist, a scholar who—I gradually understood—could not abide the vocation he thought he was training for. The more we talked, the more he spun his stories, the more vividly I saw his situation. Gene was not so much ABD—all but dissertation—as he was all but ready for desertion. He was a proud misfit who was unable to abide the lockstep procedures of academia. He was too contentious, too impatient for the life that he had imagined for himself. Charing Cross was more than a civilized amusement—which he liked to pretend—it was a way out.

Gene was an aesthete, a man for whom quality of life, down to the last detail, meant everything. He would linger over an assortment of shoelaces in a store, considering his choices. We could not have been more different. My life was so simple, so without fuss. When I opened my eyes in the morning, I got out of bed. I washed my face, rooted around for a wearable shirt, fixed a cup of simple coffee (instant if need be). I could be out the door in five minutes.

Not so Gene. On the mornings when I was supposed to pick him up—if we were scheduled to go on a buy, say—I would very nearly lose my mind waiting for him to get ready. The shower, the beard-trimming, the fussing with the cappuccino maker . . . I would patrol his library, trying to fall in with this more civilized pace. Certainly the books were there to be admired. Gene had them sorted by subject, perfectly alphabetized. Each edition, each translation, was, naturally, *the* one to have. Dust-jacketed editions wore a clear plastic wrap; pages were marked with little slips of paper, though it was true—Gene was sheepish about this—that books from an earlier era were still decorated in the margins with his immaculate tiny script.

Gene's apartment—the floor of a small house—was a world reared up defiantly against the messy world outside. What care he had expended building narrow shelves over the doors; how the morning light glittered off the wineglasses arranged in the kitchen cupboard. But it was almost impossible to get out the door. First the cup of cappuccino, then the croissant, then I would have to restrain my twitching impulsiveness while Gene introduced me to whatever was the latest prize—an Elly Ameling recording, a new edition of *Daniel Deronda* he'd found somewhere. And so it went through the day, as we hunkered over boxes in someone's garage, treated ourselves to lunch in a new Indian place Gene had heard about, or unpacked our spoils in the basement of the store—my education. . . .

My life at Charing Cross lasted for a year and a half. Working with Gene, discovering for the first time in my life the satisfaction of applying myself to something and having it pay off—this pulled me out of the melancholy I had been floundering in. I had never thrown myself at anything so zealously before, nor had I ever let myself be quite so consumed by anything. As soon as I woke up in the morning, I was off to the store. I bought a muffin and a large coffee at Kresge's across the street, turned off the alarm, and let myself in. Often it was hours before opening time. I liked turning on the classical station and then drinking my coffee downstairs at the sorting table, looking over our recent acquisitions. There was always work to be done—pricing books, looking up values in catalogs, arranging the display tables . . .

More and more, too, I was taking inspiration from Gene, picking up books in areas outside my immediate literary interest—books in history, classics, anthropology, art history. It was inevitable that I would begin to amass a library of my own. And this I did—at first almost reluctantly, as if this signaled that I was settling down—then with growing zeal. My new apartment, just around the corner from the store—I moved out of the other room shortly after my landlord's suicide—had space for bricks and boards. And foot by foot I covered the bare walls with the spines of my new finds. It would be a long time before I was anywhere near being in Gene's league, but I was making a start, somehow reconnecting with those afternoons I'd spent years before at the Wooden Spoon and the evenings I'd sat in my dilapidated armchair perusing whatever I'd found that day. . . .

One rainy Sunday that first spring back, when my entrepreneurial pride was just cresting, I wandered around the corner to Borders to buy a Sunday newspaper. As I was walking through the door, I noticed Joseph Brodsky standing by the front counter. He was trying to explain something to one of the clerks and judging by his expression—and the clerk's—was not having much success. I ventured closer, at first just eavesdropping and then, as soon as I made out what the poet was looking for, butting in. "You want a copy of *The Education of Henry Adams?*"

"Ya, that's it." Brodsky flashed a vindicated glance at the clerk.

"It's out of print," I said.

"How 'out of print'?" He looked genuinely baffled.

"But"—and now I felt the rush of things falling beautifully into place—"I can get you a copy. Follow me."

Brodsky made a startled surmising grimace but asked no questions. I pointed out the door and across the street. He followed me in the drizzle. How can I convey the pride and self-importance I felt as I fetched forth my bundle of keys, first deactivating the alarm, then unlocking the heavy door? "Come in."

The poet waited at the front while I loped through the dark room to the American history shelves, where, for some reason, we usually shelved the Adams. I was now hoping fervently that my memory had not played me wrong. I had such a clear picture in my mind of that oversize blue volume.

My luck held. The book was there. I could see it protruding from the top shelf even as I crossed the room in the dark. And it was with a sense of lordly beneficence—as though I were furthering some collective cultural project—that I presented it to Brodsky. "On the house."

"What house?" He looked puzzled.

"A gift." I paused for a second, then added, "From a fan."

He smiled sheepishly, accepted. And then we stood together awkwardly in the darkened front of the store.

"You know this Adams?" he asked. I wished more than anything in the world that I could say yes, strike off some startling observation. Gene could have. Gene could have kept the poet there half the afternoon with his striking observations. I could only shake my head.

"Well, do read him," said Brodsky.

To which I could only nod. I had lost all powers of speech just then. Here was one of life's gift moments: I was alone, in my store, with one of my heroes, a writer I had read and pondered, whose terrible sorrow I thought I knew, and my speaking powers were suddenly vaporized. But then, as I was turning to unlock the door again, I had an inspiration.

"I live around the corner," I said. "Would you like a cup of coffee?" And before I could even begin to worry about what he might be thinking of me, Brodsky agreed.

It was a strange two hours that followed. We did not break all the barriers of awkwardness and have the conversation I would have dreamed. But we did talk. I had only to mention a poet, any poet, and Brodsky would promptly assign a ranking. "Terrific!" he would say, fishing out another L&M from his pack ("Wystan smoked these," he said at one point). Or else: "He's shit." I was nervously matching him smoke for smoke, until it looked like we had been burning leaves in the apartment. When my sister walked in halfway through our conversation, she made a big show of fanning the air with a magazine.

With the arrival of a young woman, Brodsky's mood changed instantly. Where he had been tersely intense before, he now grew voluble. Everything turned comic. He began to laugh eagerly at his own gibes, eyeing the two of us with a kind of mischievous encouragement. Until it came out, as it was bound to eventually, that we were Latvian.

"Latvia . . ." He scrunched up his brow in mock concentration, and then, bright with malice, said: "In *dibens*."

My sister and I looked at each other. "In" was English, we got that. And *dibens* meant "butt" or "ass" in Latvian.

"Up your ass?" I ventured.

"Ya, exactly." Brodsky guffawed. I had no idea how to take this. I knew there was no love lost between Russians and Latvians, but there was no love lost between Brodsky and Russians, either. Was it a slight, or was the poet simply offering us his only half-remembered idiom? As he was sitting in my apartment, drinking my coffee, I went with the more charitable explanation. "In *dibens*," I repeated, and Andra and I both laughed.

But then, later, I did ask Brodsky if he knew any Latvian poets.

"There are no Latvian poets."

"Rainis—"

"*Rainis* . . ." He laughed cruelly and I cringed. "Ya, Rainis." That was all.

At that moment I surprised in myself a spark of ancient chauvinism. I felt the ancestral culture being mocked, and I—who had so resolutely refused all things Latvian—felt hurt. I wanted to rush forth in defense. I should have, though I can't imagine what I might have said. But instead I let it go. So eager was I to claim the poet as a friend that I let his cynical posturing silence me. I carefully steered the conversation back to safer ground.

Brodsky would have been in his mid-thirties then. He had not yet gone stocky and still had most of his hair, which was then reddish brown and wonderfully disheveled. But it was the face that held you, the strong blade of the nose and the wide, ironic, sinisterly sensuous mouth. I watched it at every moment, how it worked its way from cruel Caligula to what could feel like an unrestrained comic rapture. It was the mouth of an old Jewish sultan, if there could be such a hybrid creature.

Though Brodsky and I never became fast friends, our paths did begin to cross more often. He would stop in the store every so often. I would set aside odd volumes of poetry to show him. Sometimes he would ask, encouragingly, whether I was writing anything. And though I had, since meeting him, written a few pleasingly desolate lyrics, I shook my head. It would be a very long time before I would dare show him anything.

From My *Sky Blue Trades: Growing Up Counter in a Contrary Time* (New York: Viking Press, 2002).

Part Five

On the Edge of Academe

Ann Arbor Variations

I

Wet heat drifts through the afternoon
like a campus dog, a fraternity ghost
waiting to stay home from football games.
The arches are empty clear to the sky.

Except for leaves: those lashes of our
thinking and dreaming and drinking sight.
The spherical radiance, the Old English
look, the sum of our being, "hath perced

to the roote" all our springs and falls
and now rolls over our limpness, a daily
dragon. We lose our health in a love
of color, drown in a fountain of myriads,

as simply as children. It is too hot,
our birth was given up to screaming. Our
life on these street lawns seems silent.
The leaves chatter their comparisons

to the wind and the sky fills up
before we are out of bed. O infinite
our siestas! adobe effigies in a land
that is sick of us and our tanned flesh.

The wind blows towards us particularly
the sobbing of our dear friends on both
coasts. We are sick of living and afraid
that death will not be by water, o sea.

2

Along the walks and shaded ways
pregnant women look snidely at children.
Two weeks ago they were told, in these

selfsame pools of trefoil, "the market
for emeralds is collapsing," "chlorophyll
shines in your eyes," "the sea's misery

is progenitor of the dark moss which hides
on the north side of trees and cries."
What do they think of slim kids now?

and how, when the summer's gong of day
and night slithers towards their sweat
and towards the nests of their arms

and thighs, do they feel about children
whose hides are pearly with days of swimming?
Do they mistake these fresh drops for tears?

The wind works over these women constantly!
trying, perhaps, to curdle their milk
or make their spring unseasonably fearful,

season they face with dread and bright eyes.
The leaves, wrinkled or shiny like apples,
wave women courage and sigh, a void temperature.

3

The alternatives of summer do not remove
us from this place. The fainting into skies
from a diving board, the express train to
Detroit's damp bars, the excess of affection
on the couch near an open window or a Bauhaus
fire escape, the lazy regions of stars, all
are strangers. Like Mayakovsky read on steps
of cool marble, or Yeats danced in a theatre
of polite music. The classroom day of dozing
and grammar, the partial eclipse of the head

in the row in front of the head of poplars,
sweet Syrinx! last out the summer in a stay
of iron. Workmen loiter before urinals, stare
out windows at girders tightly strapped to clouds.
And in the morning we whimper as we cook
an egg, so far from fluttering sands and azure!

4

The violent No! of the sun
burns the forehead of hills.
Sand fleas arrive from Salt Lake
and most of the theatres close.

The leaves roll into cigars, or
it seems our eyes stick together
in sleep. O forest, o brook of
spice, o cool gaze of strangers!

the city tumbles towards autumn
in a convulsion of tourists
and teachers. We dance in the dark,
forget the anger of what we blame

on the day. Children toss and murmur
as a rumba blankets their trees and
beckons their stars closer, older, now.
We move o'er the world, being so much here.

It's as if Poseidon left off counting
his waters for a moment! In the fields
the silence is music like the moon.
The bullfrogs sleep in their hairy caves,

across the avenue a trefoil lamp
of the streets tosses luckily.
The leaves, finally, love us! and
moonrise! we die upon the sun.

From *The Collected Poems of Frank O'Hara*, edited by Donald Allen
(circa 1951; Berkeley: University of California Press, 1995).

Ross Macdonald

from The Dark Tunnel

I knew the door. It opened onto a concrete stair leading down into the steam-tunnels which branched all over the campus like arteries in a body, carrying steam from the university powerhouse to heat the buildings. One of the janitors must have left the light on. I crossed the hall and unlocked the door to turn out the light, but I couldn't find the switch. I left the door open so a janitor would see it in the morning.

The elevator was waiting and I got in and went up to the fourth floor. All the lights were out but the door of the Dictionary office was still open. I had the air-raid warden's flashlight, and I switched it on and entered the office, closing the door behind me.

The making of a historical dictionary is a long process. For five years Alec had been co-editor of the *Middle English Dictionary*, with a dozen people working under him. One thing his death meant was that the Dictionary would have to find a new editor. I had never had anything to do with the Dictionary directly, but Alec had given me a general idea of it.

It was intended to put in print for the first time, in ten handy volumes weighing about fifteen pounds each, all the meanings of all the words written in English between the death of William the Conqueror and the time of Caxton, the first English printer. This meant that the editors and subeditors and infra-editors had to read all the books and manuscripts remaining from four hundred years of English writing. They had to keep a file of every word read and examples of every use of every word. That is the first half of the process of making a historical dictionary.

The second half is the actual writing of the dictionary, listing every meaning of every word and at least one example of each meaning.

Since the reading in the Midwestern Dictionary office had been going on for a mere seven years, and not more than a dozen people spent only six or seven hours a day reading, the first half of the process was not yet complete. But there was already a roomful of tall steel filing cabinets filled with examples of the uses of Middle English words filed in alphabetical order. . . .

I thought of the open door leading into the steam-tunnels and ran back into the building. When I got to the door it was closed and the light behind it was out. Could there be a janitor here this early? Maybe Sale closed it and turned out the light.

The door wasn't locked and I opened it. Nothing but darkness. I still had the flashlight and turned it on and flashed it down the steps. The concrete basement room at the foot of the stairs was bare and the door in the grey wall which led into the tunnel was closed.

I heard a sound of running feet behind and above me on the first floor of the building and put out my light. The bulb which lit the stairs from the first floor into the basement corridor was switched on. I stepped inside the door and closed it except for a crack through which I could watch the lighted stairs. A bareheaded man with a gun in his hand came down the stairs two at a time.

I recognized the wide grey shoulders and the sullen Indian face. He paused at the foot of the stairs and looked up and down the basement corridor, his gun following his glance. Then he turned and ran out the back of the building.

Christ, was Gordon after me already? I thought of following him and throwing myself on his mercy—he was probably more intelligent than the local police—but I dropped the idea as soon as I picked it up. I was in a box that it would be hard to argue myself out of. The only way to get out was by running.

There was a pounding on the double doors at the west end of the corridor, and then the crash of glass. The police. I closed the door quietly and went down the concrete stairs into the steam-tunnel.

The basement was hot—perhaps the steam was on: it was just past the equinox and the weather was turning cold. As soon as I opened the second door, I knew the steam was on. It was like opening the door of a moderate hell. The air rushed out to take me like black flames. I closed the second door behind me and switched on the flashlight.

The two huge steampipes, green-painted, hung before me like twin segments of impossible serpents glowing with impossible energy. To my right and left they were lost in darkness in the endless man-made cave. I chose the left at random and started down the tunnel, the flashlight beam dancing before me like a wild hope. Then I remembered the closed door I had left open and the dark light I had left on.

Somebody might be waiting for me at the first turning. I put out the light and, with the unlit flashlight in my left hand and the gun in my right, went on in darkness. The concrete roof nearly brushed my hair as I walked and I felt the whole building above me like a weight on my neck. The sweat ran down in my eyes from the heat and I couldn't stop to take off my coat.

I went faster as my senses grew used to the darkness. At least I heard no one following. I half-turned my head to listen and walked into a wall. The clang of my flashlight against the concrete sounded like a gong.

I switched it on—it wasn't broken—and saw that the tunnel jogged to the left. Something on the tunnel floor caught my eye, a shining object. I picked it up and looked at it. It was a small metal cylinder, a lipstick. Women go everywhere nowadays, I thought. I put the lipstick in my pocket in case I should meet a woman, and held my gun cocked for the same reason as I went on.

I turned out the flash and went on in the hot darkness of the forest-floor of the twentieth-century jungle. The forest that bears no fruit, the rivers of steam and brooks of sewage that quench no thirst. I remembered something Alec had said about the carnivores creeping on rubber tires in the urban valleys. The blessings of civilization, I thought.

Not that I couldn't have done with a small armored motorcycle. Or even my car would do. If I could get to my car, I could get away into the country. But my car was parked on the campus and I didn't dare try to reach it.

I barely raised my feet and my leather soles hissed along the concrete. I walked with my hands held out to protect my face, like a blind man in an unfamiliar room. I felt as if I had walked a mile; the hot air was palpable and seemed to resist movement like water.

I switched on the flash for a moment and saw a dark open arch in the left wall about fifty feet ahead of me. I walked to it with the light on and the gun ready.

There was a sign stencilled on the wall in black letters at the side of the opening: Natural History Museum. It was nice to know where I was but I hadn't gone as far as I thought. Hardly more than a quarter-mile. At least the museum wasn't on the campus, which might now be surrounded by police. It stood in its own grounds across the street from the campus on the north side. It was a chance to get away.

I found the door out of the tunnel and beyond it the stairs leading up into the museum. I mounted them cautiously and opened the door at the head of the stairs. No light and no noise. I stepped out into the hall.

Across and down the hall from where I stood, there was pale light like moonlight falling through a great arched doorway. I tiptoed to the doorless arch and looked in.

Fixed lights from outside, street-lights probably, shone through the high windows into a huge hall that seemed to have no ceiling. Impossible monsters, one of them twenty feet high, watched me from every side. You've got the jungle on the brain, I said to myself. Out of one jungle into another.

I recognized the room. The tall monsters were the mounted skeletons of prehistoric saurians. I could see the light shining bleakly through their ancient ribs.

There was a slight rustle on the other side of the room and I stepped out of the doorway and sidled along the wall into dark shadow. I heard no other sound. Probably the noise was a prehistoric mouse no more than five feet tall.

I shifted my position and looked along the opposite wall. In a dark corner, almost facing me, four human figures crouched. I huddled down against the wainscotting like a six-foot mouse. Then I remembered the exhibition in that corner of the room, several life-size dummies painted and dressed like Neanderthal men, holding stone weapons and squatting over a cold fire in an imitation cave.

But I didn't remember *four* dummies. I levelled my gun and walked to the roped enclosure where the cavemen sat on their heels. They didn't move.

I stepped closer and looked down at the bushy papier-mâché heads. The light was weak, but I could see that two of the heads were black and one was lighter and one was almost white. I felt as if I jumped a foot but I didn't move. My back was to the windows and my face was in shadow.

I lingered a moment, reining the wild horses in my legs, and then moved away. As I moved I saw with the edge of my retina that the caveman at the end was looking at me from under tousled red locks, out of live green eyes. He held a stone hatchet shaped like a gun.

I sauntered back to the other side of the room, feeling I had a fifty-fifty chance of not being shot. Peter and Ruth could have shot me then, but I was their scapegoat for Dr. Schneider's death. And they didn't know I'd seen them.

I stepped into the striped shadow of a brontosaurus skeleton, drew a quick bead on the head at the end of the roped enclosure, and fired. I must have missed because two flashes answered my shot simultaneously and two shadows came over the ropes towards me.

I turned and ran through the arch and heard two more shots as I turned the corner. I clattered down the tiled hall and found another corner to turn and then another. The feet behind me were light and quick like cats' feet.

I ran into a door with a bar across it like an exit and it flew open under my weight. I staggered out onto a concrete loading-platform at the back of the museum, slammed the door behind me, and jumped to the ground.

The corner of the building was quite near and I turned it as I heard the door spring open. I sprinted across a lawn, keeping in the shadow of bushes and trees, towards the circular building surrounded by cages, where the museum kept its live animals. I put this building between me and the cave-dwellers, but I heard their light feet running towards me on gravel.

I passed a fox curled up asleep behind his wire netting, and I envied him his nice, safe cage. I wanted one of my own. I could have one if I could get into it before the feet came around the animal-house. Across from the fox-cage there was a pit perhaps four feet deep where the snakes and turtles were kept. I vaulted the iron fence around it and landed on my hands and knees on the gravel floor. I scuttled against the concrete wall like a frightened crab and a black snake slithered away from under my hands. I crouched there trying to control my panting, and heard the running feet go by above my head.

When the sound had ceased, I climbed out of the pit like an ambitious turtle and ran back to the museum. The back door was still open and I scrambled up on the loading-platform and went in, leaving the door open behind me. The corridor I had dashed through three minutes before seemed longer on the way back. I found the door at last and went down into the tunnels again. They wouldn't come back to the museum. Someone must have heard the shots and the police would soon be here.

I flashed my light in the sub-basement and saw a chart on the wall. McKinley Hall, the Little Theatre, the Women's Building, the Graduate School, the Natural History Museum circled in red. A network of blacklines crisscrossed the chart. It was a map of the steam-tunnels.

The university powerhouse was about as far from the museum as McKinley Hall, but in the opposite direction. I got my bearings and went into the tunnel. As I closed the door behind me, I heard loud feet like policemen's feet on the floor of the building above me, and a sound of voices. I set out for the powerhouse. Powerhouses have always interested me.

My shirt was still sopping and my coat began to get wet. My heart was beating hard from the sprint and the darkness swelled and contracted around me like black blood in an artery. It slithered like a snake past my sightless eyes. Suddenly, I noticed that I had no gun. I must have left it in the reptile-pit.

As soon as I bumped into a wall and turned a corner, I used my flashlight. There could be no one in front of me now until I reached the powerhouse. I quickened my pace and trotted along on the left side of the green pipes, sweating like a wrestler. My feet clattered on the paved floor and I let them clatter.

I heard feet behind me far down the tunnel and I stopped for an instant and looked back. There was a faint light on the wall where the tunnel turned and shadows like grey fingers reached out towards me. I switched out my light and ran on blindly in the dark with heavy footsteps reverberating behind me.

Something struck me across the chest like a falling tree and I leaned against it gasping for breath. I felt searing heat against my body: it must be the steampipe. I crawled under the pipes where they turned into the wall and ran on with one hand scraping the wall, feeling for the door that must be there.

Flashlights came around the corner on pounding feet a hundred yards behind me. I saw my shadow leaping ahead of me like a frantic mimic of my fear. And I saw a door.

A man's voice shouted, "There he is," and a gun went off with a sound like vessels bursting in my brain. The bullet ricocheted from the wall behind me and passed me like a droning bee. I have always hated bees.

I dived for the door and it opened under my hand. I ran out on the floor of a great concrete vault lined on one side with black iron boilers. By the light of the few unshaded bulbs that hung in the furnace-room I could see no one, but the footsteps sounded through the door at my back like pounding fists. To my right were windows and an iron ladder leading up to a door in the wall.

I dropped my flashlight and scrambled up the ladder and got the iron door at the top open. The door from the tunnel sprang open below and I slammed the iron door shut. Two bullets rang flatly against it like the knocking of iron knuckles, and I jumped onto a black hill which loomed outside the door.

I was halfway up the side of the university coal-pile. Anthracite is not good to run in but there was nowhere to hide and nothing to do but run.

I leaped and scrambled down the side of the coal-pile towards a railway track which gleamed faintly in the starlight. I heard the iron door open behind me and the sound of another shot but I didn't look back.

When I reached the track it was easier to run, and there were buildings on each side which helped to shadow me. I heard scrambling and cursing behind me but I ran straight on down the track to the end of the buildings. By now the feet behind were ringing on the ties and I turned to my left and jumped down the embankment.

There was a board fence in front of me and beyond it the clotted darkness of a clump of trees. Before the flashlights behind me reached the end of the buildings, I flung myself over the fence and landed on my side in weeds.

I got to my feet crouching low and ran into the patch of trees. When I reached the other side with my face scratched by low branches, I stopped and listened. There was no sound behind me, but I had to get away from there. I remembered newspaper stories of police cordons thrown around trapped killers. To the police, I was a killer. But I wasn't trapped yet.

The grove was in a valley, and on the hillside opposite me there was a huge dark building punctured with a few lighted windows. I knew the building—it was the hospital—and it helped me to get my bearings. Helen Madden lived near the hospital. If I could get to her she would help me.

Keeping close to the edge of the trees I ran along the valley, stumbling over hummocks and rubbish. With the lights of the great hospital above me, I felt more than ever like an outlaw, and I felt self-pity that other men should make me run like an unwanted dog among rubbish-heaps. But I felt pleasure, too, in running for my life. My two enemies were running in the same darkness.

From *The Dark Tunnel* (1944; Boston: Gregg Press, 1980).

The Little Boat

As soon as spring peepers sounded from the stream
and boggy lower barnyard across the road
Mother let us bring out the cots,
and sleeping bags—red and gray and black
plaid flannel, still smelling of the cedar chest.

How hard it was to settle down that first night
out on the big screened porch: three times
trains passed the crossing, and the peepers' song
was lost under the whistle (two long,
two short), the rumble and clacking,
and clang of the crossing bell. The neighbor's
cocker spaniel howled the whole time
and for a full two minutes after. . . . Or rain
sluiced from the eaves, and we saw black limbs
against a sky whitened by lightning.
The gloom was lavish and agreeable. . . .

August came. Mother took us to Wahr's on State Street,
bought each of us a reader, speller, Big 10 Tablet,
a bottle of amber glue with a slit like a closed eye,
pencils, erasers of a violent pink, a penmanship workbook
for practicing loops that looked to me
like the culvert under the road, whose dark and webby length
Brother and I dared each other to run through . . .
and crayons, the colors ranging from one to another
until what began as yellow ended amazingly as blue.

One morning we walked to the top of Foster Road,
and stood under the Reimers' big maple.
Ground fog rose from the hay stubble.

We heard gears grinding at the foot of the hill;
the bus appeared and we knew we had to get in.
All day in my imagination my body floated
above the classroom, navigating easily
between fluorescent shoals. . . . I was listening,
floating, watching. . . . The others stayed below
at their desks (I saw the crown of my own head
bending over a book), and no one knew I was not
where I seemed to be. . . .

From *The Boat of Quiet Hours* (Saint Paul: Graywolf Press, 1986).

Robert Hayden

The Performers

Easily, almost matter-of-factly they step,
two minor Wallendas, with pail and squeegee along
the wintry ledge, hook their harness to the wall
and leaning back into a seven-story angle of space
begin washing the office windows. I
am up there too until straps break
and iron paper apple of iron I fall
through plateglass wind onto stalagmites below.

But am safely at my desk again by the time
the hairline walkers, high-edge
balancers end their center-ring routine
and crawl inside. A rough day, I remark,
for such a risky business. Many thanks.
Thank *you*, sir, one of the men replies.

From *Collected Poems*, edited by Frederick
Glaysher (New York: Liveright, 1985).

Macklin Smith

Two Views

Before you check into 8–A, where you will
Either die or walk out with

Reasonable prospects, you are told that
Your room will be either riverview or helipad,

Depending on the discharge schedule. Nothing
You can do about it, it's heads or tails

And why did I even care? The river is
Invisible from riverview. What I saw was

Streams of blood, painkillers, and chemotherapy,
And let's face it, the health care

Management considerations have to outweigh a patient's
Personal preference

About his room assignment. I got helipad,
Which bummed me out, but actually it wasn't such a bad

Room, it was exciting to watch the paramedics run
Out from the chopper with their gurneyed victim

Toward a door I couldn't see from there;
And they showed such intense care

That I felt somehow reassured, institutionally,
All of the traumas and burns set down outside my

Room as expeditiously as a Peregrine's pigeon
On its nest ledge. Someone

Died next door to me, day ten, I can't even remember
His name. He had a graft-versus-host problem

In his lungs, and suddenly his room was empty,
Briefly. I would pace at night looking for other empty

Rooms overlooking the Huron River,
Dead patients and those who had just been discharged.

You could see the swath of woods
Along the river, lit by the arc lights from Fuller Road,

You knew it was there. Remembering a Connecticut Warbler
Years ago, not far downstream in the Arb,

Walking through jewelweed. My one-month 8–A bird list
Pathetic, even given my situation:

Rock Dove, House Sparrow, Starling, Crow—
Missing the Mallard that Lynette saw,

I was probably throwing up at the time
Or sleeping. I would walk the halls trying

To find an empty riverview
Window, to watch the trees along the river,

And night after night the Hale-Bopp
Comet sped slowly east with its tail of suicidal devotees.

I would pass around my binoculars
To all the residents and night nurses. Everyone saw it.

From *Transplant* (Ann Arbor: Shaman Drum, 2002).

Linda Gregerson

ф

An Arbor

1.

The world's a world of trouble, your mother must
                    have told you
            that. Poison leaks into the basements

and tedium into the schools. The oak
                    is going the way
            of the elm in the upper Midwest—my cousin

earns a living by taking the dead ones
                    down.
            And Jason's alive yet, the fair-

haired child, his metal crib next
                    to my daughter's.
            Jason is nearly one year old but last

saw light five months ago and won't
                    see light again.

2.

Leaf against leaf without malice
                    or forethought,
            the manifold species of murmuring

harm. No harm intended, there never is.
                    The new
            inadequate software gets the reference librarian

fired. The maintenance crew turns off power one
                    weekend
            and Monday the lab is a morgue: fifty-four

rabbits and seventeen months of research.
                    Ignorance loves
            as ignorance does and always

holds high office.

        3.
Jason had the misfortune to suffer misfortune
                    the third
            of July. July's the month of hospital ro-

tations; on holiday weekends the venerable
                    stay home.
            So when Jason lay blue and inert on the table

and couldn't be made to breathe for three-and-a-
                    quarter hours,
            the staff were too green to let him go.

The household gods have abandoned us to the gods
                    of juris-
            prudence and suburban sprawl. The curve

of new tarmac, the municipal pool,
                    the sky at work
            on the pock-marked river, fatuous sky,

the park where idling cars, mere yards
                    from the slide
            and the swingset, deal beautiful oblivion in nickel

bags: the admitting room and its stately drive,
                    possessed
            of the town's best view.

        4.
And what's to become of the three-year-old brother?
                    When Jason was found
            face down near the dogdish—it takes

just a cupful of water to drown—
               his brother stood still
          in the corner and said he was hungry

and said that it wasn't his fault.
               No fault.
          The fault's in nature, who will

without system or explanation
               make permanent
          havoc of little mistakes. A natural

mistake, the transient ill will we define
               as the normal
          and trust to be inconsequent,

by nature's own abundance soon absorbed.

   5.
Oak wilt, it's called, the new disease.
               Like any such
          contagion—hypocrisy in the conference room,

flattery in the halls—it works its mischief mostly
               unremarked.
          The men on the links haven't noticed

yet. Their form is good. They're par.
               The woman who's
          prospered from hating ideas loves causes

instead. A little shade, a little firewood.
               I know
          a stand of oak on which my father's

earthly joy depends. We're slow
               to cut our losses.

From *The Woman Who Died in Her Sleep* (Boston: Houghton Mifflin, 1996).

Thomas Lynch

Still Life in Milford—
Oil on Canvas by Lester Johnson

You're lucky to live in a town like this
with art museums and Indian food
and movie houses showing foreign films
and grad students and comely undergrads.
Years back I'd often make the half-hour trip.
It was good for my creative juices
to browse the holy books at Shaman Drum.
Still, life in Milford isn't all that bad.

We have two trendy restaurants and a bar
well known by locals for its Coney dogs.
We have a bookshop now. We even have
a rush hour, art fairs and bon vivants.
And a classic car show every October—
mostly muscle cars—Dodges, Chevys, Fords.
No psychic healers yet or homeopaths.
Still, life in Milford has a certain ambiance,

more Wyeth than Picasso, to be sure,
more meatloaf and potatoes than dim-sum. Fact is,
at first I thought this Lester Johnson was
a shirttail cousin of the Johnson brothers—
long-standing members of the Chamber of Commerce
in Milford, Michigan, like me. In fact
his only connection to these parts was
Still Life in Milford, gathering dust here

in the basement of the art museum.
His own Milford's somewhere back east, near Yale—
the day job, teaching, he could never quit
the way that Robert Frost taught English here

and Donald Hall before the muse in them
escaped their offices in Angell Hall.
They were last seen running and maybe running still.
Life in Milford, Michigan, is similar.

I have steady work, a circle of friends
and lunch on Thursdays with the Rotary.
I have a wife, unspeakably beautiful,
a daughter and three sons, a cat, a car,
good credit, taxes and mortgage payments
and certain duties here. Notably,
when folks get horizontal, breathless, still:
life in Milford ends. They call. I send a car.

Between the obsequies I play with words.
I count the sounds and syllables and rhymes.
I try to give it shape and sense, like so:
eight stanzas of eight lines apiece, let's say
ten syllables per line or twelve. Just words.
And if rhyming's out of fashion, I fashion rhymes
that keep their distance, four lines apart, like so.
Still, life in Milford keeps repeating. Say

I'm just like Lester, just like Frost and Hall:
I covet the moment in which nothing moves
and crave the life free of life's distractions.
A bucket of flowers on a table.
A vase to arrange the flowers in. A small
pipe—is it?—smoldering in an ashtray to
suggest the artist and impending action.
Still Life in Milford seems a parable

on the human hunger for creation.
The flowers move from bucket to vase
like moving words at random into song—
the act of ordering is all the same—
the ordinary becomes a celebration.
Whether paper, canvas, ink or oil paints,
once finished we achieve a peace we call
Still Life in Milford. Then we sign our names.

From *Still Life in Milford* (New York: Norton, 1999).

Laurence Goldstein

Ann Arbor Solitary

Brawling in the bush with himself
our schnapps-bloated German
punches free to the sidewalk,
mock orange blossoms in both fists.
His bright yellow blazer, a sign
of bad conscience—for we know
his taste is good, and bottomless—
turns every human head.
It's twilight, his only happy hour.

New faculty have made Germantown
a ghetto of sorts, him a survivor.
He once let drop that my house
havened a devotee of the Führer,
who carpentered for the old families.
I imagine these compatriots in song—
swelling the *Horst Wessel Lied*, and
chiming steins at the Old Heidelberg.

Having nothing on these blocks
to remember, I remember a ghost
who safeguarded the pine floors
and surely gazed with pleasure upon
the celtic patterns of the woodwork,
the chalet-style gingerbread,
the Nordic newel post and moldings
he mined with coverage of the Last Days
when he repaired what I re-repair.

Often I fancy a bull shape
snorting like my sodden neighbor's,

a distemper passionate as his,
eager to trespass and reclaim,
their voices mingled into one
that calls to my boys at catch
across the battlement of spirea:
"Here was a piece of the Fatherland."

From *The Three Gardens* (Providence: Copper Beech Press, 1987).

Courtney Mandryk

☐

Flat (*Ann Arbor*)

Give me orange. Opera. Cursive. Thick leg. Balloon.
Give me lampshade. Church window. Mouth. Question mark.

A collection of consolations:
homesick eyes find phantom
mountains, surrogate curves in thin air.

If the land here is ocean
then the waves are the Appalachians
and I'm midwaist deep in the midwest sea.

I hear whale songs at night
in groaning trains and truck brakes,

and am even glad to see a jackknifed
tractor trailer belly-up on the highway.

I watch waves on the big screen.
Quick by water. Slow by rock.
Hip's horizon. Any curve will do.

Please do you have for me a glass bowl? Cumulonimbus cloud?
Raised eyebrow? Soap dispenser? Soap? Parentheses?

Michigan Quarterly Review 44, no. 2 (spring 2005).

Envoi

❦

Two Columns from the *Michigan Daily*

Johanna Hanink

Dishonoring Those We've Lost by Shouting

September 24, 2001

The burden of my last summer at home began to weigh more heavily as the final days of July slipped into August. I had come home in June unenthusiastic, even averse, to seeing any of the people to whom I'd ever applied the title "best friend." I'd fallen out of touch to some degree with everybody, a separation compounded by this same "everybody's" choice to stay in New England and therefore together. Everybody, that is, except me.

But as June gave way to July I had forgotten Ann Arbor and remembered to ask for marshmallow instead of whipped cream on my chocolate-raspberry-truffle ice cream from Kathy John's, the restaurant where every night, whether we were hungry or had no other place to go, we'd avoid the unavoidable upcoming semester. And then we became coherent again as, determined to avoid any cliched "nothing left in common," I found in my friends people changed just like I had been changed by our first year at school.

Our complaints had turned from calculus labs to sweatshop labor as our concept of "sit-in" adjusted to include the term "living wage." Some evenings we'd sit on the soccer fields of our old middle school and plan the revolution until someone would drop the loaded declaration, "Well, I've got work tomorrow" and soon a caravan of cars would disperse from the parking lot, each one honking softly as it turned out of sight. Midnight had become late again.

It was, therefore, a given that I'd call one of these re-found friends on the evening of Sept. 11 to discuss and dissect the beyond-tragic, beyond-human, morning attacks. "Isn't it awful?" I asked him, hating myself for thinking of no more eloquent way to define what I now euphemistically refer to as "the events of the 11th." "Yeah," he replied. "But you know what? The United States has already killed half a million Iraqi children with its sanctions. That's awful."

This person is one of the most compassionate I have ever met and I don't think he realized what he was saying. The thought of half a million

237

children gone because of my country breaks my heart. But so does the thought of the 6,000-plus children, mothers, fathers, sisters and brothers buried in fallen rubble across New York, Washington and Pennsylvania. The two feelings are not mutually exclusive.

It is in situations like this, when the dichotomy between extreme right and extreme left blurs into nothingness, that the political spectrum gives its secret away: It is a circle rather than a line. Soon many more people, many more children, will die in Afghanistan because of some people's hate for the "Other." But the deaths of thousands in New York have been met with the complacency of a few, because of the hate some people feel for themselves and their country. Nobody worth mentioning celebrates these deaths, but from both sides comes the language of reservation and justification.

And in the midst of our struggle to determine and direct what is right, to decide how the United States should proceed with Afghanistan or reflect on the evils of our own foreign policy, some find themselves forgetting the children who will lose parents and the parents who will lose children in a part of the world that for most of us, until now, existed only in buried headlines. And harder to understand, but still true, some will find themselves forgetting that nobody on that missing persons list, now topping 6,000, deserved to die for the failings of a nation.

On Friday, the Daily reported that, "Chanting 'stop the war' and 'U-S-A,' anti- and pro-war student groups clashed verbally yesterday on the Diag over the subject of U.S. military actions and policy." This kind of display does nothing but garner media attention for the shouting antagonists and degrade the memory of the dead.

As we plan our rallies and strategize over dinner we have to carry with us at all times the reality of death. And for those of us who ardently advocate peace and oppose more senseless loss of life, it is okay to make some people feel uncomfortable, but not to marginalize with hostility and antagonism regardless of to whom these feelings are directed any potential advocate for peace.

At this university, we have a constant inferiority complex when we compare ourselves to the legendary names and groups of the over-romanticized 1960s and '70s student activism. But it's been more than 30 years and we should have learned that we do not need to shout to be heard. It's been more than 30 years and we should have learned that some struggles are too sad to romanticize.

Michigan Daily, September 24, 2001.

Michael Grass

✝

A², a Training Ground for Life's Finer Experiences

September 3, 2002

There are few cities in the Midwest that measure up to Ann Arbor. Aside from Madison, our fair city, compared to any other Big Ten college town, is the best around.

Columbus is large, but lacks character. West Lafayette is in the middle of nowhere. Evanston, with Ivy-envy, is much like New Haven: Dead. And everyone in East Lansing is grain-fed. Or so the theory goes.

Ann Arbor is simply different. Instead of strip malls lining the main drag, we have an Art Deco theater and used bookstores. Instead of going to Taco Bell for late-night munchies, we go to the Fleetwood Diner. Instead of going to an Olive Garden for a romantic Italian dinner, we go to Gratzi or Bella Ciao. Instead of any run-of-the-mill suburban franchise like Applebee's, we have "real" neighborhood hangouts, like Ashley's Pub and the Brown Jug.

Bottom-line: We live, work, study and party in a real city.

Although Ann Arbor can be very isolating at times, the best thing about this city is that it looks outside its borders for inspiration and self-improvement. We have great architecture, vibrant neighborhoods and establishments that have history and tradition.

And Ann Arbor is a stepping stone to better things in life. Our critics say that we're stuck-up, arrogant and trapped in six square miles surrounded by reality.

But is that something to be ashamed of? No. We should celebrate it.

One of Ann Arbor's greatest fans, public radio personality, Midwestern icon and writer Garrison Keillor aptly described Ann Arbor's residents—including its students—during a live broadcast of "A Prairie Home Companion" in December at Hill Auditorium: "People in expensive scruffy clothing, talking like socialists, in expensive restaurants."

While Keillor's description may paint Ann Arbor as a superficial city, propped up by a pretentious and pompous facade, it is a training ground for the real world—a cross-section of society with all of its problems crammed into a city with 110,000 people who embrace the diversity and ideas that shape our world.

If you're an in-stater, Ann Arbor is a great training ground for social mobility and provides a large number of options for choosing a path in life. It's a place where you can learn to enjoy a good single-malt scotch, progressive jazz, inventive vegan food or an excellent microbrew.

It's a place that is a stopping-off point for the world's greatest orchestras and speakers. It's a nexus for debate, philosophy and issues. It's a place to tap a keg, find out the difference between New York and Chicago-style pizza, go see a foreign film, understand Kant, question authority, stay up all night with friends and play video games, realize that your high school English teacher was an idiot for embracing the philosophy of Ayn Rand and eat the best damn Buffalo wings this side of Lake Erie (at Mr. Spot's of course).

It's a place to hang out and a place to be serious. In Michigan, only Ann Arbor provides such an environment; you won't find that in East Grand Rapids (where I'm from), Farmington Hills or Traverse City (or up the road in East Lansing for that matter).

For an out-of-stater, Ann Arbor provides those same opportunities, but also offers something else—a reality check. Let's say you're from Nassau County, N.Y. and you're coming to Ann Arbor because of Michigan sports and a chance of getting into the Business School. You think that since your home, let's say Dix Hills, Great Neck or Jericho, is located near New York City, you are all-knowing and have the right to inherit the earth. While New York is arguably the world's greatest urban environment, it isn't the only one. "Doing one's time in the Midwest" as one out-of-state friend once told me, is probably one of the most important things for an East Coaster.

"It has made me a better person," she said. "Ann Arbor will do that to you."

She's right. In such a small but vibrant and global environment, students in Ann Arbor get to douse themselves in a city that is built on a human scale and has developed into a place where people open up their minds and reshape themselves and are better for it.

And that isn't just limited to the out-of-staters.

This happens to all people who come through this place—whether you are from northern New Jersey, Detroit's east side or Indonesia. Then when you move away, as my friend put it, "you keep your experience in Ann Arbor in your back pocket and refer back to it when you need to . . . just to make sure that you are appreciating not only where you are in life but what you can do with it."

Of course, any college town is supposed to do that. It's just that the University of Michigan, because of Ann Arbor, does it better than most places.

The integration of "town and gown" as it is called, makes Ann Arbor what it is. And it is what makes me miss the city now. Some people never move away. Others who do move on wish they never did. Everybody who happens to come through Ann Arbor appreciates the city both for its benefits and its downfalls.

Yes, there are better places than Ann Arbor. No doubt. But it is places like Ann Arbor that prepare people to appreciate those better places and the finer things in life. That is what makes Ann Arbor so great. Enjoy.

Michigan Daily, September 3, 2002.

∯

Contributors

Olive San Louie Anderson (1852–86) graduated from the University of Michigan in 1875 and published her novel, *An American Girl, and Her Four Years in a Boys' College*, under the pen name SOLA in 1878. She became a teacher and school administrator in San Rafael, California, and died in a drowning accident. An edition of her novel, edited by Elisabeth Perry and Jennifer Price, will be published by the University of Michigan Press in 2006.

Max Apple, born in 1941 in Grand Rapids, Michigan, received a B.A. in 1963 and a Ph.D. in 1970 from the University of Michigan, where he wrote the first of his stories for *The Oranging of America* (1976). His two books of memoirs contain scenes of Ann Arbor. He teaches at the University of Pennsylvania.

Charles Baxter, born in 1947, taught at the University of Michigan from 1989 to 2003 and is currently Edelstein-Keller Professor of Creative Writing at the University of Minnesota. *The Feast of Love*, nominated for the National Book Award, is one of the few novels set entirely in the nonacademic milieu of Ann Arbor. Much of his fiction is centered in the mythical town of Five Oaks, Michigan. He has also published books of essays and poetry.

Sven Birkerts, born in 1951, graduated from the University of Michigan in 1973. After publishing collections of essays on modern poetry and on fiction, he wrote his best-known book, *The Gutenberg Elegies: The Fate of Reading in an Electronic Age* (1994). He is currently the editor of the literary journal *Agni*.

John Dewey (1859–1952) was one of the greatest American philosophers of the twentieth century, whose theories on democracy, education, and art, first formulated during the 1890s when he taught at the University of Michigan, profoundly influenced social reformers.

Laurence Goldstein, born in 1943, is Professor of English at the University of Michigan and, since 1977, editor of *Michigan Quarterly Review*. His fourth book of poetry, *A Room in California*, appeared in 2005. He is also the author of *The American Poet at the Movies: A Critical History* (1994).

Peggy Goodin (1923–83) based her novel *Take Care of My Little Girl* on her experience of sororities at the University of Michigan during her undergraduate years, 1942–46. The novel was filmed in 1951 by Jean Negulesco, featuring Jeanne Crain, Mitzi Gaynor, and Jean Peters. Her first novel, *Clementine* (1945), was filmed in 1948 as *Mickey*.

Richard Goodman, born in 1945, is the author of *French Dirt: The Story of a Garden in the South of France* (1991). A resident of New York City, he teaches creative nonfiction at Spalding University's Brief Residency MFA in Writing program.

Michael Grass, born in 1979, received a B.A. from the University of Michigan in 2002. He covered the university administration and served as a news editor and editorial page editor during his time at the *Michigan Daily*. He is now working as a journalist in Washington, D.C.

Linda Gregerson, born in 1950, began teaching at the University of Michigan in 1987. She is the author of three collections of poetry; the most recent, *Waterborne*, won the 2003 Kingsley Tufts Poetry Award. She has also published books of commentary on Renaissance literature and contemporary American poetry.

Donald Hall, born in 1928, taught at the University of Michigan from 1957 to 1975. His many books include *Old and New Poems* (1990) and several volumes of essays, including *Breakfast Served Any Time All Day* (2003). His most recent book is a memoir of his life with Jane Kenyon, *The Best Day the Worst Day* (2005).

Alice Hamilton (1869–1970), considered the founder and foremost practitioner of occupational medicine, was the first woman professor at Harvard Medical School. She received her medical degree from the University of Michigan in 1893; worked at Hull House; published widely in the field of industrial toxicology; and wrote an autobiography, *Exploring the Dangerous Trades*.

Johanna Hanink, born in 1982, attended the University of Michigan from 2000 to 2003 and served as the editorial page editor of the *Michigan Daily* in 2002. She is pursuing a Ph.D. in Classics at the University of California, Berkeley.

Karl Edwin Harriman (1875–1935), born in Ann Arbor, wrote popular fiction such as *The Girl and the Deal* (1905) and edited *Red Book* and *Blue Book* magazines, 1919–27.

E. O. Haven (1820–81) served as Chancellor of Syracuse University before becoming President of the University of Michigan in 1863 and thereafter was President of Northwestern University from 1869 to 1872. *The Autobiography of Erastus O. Haven* appeared in 1883.

Robert Hayden (1913–80) studied with W. H. Auden at the University of Michigan in 1941 while a graduate student and returned there to teach in 1970. He was appointed Consultant in Poetry at the Library of Congress in 1976, and his volume *Collected Poems* appeared in 1985.

Tom Hayden, born in 1939 in Detroit, drafted the Port Huron Statement in 1962 shortly after graduating from the University of Michigan. A cofounder of Students for a Democratic Society, a defendant at the Chicago Seven trial in the late 1960s, and a husband of Jane Fonda, he served in the California assembly and senate till his retirement in 1999.

Lawrence Joseph, born in 1948, earned his B.A. from the University of Michigan in 1970 and a degree in law in 1975. His collected poems, *Codes, Precepts, Biases, and Taboos*, and a new volume, *Into It*, appeared in 2005. He teaches at St. John's University School of Law in New York City.

Jane Kenyon (1947–95) was born and raised in Ann Arbor and won a Hopwood Award at the University of Michigan. Her poetry has been increasingly acclaimed since the publication of her selected lyrics, *Otherwise* (1996), and the memorial volume by her husband, Donald Hall, *Without* (1998).

Thomas Lynch, born in 1948, is the author of three books of poetry, *Sailing with Heather Grace* (1986), *Grimalkin and Other Poems* (1994), and *Still Life in Milford* (1998), and two books centered on his occupation as a mortician in Milford, Michigan, *The Undertaking* (1997) and *Bodies in Motion and at Rest* (2000). He is an adjunct professor in the creative writing program at the University of Michigan.

Ross Macdonald (1915–83) was the pen name of Kenneth Millar, who earned an M.A. in 1943 and a Ph.D. in 1951 from the University of Michigan. As a teaching fellow in 1943 he wrote his first novel, *The Dark Tunnel,* and afterward crafted a series of masterful novels and short stories set in California featuring the detective Lew Archer. *The Galton Case* (1959), arguably his greatest novel, returns to Ann Arbor in significant scenes.

Courtney Mandryk, born in 1979, studied in the M.F.A. program at the University of Michigan from 2003 to 2005 and won a Hopwood Award in Poetry. She is enrolled in the M.F.A. program at the Cranbrook Academy of Art.

Justin McCarthy (1830–1912) was an Irish journalist, novelist, and historian, best known for his service in the British parliament, his lecture tours in America, and the seven-volume *History of Our Own Times* (1879–1905).

Dorothy Gies McGuigan (1914–82) was born in Ann Arbor and graduated from the University of Michigan in 1936. Her best-known books are *The Habsburgs* (1966), *A Dangerous Experiment: 100 Years of Women at the University of Michigan* (1970), and *Metternich and the Duchess* (1975). She served as program director at the University of Michigan Center for the Continuing Education of Women.

Richard Meeker (1901–96) was the pseudonym used by Forman Brown when he published his novel *Better Angel* in 1933. He recorded his life in Los Angeles as a songwriter, puppeteer, and playwright in *Small Wonder: The Story of the Yale Puppeteers and the Turnabout Theatre* (1980), with an introduction by Ray Bradbury.

Arthur Miller (1915–2005) was one of the greatest playwrights of the twentieth century, best known for *All My Sons, Death of a Salesman, The Crucible, A View from the Bridge,* and *After the Fall.* He also wrote a novel, books of short fiction, and the screenplay for *The Misfits.*

Joyce Carol Oates, born in 1938, has written extensively in her fiction about southeast Michigan and western Ontario, as well as the upstate areas of New York where she grew up. She teaches at Princeton University and is a coeditor of *Ontario Review* with her husband, Raymond Smith. Greg Johnson has published a biography of Oates, *Invisible Writer* (1998).

Frank O'Hara (1926–66), a graduate student at the University of Michigan during 1950–51, became an important member of the New York School of poets, writing the first study of Jackson Pollock and the experimental volumes *Meditations in an Emergency* (1957) and *Lunch Poems* (1964).

Marge Piercy, born in 1936, was born in Detroit and matriculated at the University of Michigan during the 1960s. She has written books of fiction and poetry, and her novel *Woman at the Edge of Time* (1976) has been studied in several academic disciplines. She lives in Wellfleet, Massachusetts.

Dudley Randall (1914–2000), poet and essayist, founded Broadside Press in Detroit in 1965. "The Ballad of Birmingham" and his volume *Cities Burning* (1968) established him as an important voice in the African American community. Melba Boyd wrote a biography of him and the Press.

Ruth Reichl, born in 1948, received her B.A. in 1968 and her M.A. in 1970 from the University of Michigan. A chef, a restaurateur, and restaurant critic for the *Los Angeles Times* and *New York Times,* she has written several books on the culinary arts, including *Comfort Me with Apples: More Adventures at the Table* (2001), *Tender at the*

Bone: Growing Up at the Table (1998), and *Garlic and Sapphires: The Secret Life of a Critic in Disguise* (2005).

Elwood Reid, born in 1966, attended the University of Michigan on a football scholarship from 1985 to 1989 and subsequently earned an M.F.A. He is the author of three novels— *If I Don't Six* (1998), *Midnight Sun* (2000), and *D.B.* (2004)—as well as a book of stories, *What Salmon Know* (1999).

Allan Seager (1906–68) was born in Adrian, Michigan, and earned his B.A. from the University of Michigan in 1930. He returned to his alma mater in 1945 to teach until his death. His biography of Theodore Roethke, *The Glass House* (1967), recalls their friendship as undergraduates. His other books include the novels *Amos Berry* (1953), *Hilda Manning* (1956), and *A Frieze of Girls: Memoirs as Fiction* (1964; 2004).

Grace Shackman, born in 1943, received her B.A. from the University of Michigan in 1965. She is the author of *Ann Arbor in the 19th Century: A Photographic History* (2001) and *Ann Arbor in the 20th Century: A Photographic History* (2002) and is a regular columnist for the *Ann Arbor Observer,* the *Community Observer,* and the *Old West Side News.* She teaches local history classes at Washtenaw Community College.

Macklin Smith, born in 1944, began teaching at the University of Michigan in 1976. He chronicles his bone marrow transplant in the volume *Transplant* (2002). When not birding, he teaches critical and creative courses in poetry and works on early poetics.

Ted Solotaroff, born in 1928, earned a B.A. in 1952 from the University of Michigan. A literary critic specializing in contemporary fiction, he published a collection of essays, *The Red Hot Vacuum and Other Pieces on the Writing of the Sixties,* in 1970. He has been the editor of two distinguished series of anthologies, *New American Review* and *American Review.*

Anne Stevenson, born in 1933, grew up in Ann Arbor and won several Hopwood Awards during her undergraduate years at the University of Michigan. Her first book of poems, *Living in America,* was published in 1965 by the Ann Arbor publisher Generation. She has published many volumes since, as well as books of literary criticism and a biography of Sylvia Plath.

Bob Ufer (1920–81) was the radio voice of Michigan (he pronounced it Meeee-shegan) football for four decades. A CD set "The Best of Bob Ufer" (proceeds go to charity) can be purchased from www.uferfoundation.org.

Pete Waldmeir, born in 1931, spent fifty-five years at the *Detroit News* and covered sports for about twenty-five of them. In 2000 he was inducted into the Michigan Journalism Hall of Fame. He lives in Grosse Pointe Woods.

Wendy Wasserstein, born in 1950, is one of America's leading playwrights. Her works include *Uncommon Women and Others* (1975), *Isn't It Romantic* (1981), *The Heidi Chronicles* (1988), and *The Sisters Rosenzweig* (1992), as well as a book of essays, *Bachelor Girls* (1990).

Stanley Waterloo (1846–1913) grew up in St. Clair, Michigan, and specialized in Jack London–like novels about the primitive and apocalyptic such as *The Story of Ab* (1897), *Armageddon* (1898), and *The Wolf's Long Howl* (1899).

Nancy Willard, born in 1936, grew up in Ann Arbor and earned a B.A. from the University of Michigan in 1958. Her first book of poems, *In His Country,* was published in 1966 by the Ann Arbor publisher Generation. Since then she has written many volumes of poetry, fiction, essays, and children's stories. She is Emeritus Professor of English at Vassar.

⚓

Acknowledgments

Every attempt has been made to secure permission to reprint works contained in this volume. Grateful acknowledgment is made to the following authors, publishers, and journals for the use of previously published materials.

Olive San Louie Anderson (SOLA), from *An American Girl, and Her Four Years at a Boys' College*, D. Appleton and Company, 1878. Max Apple, from *Roommates: My Grandfather's Story*, © 1994 by Tov Sheyni, Inc. Reprinted by permission of Warner Books, Inc. Charles Baxter, from *The Feast of Love*, © 2000 by Charles Baxter. Used by permission of Pantheon Books, a division of Random House, Inc. Charles Baxter, "Hybrid City" from *Ann Arbor (W)rites: A Community Memoir*, edited by Nicholas Delbanco, The Ann Arbor District Library, 2004. Gorman Beauchamp, "Dissing the Middle Class: The View from Burns Park" from *The American Scholar*, reprinted by permission of the author. Sven Birkerts, from *My Sky Blue Trades*, © 2002 by Sven Birkerts. Used by permission of Viking Penguin, a division of Penguin Group (USA) Inc. John Dewey, "A College Course: What should I Expect From It?" from *The Collected Works of John Dewey, Early Works: Volume 3, 1889–1892*, © 1969 by Southern Illinois University Press, reproduced by permission of the publisher. Lela Duff, from *Ann Arbor Yesterdays*, 1962, reprinted by permission of the Friends of the Ann Arbor District Library. Laurence Goldstein, "Ann Arbor Solitary" from *The Three Gardens*, Copper Beach Press, 1987, reprinted by permission of the author. Peggy Goodin, *Take Care of My Little Girl*, © 1950 by Peggy Goodin. Used by permission of Dutton, a division of Penguin Group (USA) Inc. Richard Goodman, "Homage to Cazzie Russell" reprinted by permission of the author. Michael Grass, "A², Training Ground for Life's Finer Experiences" from *The Michigan Daily*, September 3, 2002, reprinted by permission of *The Michigan Daily*. Linda Gregerson, "An Arbor" from *The Woman Who Died In Her Sleep*, © 1996 by Linda Gregerson. Reprinted by permission of Houghton Mifflin Company. All rights reserved. Donald Hall, "Kicking the Leaves" from *Old And New Poems*, © 1990 by Donald Hall. Reprinted by permission of Houghton Mifflin Company. All rights reserved. Alice Hamilton letters from *Alice Hamilton: A Life in Letters*, Harvard University Press, 1984. Johanna Hanink, "Dishonoring Those We've Lost by Shouting" from *The Michigan Daily*, September 24, 2001, reprinted by permission of *The Michigan Daily*. Karl Edwin Harriman, from *Ann Arbor Tales* by Karl Edwin Harriman, George W. Jacobs and Company, Philadelphia, 1902. E.O. Haven, "Address Delivered to the Medical Class at the University of Michigan, 1869" from a pamphlet published by Dr. Chase's Steamfitting House, 1869. Robert Hayden, "The Performers" from *Collected Poems of Robert Hayden*, edited by Frederick Laysher, © 1985 by Emma Hayden. Used by permission of Liveright Publishing Corporation. Tom Hayden, "The Conversion: Ann Arbor 1957–61" from *Reunion: A Memoir*, Random House, 1988, reprinted by permission of the author. Lawrence Joseph, "An Awful Lot Was Happening" from

Curriculum Vitae, University of Pittsburgh Press, 1988, reprinted by permission of the author. Jane Kenyon, "The Little Boat," © 2005 by the Estate of Jane Kenyon. Reprinted from *Collected Poems* with the permission of Graywolf Press, Saint Paul, Minnesota. Thomas Lynch, "Still Life in Milford—Oil Canvas by Lester Johnson" from *Still Life in Milford*, © 1998 by Thomas Lynch. Used by permission of W.W. Norton & Company, Inc. Ross Macdonald, from *The Dark Tunnel*, Gregg Press, 1980. Courtney Mandryk, "Flat" from the *Michigan Quarterly Review*, 2005, reprinted by permission of the author. Justin McCarthy, from *Dear Lady Disdain*, Collins' Clear Type Press, 1908. Dorothy Gies McGuigan, "A College Romance" from *Our Michigan: Anthology Celebrating the University of Michigan's Sesquicentennial*, edited by Erich A. Walter, The University of Michigan, 1966. Richard Meeker, from *Better Angel* by Richard Meeker, Alyson Publications, 2000. Reprinted by permission of Alyson Publications. Arthur Miller, "University of Michigan" from *Echoes Down the Corridor: Collected Essays, 1944–2000*, edited by Stephen Centola, © 2000 by Arthur Miller. Used by permission of Viking Penguin, a division of Penguin Group (USA) Inc. Joyce Carol Oates, from *All the Good People I've Left Behind*, © 1979 by the Ontario Review, Inc. Frank O'Hara, "Ann Arbor Variations" from *Collected Poems*, © 1971 by Maureen Granville-Smith, Administratrix of the Estate of Frank O'Hara. Used by permission of Alfred A. Knopf, a division of Random House, Inc. "Old Okemos" from *The History of Washtenaw County*, Chas. C. Chapman, Chicago, 1881. Marge Piercy, from *Braided Lives*, Ballantine Books, 1997. Reprinted by permission of the Wallace Agency. "The Port Huron Statement of the Students for a Democratic Society, 1962" reprinted by permission of Tom Hayden. Dudley Randall, "Winter Campus, Ann Arbor" reprinted by permission of the Estate of Dudley Randall. Ruth Reichl from *Tender at the Bone*, © 1998 by Ruth Reichl. Used by permission of Random House, Inc. Elwood Reid, from *If I Don't Six*, © 1998 by Elwood Reid. Used by permission of Doubleday, a division of Random House, Inc. Allan Seager, from *Amos Berry* reprinted by permission of the Estate of Allan Seager and the Watkins/Loomis Agency. Grace Shackman, "The Underground Railroad in Ann Arbor" from *The Ann Arbor Observer*, December 1998, reprinted by permission of *The Ann Arbor Observer*. Macklin Smith, "Two Views" from *Transplant*, Shaman Drum, 2003, reprinted by permission of the author. Ted Solotaroff, from *First Loves: A Memoir*, Seven Stories Press, 2004. Anne Stevenson, "Ann Arbor (A Profile)" from *The Collected Poems 1955–1995*, Oxford University Press, 1996, reprinted by permission of the author. Bob Ufer, "Burying Woody Hayes" reprinted by permission of the Bob Ufer Foundation. Pete Waldmeier, "Michigan's Great Victory Makes Football Worthwhile" from *The Detroit News*, November 22, 1969, reprinted by permission of *The Detroit News*. Stanley Waterloo, from *The Launching of a Man*, McNally & Company, 1899. Wendy Wasserstein, from *The Heidi Chronicles and Other Plays*, © 1990, reprinted by permission of Harcourt, Inc. Nancy Willard, from *Sister Water*, Random House, 1993. Reprinted by permission of Nancy Willard and the Jean V. Naggar Agency. Nancy Willard, from *Things Invisible to See*, Random House, 1984. Reprinted by permission of Nancy Willard and the Jean V. Naggar Agency.